BRITISH FORCES MOTORCYCLES 1925–45

C.J. ORCHARD
&
S.J. MADDEN

Budding BOOKS

A Budding Book

First published in 1995 by
Alan Sutton Publishing Ltd, an imprint of Sutton Publishing Ltd
This edition published in 1997 by Budding Books, an imprint of Sutton Publishing Ltd, Phoenix Mill · Thrupp · Stroud · Gloucestershire · GL5 2BU

British Library Cataloguing in Publication Data

Orchard, Chris
British Forces Motorcycles, 1925–45
I. Title II. Madden, Steve
623.7472

ISBN 1-84015-012-2

Typesetting and origination by
Sutton Publishing Limited.
Printed in Great Britain by
WBC Limited, Bridgend.

Contents

Abbreviations

AFEE	Airborne Forces Experimental Establishment
AD	Admiralty Dept (Government office for the Navy)
AM	Air Ministry (Government office for the RAF)
AMC	Associated Motor Cycles
IWM	Imperial War Museum
JAP	J.A. Prestwich
LP	Local Purchase
MEE	Mechanization Experimental Establishment
MOA	Ministry of Agriculture
MOS	Ministy of Supply (Government office for provision and demand of military, Government and war produce)
MVT	Military Vehicle Trust
MWEE	Mechanical Warfare Experimental Establishment
OHV	Overhead-valve
PRO	Public Record Office
RAF	Royal Air Force
RAOC	Royal Army Ordnance Corps (principally in control of supply and distribution of motorcycles from manufacturers. MOS did the initial ordering)
REME	Royal Electrical & Mechanical Engineers
RN	Royal Navy
SV	Side-valve
SWD	Sidecar wheel drive
VMCC	Vintage Motor Cycle Club
WD	War Department } Government office for the Army
WO	War Office } Government office for the Army

Acknowledgements

The origins of this book date back to the late 1970s when Chris Orchard's interest in military motorcycles of the Second World War period started, and he contacted John Marchant of the Military Vehicle Trust (MVT; formerly the Military Vehicle Conservation Group) who was kind enough to supply him with motorcycle contract information from a 1944/5 census record. This material together with the information from original parts lists, drivers' handbooks, ledgers held by the Science Museum Library, contract details in various volumes held by the Public Record Office at Kew (PRO), records held by the Army Museum of Transport at Beverley, and additional census details obtained in 1990 from the REME Museum (missing from the original census details obtained), constitute the tabular information at the end of this book.

Help must also be acknowledged from all the private individuals who have sent in details to both authors over the years and who are too numerous to mention individually by name. (If anyone can help with any missing information, the authors would be pleased to hear from you.)

In about 1988 Chris met Steve for the first time when he contacted him for details on his BSA M20. Many months later, Steve convinced Chris to use this information as the basis for a book and turn it into a 'bible' and reference source for WD motorcycle enthusiasts. Steve then added further information to the details that had already been collected over the years.

The following clubs, individuals and museums are to be thanked for their help in providing substantial information for this book:

AJS John Allen of the AJS and Matchless Owners' Club, Science Museum Library; **ARIEL** Ralph Hawkins of the Ariel Owners' Motor Cycle Club, Dragonfly Motorcycles, PRO, Science Museum Library; **AVELING BARFORD** PRO; **BMW** John Lawes of the VMCC; **BSA** Steve Foden of the BSA Owners' Club, N.W. Lewis of the VMCC, PRO, Science Museum Library, A.G. Jeal; **DOUGLAS** Reg Holmes of the London Douglas Owners' Club, David Fletcher of the Tank Museum, PRO, F.L. Dolman of the VMCC; **EXCELSIOR** A.D. Mellor; **FRANCIS BARNETT** PRO, John Harding of Francis Barnett Owners' Club; **GILLET-HERSTAL** Bart Vanderveen, PRO; **HARLEY-DAVIDSON** Iain Cottrell of the MVT, D. Sarafan; **INDIAN** J. Reed of the VMCC, M. Hitchens; **JAMES** C.P. Penny; **LEVIS** PRO and David Fletcher of the Tank Museum; **MATCHLESS** (See AJS); **MOTO-CHENILLE** PRO; **NEW HUDSON** Eric Londesborough of the VMCC; **NEW IMPERIAL** Fred Pateman of the New Imperial Owners' Association; **NORMAN** J. Sampson of the British Two Stroke Club; **NORTON** W. Flew of the VMCC, Science Museum Library, N. Hinton of the Norton Owners' Club; **OEC** M. Shelley of the VMCC; **PANTHER** Barry Jones of the Panther Owners' Club, Imperial War Museum; **ROYAL ENFIELD** Steve Mayhew and Doug Young of the Royal Enfield Owners' Club, A.D. Mellor; **RUDGE WHITWORTH** Dave McMahon of the Rudge Enthusiasts' Club; **STEWART-EHRLICH** PRO and Dr J. Ehrlich; **SUNBEAM** Derek Beddows of the Marston Sunbeam Register; **TRIUMPH** Martin Jones of the Triumph Owners' Motor Cycle Club; **VELOCETTE** R. Franklin of the Velocette Owners' Club, and J. Clew of the VMCC; **SIDECARS** Various sources; **MISCELLANEOUS MOTORCYCLES** Various sources; **COLOUR SCHEMES** Various sources, Steve Madden.

Particular thanks must also be given to Peter Watson our close friend at the offices of EMAP; Brian Baxter and David Ross (photographer) of the REME Museum at Arborfield, Berkshire; Michael Ware and Jonathan Day of the National Motor Museum Museum at Beaulieu, Hampshire; Nick Nicholson of the Aircraft & Armament Evaluation Establishment, Boscombe Down, Wiltshire; members of the MVT (PO Box 6, Fleet, Hants GU13 9PE); David Fletcher of the Tank Museum, Bovington Camp, Dorset; G. Blewett of the Museum of Army Transport, Beverley, N. Humberside; Bill Phelps of the VMCC; Bob Whistler (photo reproduction), Diane Andrews, Alan Brown and others at the Airborne Forces Museum, Aldershot, Hampshire; Bart Vanderveen; C.P. Penny; the Trustees of the Imperial War Museum, London, and of the Public Record Office, Kew, Surrey; and John Underwood of the Science Museum Library. To all, a big thank you for their help on many matters.

Special thanks go to both our wives, Gill Orchard and Jamie Madden, for putting up with us during the writing of this book. Thanks also to Gill's mother, Mrs Paula Smith, for typing numerous letters and chapter drafts over the past few years.

Suitable for WD Requirements?

The First World War witnessed the first large-scale employment of vehicles and other forms of mechanized transport in the history of conflict. Acting as a proving ground for mechanization, the war highlighted the advantages and disadvantages of machines and, in some instances, their total unsuitability for military usage. Drawing on the experiences of the First World War, the long-term aim in the interwar period was towards the total mechanization of the armed services and the ultimate replacement of horse-drawn transport. To this end the military authorities created the Mechanical Warfare Experimental Establishment in 1926 (later to become the Mechanization Experimental Establishment in 1934, and referred to hereafter as the MWEE and MEE respectively) located at Cove, near Farnborough in Hampshire. Later, in 1940, the MEE underwent a further change of name, to 'TT2'.

The purpose of this establishment was to test and assess the suitability of all forms of mechanized transport, including motorcycles, offered to or acquired by the military authorities for potential service use. Each class of equipment had a standardized evaluation period applied to it. In the case of the motorcycle, the establishment considered that all models should be subjected to a comprehensive 10,000 mile test period consisting of both on- and off-road mileages, the initial 500 miles of the test mileage being a running-in period. During the course of the test period an interim inspection of the motorcycle was carried out, usually following the completion of at least 5,000 miles, in order to note the degree of wear and endurance of individual components. A variety of performance checks were also carried out, but which generally employed ¼ mile standing-start times and fuel consumption figures over 100 mile distances. The machine's off-road ability was also reviewed, including its ability to travel across rough ploughed fields, wet clay, bogs, sandy ditches and loose stone surfaces. Its ability to successfully stop and start on a gradient was also assessed.

Following completion of the 10,000 mile test period, the motorcycle was completely stripped down to measure all components for wear and damage. All the relevant details were added to the interim 5,000 mile report, together with any notable points of concern that had arisen during the entire test period, principally mechanical and electrical faults. The final stage of the test period involved the collation of all the information that had been gathered, resulting in a detailed report on the motorcycle concerned. It noted whether the machine was considered suitable, or unsuitable, for War Office requirements and the completed report was then sealed and classified 'Top Secret'.

Military thinking towards both the type and specification of motorcycles required for service use, together with their intended role and applications was to vary considerably during the interwar period. This was particularly so during the 1930s, although policy changes were to continue throughout the Second World War and beyond. These revisions in thinking were due to a number of factors, not least the changes in hierarchy at the War Office, improvements and advances in motorcycle design, operational experience and the necessary economies arising in wartime.

The situation concerning motorcycle combinations can be used to illustrate some of the above points. Proven to be of considerable military value during the First World War, the motorcycle combination was initially thought to be an ideal step towards the concept of a mechanized army, principally as a lightly armed scouting or reconnaissance vehicle. Design limitations, such as the lack of protection from the elements, inadequate equipment stowage and doubtful cross-country abilities became apparent during the late 1920s after the introduction of the Austin Seven 2-seater car. This vehicle successfully addressed many of the motorcycle combination's deficiencies and as a result, the Austin Seven began to take over the role previously the sole domain of the combination. However, it was not entirely superceded, for in the late 1930s the motorcycle combination once again attracted War Office interest in the form of the Norton 'Big 4'. This machine incorporated a driven sidecar wheel and proved to be a major improvement across country over previous sidecar designs.

However, by 1942 the sidecar machine was once again declared to be obsolete, thanks to the arrival of American-manufactured light-utility 4x4 cars supplied under Lend-Lease arrangements. Produced by both Willys-Overland and the Ford Motor Company, these vehicles became known universally as the 'Jeep'. They were vastly superior to extant motorcycle combinations in virtually every aspect, being more rugged and with a greatly increased carrying capability, a superior performance and a better off-road capability amongst other things. Anyone who could drive a car would have little difficulty in driving the Jeep, whereas the Norton 'Big 4' combination, in particular, took an experienced sidecar rider to competently drive the combination across country, more so over difficult terrain. Yet again, the motorcycle combination was downgraded by the military.

No longer required for off-road duties, the War Office still regarded the motorcycle combination as a useful and cheap form of passenger and stores transportation. It therefore continued to order under contract small quantities of machines fitted with sidecars, primarily BSA M20 and Norton 16H models, until near to the end of the Second World War. Principal recipients were the Royal Air Force, where the combination was a useful mode of transport on airfields with far-flung dispersals, and civil defence organizations including some units of the Home Guard where the machines were frequently employed on road-patrol duties in rural areas.

The situation concerning solo motorcycles and the War Office was a very different matter however, with the MWEE/MEE constantly looking for better machines than the examples of the time. It is not widely realized that from its formation in 1926, up to the Second World War and beyond, the MWEE/MEE tested and evaluated countless motorcycles. Almost every machine produced during this period, even if not ultimately tested by the War Office for military suitability, was invariably considered for possible testing.

Solo motorcycles were judged by the War Office to have distinct advantages

REME workshop assembly line, probably North Africa, sometime after 1942. Note the pile of engines in the foreground. (REME Museum)

No. 1 Workshop Group (REME), Chilwell, busy repairing forks and frames. The completed forks in the foreground are for Matchless G3/L, Triumph and Indian models. (REME Museum)

over most other forms of mechanized wheeled transport of the period. These advantages were of considerable value and included: small overall size which favoured manoeuvrability and concealment; a good overall performance from the engine; a limited off-road capability and the ability to proceed across, through and around obstacles which impeded larger vehicles; overall cheapness in value and running costs; and, in the main, ease of maintenance. The First World War and the years that followed revealed that certain motorcycles were more suited to military requirements than others. With the War Office looking towards the mechanization of the British Army, motorcycles for the military was one of the many areas to be assessed. The search for the most suitable solo motorcycle for War Office requirements was put in the hands of the MWEE during 1927, a year after the establishment had been formed. At this time, the British Army was still using a number of mechanized vehicles dating from the First World War some nine years earlier, including some motorcycles.

The MWEE was charged with looking at every possible feature of a motorcycle and testing commenced with experiments using lightweight 2-stroke motorcycles and 3-wheels-in-line machines. Initial results of these first tests tended to reveal that a machine's lightness in weight was important for cross-country use, but this appeared to be at the expense of robustness. Speed on the road was also poor with the 2-stroke engines often showing a tendency to seize. Experiments with the 3-wheel machines showed the type to be extremely heavy and complex in design. The additional expense incurred by the design outweighed the moderate gain in cross-country ability, particularly so as by now conventional solo machines fitted with bigger section tyres were displaying considerably improved off-road performance. Other problems arising with the heavy 3-wheel machines included poor reliability and ride quality which made them tiring for the riders.

Still attempting to find a suitable motorcycle for the military, a committee of War Office representatives visited the 1928 Olympia Motorcycle Show with the objective of finding the most suitable machine of standard design for military purposes. However, not one single machine at the Show appeared to meet all of the stringent service requirements, particularly at a weight appreciably less than 300 lb. In December that same year it was decided to obtain detailed particulars of machines manufactured by leading British manufacturers, with those showing most promise to be submitted for testing by the MWEE and/or in the hands of selected units within the Army's Royal Corps of Signals. The result of this decision saw seven different makes of motorcycle purchased during 1929 for comparative trials against one another, these being the products of OEC, Francis Barnett, BSA, AJS, New Hudson, Matchless and Douglas. Every one of the motorcycles supplied was of 350 cc engine capacity (or 2¾ hp), the maximum engine size the military authorities deemed necessary for solo use at the time.

However, before the tests had been completed the need for a new type of motorcycle for the War Office became so urgent that the authorities stepped in, ordering an irregular and hasty comparison test between the products of Douglas and Triumph, both companies having held considerable favour with the War Office up to then. Ultimately, the Douglas machine, the model L29, was to be chosen in preference to the Triumph machine, the model NL3. Interestingly, the Triumph NL3 was not even part of the seven-make trial, although later on it was to be tested overseas in Egypt in company with an OEC 3-wheel machine and the Levis.

By November 1929 the trials were concluded and the MWEE had formed the opinion that the heavier machines should be dropped due to the considerable difficulty in riding them across country. The lightweight machines fared little better and they too were dropped due to their poor performance and susceptibility to damage. This decision left the War Office with three models available for further testing – the AJS model M6, the Matchless T/4, and the Douglas L29, although even these were heavier than the preferred upper limit set by the authorities. Further testing of these machines resulted in little progress and led to a hardening of the viewpoint that no commercial motorcycle then available could meet all necessary military requirements without drastic modification. In order to meet all these requirements it would be more practical if a dedicated military machine was designed and built, specifically with an upper weight limit of 300 lb or less, yet still retaining performance and durability.

Other points of desirability to arise from the testing of machines for military use included such features as enclosed valve operating mechanisms, dry-sump lubrication, general weatherproofing of vulnerable components and twin exhaust-ports with dual-silencing. Also deemed a necessary feature in all future military motorcycle contracts was a standardized pattern of controls, as proposed by the British Cycle and Motor Cycle Manufacturers and Traders Union in February 1929, and endorsed and supported by the authorities.

However, the War Office had still not given up entirely on the idea of using a commercial production motorcycle of the time, suitably modified of course, although a visit by a group of representatives to the 1929 Motorcycle Show proved once again to be unsuccessful in establishing a model suitable for military use. Certain motorcycles at the Show did, however, incorporate various features as required by the authorities, although not sufficient to justify purchase. In the following year thinking changed at the War Office in favour of twin-cylinder motorcycles which it was thought were generally quieter than single-cylinder versions. The recently acquired Douglas machines remained in service throughout this period, although they were subjected to modification at various intervals. The other remaining machines were quietly, and conveniently, forgotten.

With twins now in favour, Matchless was to supply the War Office with its Silver Arrow model and BSA was to supply its new 500 cc overhead-valve (OHV) V-twin model. In due course, the authorities were to favour the BSA twin over the Matchless, and were to purchase quantities of the type at various stages throughout the 1930s. However, the model was prone to excessive cylinder wear throughout its service life, a problem which was never fully corrected.

Another requirement for military motorcycles was an efficient silencing system. Throughout this period the MWEE evaluated a number of different silencers in an attempt to establish the most effective example – the products of Howarth, Premier and Woodvan were investigated but ultimately none proved effective. (In later years, notably during 1938, the War Office was to work with Norton Motors on the silencing problem, only to conclude that it was difficult to silence motorcycles!) By now, attention was also being focussed on mechanical noise and some improvements were made in this area. Even by 1934 it was realized that twin-cylinder machines were actually no quieter than single-cylinder variants and considerably more expensive, notably on running costs.

Still seeking motorcycles suitable for military purposes, by 1935 the War Office was once again looking at single-cylinder machines. The basic requirements were for a machine of 350 cc or more and of either side-valve (SV) or OHV configuration. Accordingly, a trial period was arranged and seven makes of machine were purchased for evaluation purposes, these being the products of Ariel, BSA, Matchless, New Imperial, Norton, Royal Enfield and Triumph. Once the trial was underway, the Ariel machine, which up until then had proved to be the best both in terms of performance and reliability, became obsolete and was dropped from the testing programme. For the remaining models the New Imperial and Royal Enfield machines showed poorly throughout the test period while the BSA, Matchless, Norton and Triumph models all showed well – initially, that is. All testing was completed within six months unlike the previous trials of 1929 which ran on for many months more.

In 1936 BSA replaced its model W35/6 which had shown poor reliability during the War Office 10,000 mile test, with a new model, the ubiquitous M20. Following the company's reorganization, initially preceded by a name change, Triumph was also to replace the previously tested model 3/1 within its range with a new model, the 3S. Those machines remaining from the military trials of 1935 were now just two in number, the original 16H Norton model and the Matchless G3, small orders for both of which were to follow. Other manufacturers at this time attempted to arouse War Office interest in their products, namely newcomers Rudge and Sunbeam, along with Douglas and Ariel

fNo. 1 Workshop Group (REME), Chilwell, overhauling mainly BSA M20s. (REME Museum)

with new machines, but ultimately only Rudge was to succeed modestly in gaining contract status. The Sunbeam model offered was subsequently withdrawn from testing due to the Matchless buy-out of the company, while both the Douglas and Ariel machines ultimately proved unsuitable for service requirements.

During 1936, a need was identified for motorcycles suitable for training purposes and light communication duties. The War Office purchased a quantity of 250 cc Matchless models without the type first having been evaluated for suitability by the MEE.

With development continuing, the next official trials took place during 1939 when the various manufacturers were asked to submit a design of machine not exceeding 250 lb in weight, but retaining the performance of a standard 500 cc military motorcycle. Norton, Royal Enfield and Triumph were first to submit their respective designs, followed later by those of BSA and Matchless who were also invited to submit designs. In the end, only the BSA and Triumph designs were to reach production stage, yet neither were to survive. The bombing of the Triumph factory during November 1940 destroyed the Triumph model, and BSA's design was cancelled at the last minute by the War Office, most probably for concern over spares for yet another different model of machine to those then in service.

During the build-up to the Second World War military motorcycle production was indeed stepped up and by early 1940 supply was beginning to meet demand. Even so, many of the larger manufacturers were still producing models for the civilian market but could not guarantee immediate delivery due to the pressures of war. By May 1940 however, this was to change following the invasions of France and the Low Countries by Germany and the evacuation of the British Expeditionary Force from Dunkirk. The vast proportion of the British Army's most modern and newest equipment, including motorcycles, had been lost during the evacuation. With the threat of invasion to Great Britain itself now a very real possibility, the War Office found itself chronically short of virtually every kind of item imaginable, including motorcycles, vital for the defence of mainland Britain.

Accordingly, all major manufacturers were inundated with huge orders for motorcycles from the War Office, fresh contracts being placed prior to the completion of existing ones in some cases. To meet demand, emergency purchases were also made which principally involved the authorities impressing all suitable civilian-destined machines awaiting either completion or delivery from the factories and also from dealers' showrooms. Other machines were delivered to the War Office in the form of 'gifts' – typically suitable machines in good, serviceable condition donated by their patriotic civilian owners. Some 8,000 motorcycles of both impressed and gift status were to be accepted by the authorities at the time, the vast proportion being employed by second-line formations, training units and civil defence organizations.

To further boost the War Office's stocks, machines from Harley-Davidson and Indian, manufactured in America, were delivered to the authorities under the War-Aid scheme of Lend-Lease. The first to arrive were combination machines, soon to be followed by solo machines. Generally, the War Office disliked the American motorcycles due in the main to their size and weight; also, the rider's controls in most cases were arranged in a completely different configuration to those on conventional British military machines. This, of course, required good familiarity from a rider before one could be ridden competently and with safety.

Many of these Lend-Lease machines were sent to far-flung outposts of the British Empire or issued to UK-based second-line civil defence formations, not to mention sizeable quantities, particularly of the Indian model 741B, going to the Royal Air Force.

As the Second World War progressed, the major manufacturers continued to churn out the same basic models for the authorities that they had first supplied during 1940 or earlier. Certain manufacturers even changed from SV to OHV designs during the mid-war period in an attempt to standardize War Office motorcycles as 350 cc OHV designs and 500 cc SV machines. Motorcycle production settled into a steady, high-volume turnout of machines.

Despite this, the authorities were still concerned about the wide range of different spares required for each type of machine held on inventory, and the possible production and distribution problems that might arise. Even so, some rationalization had already taken place with the standardization of certain universal fittings, such as handlebar control levers, saddles, pillion and pannier equipment. Number plates disappeared from military machines from about 1941 onwards; rubber fittings, apart from essential items, were deleted from about 1943 onwards due to rubber shortages caused by the Japanese conquests in South East Asia. Early wartime machines were often updated during the war by fitting newer components, such as the pannier frames; yet others often lost fittings, such as lights, seat covers and front mudguards, either owing to damage or in an effort to lighten the machine. This practice was most common in North Africa, and was probably due to a shortage of spares and attendant maintenance difficulties in the region.

The supply of spare parts was always a problem throughout most of the Second World War: the more isolated the theatre of operations, the more acute the problem became. In many such instances, cannibalization of damaged machines was necessary in order to produce one serviceable machine. Frequently, the popular teledraulic front forks of the Matchless G3/L can be seen adorning the front of a more mundane, girder-forked machine in an attempt to improve handling and comfort. Other noted home-made modifications in the desert included an air filter made from an old mess tin strapped to the top of the fuel tank and sump-shields, to name but a couple.

Captured enemy machines were also frequently used whenever available. Later in the war the authorities actually reserved a series of serial numbers for allocation to such types, and they also allocated blocks of numbers for REME-rebuilt machines, those impressed, and of local purchase and gift status.

The continuing concern about spares resulted in the establishment of a standardization committee in 1944 to advise the authorities on a single motorcycle design required for future universal military service. Yet again, models were built by the various manufacturers, Triumph, BSA, Douglas, Norton and Royal Enfield who all built and submitted their designs for evaluation. Progress by the authorities was slow, however, and with the end of the war in sight the urgency for new machines was considerably lessened. Subsequently all the models offered were dropped, save for the Triumph design which lingered on for long enough to evolve into the post-war TRW model.

Following the end of the Second World War, military motorcycle development came to a virtual standstill. New designs were something of white elephants in the austere post-war years, with the country short of money, saddled with huge war debts, and overwhelmed with enormous stocks of now redundant motorcycles to sort out. Practicality and economy were the two main concerns of the period, and the machines retained were typically late or rebuilt examples, with those disposed of by the authorities usually being early production, worn-out or obsolete types. The latter category included the Royal Enfield WD/C, virtually all Triumph models, all Velocettes, the James ML, and all Lend-Lease American machines alongside all other small quantity makes, everything being disposed of through the trade or returned to the manufacturer by the end of the 1940s. By the early 1950s, the post-war armed forces accepted the BSA M20 as the standard service machine of the period alongside the Matchless G3/L. Small numbers of other wartime types could also be seen, although all had been retired by the end of the decade. As well as disposal to the trade, public or return to the manufacturer, large quantities of surplus War Office machines were disposed of to the governments of the liberated Allied countries. This was to aid the rebuilding of their armed forces, with such machines filling the gap until newer designs could be purchased.

Military motorcycles retained by the Services for post-war use were subjected to at least one, if not several, full workshop overhauls. This was particularly so in the case of the BSA M20 and Matchless G3/L, where the machines would be completely stripped down and rebuilt using any serviceable parts available, either reconditioned

No. 21 Advanced Base Workshop REME, Belgium, 1945. Note the manufacturers' names hanging above the motorcycles, showing how the REME divided its workshops to cope with all the different motorcycle brands. BSA, Norton and Ariel can be seen here. (REME Museum)

or new, followed by a repaint. In virtually all instances the engine originally fitted would be replaced by a service-exchange unit. The War Office's primary concern was a serviceable machine at minimum cost and it was none too concerned about the correct correlation between frame and engine numbers, nor the fitting of non-original parts. To the War Office, a motorcycle was a motorcycle and identified in the inventory by the serial number (later, registration number) alone. Little wonder, then, that most wartime machines still in service during the late 1950s/early 1960s bore scant resemblance to their original wartime factory specification.

As previously mentioned, the MWEE/MEE not only tested complete motorcycles (as well as countless other categories of machinery), but also component parts thereof and proprietary fitting too. Such items tested included exhausts, air filters, saddles, tyres and twistgrips. One of the many oddities tested during the period under scrutiny included the fitting of Framo skis to either side of a motorcycle. When in use they were supposed to enable the rider to transfer part of his body weight to the ground, to provide the machine with greater stability on soft sand or loose gravel when cornering. When not in use they acted as a pair of leg shields for the rider. Testing of this design was carried out in Egypt, but only to culminate in failure! Other ideas experimented with included special sidecars for specific applications, and spring frames for motorcycles. Experimental machines were also tested at various times and these oddities included the Triumph and OEC 3-wheeler machines, the Aveling Barford mini-bike, the Swiss-built Moto-Chenille Mercier model and the well-known Excelsior 'Welbike' to name but a few. Certain Axis captured machines were also investigated during the wartime period.

Motorcycle Repair Section of No. 1 Workshop Group, Chilwell. Note the tiny lens of the rear light of the early matchless G3/L undergoing repair. (REME Museum)

War Department Manufacturers

AJS

As an independent concern, the AJS company supplied few motorcycles to the War Office and a smaller amount still after the company became part of the AMC empire in 1931. During 1929 the company were involved in the seven-make trials of that year, submitting their 350 cc OHV Model M6 for War Office evaluation. Having survived the initial trial period, the model was deemed successful enough to be submitted for further testing alongside the Douglas and Matchless produced machines but ultimately, only a handful of examples of each company's models were to be procured.

It is interesting to note that, following the purchase of the AJS company by the owners of the Matchless concern in the 1930s, the products and designs of the former company generally disappeared, although the AJS name was kept alive due to carefully planned 'badge engineering' by the AMC concern. Fully aware of the loyalty of riders to individual marques, AMC discovered that some customers would not buy a Matchless model unless it carried the AJS logo, and vice-versa. Thus AMC could supply one basic model in a particular class under two different marques with, apart from the insignia, only minor differences between the two. Perhaps the most manifest of these differences was the engine's magneto-mounting position, ahead of the cylinder barrel on the AJS and to the rear on the Matchless product, which noticeably altered the shape and position of the engine's timing cover.

Following the outbreak of the Second World War it made sense to produce one named model for various reasons and the Matchless name was upheld, the AJS name disappearing from use after 1940 until the end of the war.

AJS Model M6 349 cc OHV Single-Cylinder – 1929–31

The AJS Model M6 was to be submitted for War Office testing alongside the products of six other manufacturers during the trials of 1929. The type was to prove reasonably successful throughout the initial trial period and was thus selected to continue with further evaluation, along with the Matchless Model T/4 and the Douglas L29.

After collating the results of these evaluations, the MWEE were indecisive as to which of the three machines was most suitable for military use. Ultimately, the Douglas company were to receive the principal orders for supply of their product, most probably because their machine was the lightest of the three. AJS, however, were to supply a handful of their Model M6 to the War Office up to, and

Official photograph of a 1929 AJS Model M6, as used in the 1929 trials. (PRO, WO 194 (45) – 5876)

including, 1931 although the military authorities were never really satisfied with the type and the total number supplied barely entered double figures.

The primary fault with the Model M6 in comparison to the Matchless and Douglas products was its overall weight, some 26 lb heavier than the Douglas. The weight problem was noted during testing in the desert during 1931 when it was compared against a Levis model and the Douglas L29. The M6 was described as heavy, unmanageable and unsuitably tyred for its weight, which in turn made the machine's performance seem poor and prevented comparisons with the other models.

AJS Model 8 SS 498 cc OHV Single-Cylinder – 1940

Purchased under contract during mid-1940, only two of these machines were officially supplied to the War Office. They were procured following the losses at Dunkirk, when the demand by the War Office for any remotely suitable machine was paramount, and were presumably available for immediate delivery from the AMC factory.

AJS Model 8 498 cc OHV Single-Cylinder – 1940

Purchased by the War Office under contract at the same time as the Model 26, the Model 8 SS and the Model 9, the Model 8 was purchased presumably for the same reasons; namely, that it was available for immediate delivery at a time of great need.

Only one example was supplied and, apart from the colouring, it was of standard civilian specification, although whether this was 'standard' or 'de-luxe' in specification is not known.

AJS MODEL 9 498 CC SV SINGLE-CYLINDER – 1940

The AJS Model 9 and Matchless G5 were the only SVs from the AMC company to be supplied during the war. Only two examples were officially supplied, at the same time and for the same reasons as the Model 8 SS, the Model 8 and the Model 26.

It is presumed that both were of standard 1940 civilian specification, apart from the military paintwork.

AJS MODEL 26 347 CC OHV SINGLE-CYLINDER – 1940

Only one Model 26 was officially supplied to the War Office, at the same time and under the same conditions as the AJS Model 8 SS, the Model 8 and the Model 9, although with a different contract catalogue reference number.

The Model 26 was generally the AJS-badged variant of the Matchless Model G3 and the example supplied was delivered at the time when the AMC factory was in full production with the Model G3 for the War Office.

Two impressed AJS machines. In the foreground is a Model 26 and behind it what appears to be a Model 8. (IWM, H7662)

Ariel

Ariel's first connections with the War Office following the First World War was during 1935, when the War Office purchased one of the company's VA3 models for evaluation for potential military service, along with machines from six other manufacturers. The test results were mainly favourable for Ariel's offering although the model was not chosen, because it was due for replacement.

The following year saw some key personnel at the War Office still remaining in favour of twin- or multi-cylinder machines, principally because they were still considered noticeably quieter than single-cylinder models. Ariel therefore supplied two of their model Square-Four machines for evaluation purposes, one of 1000 cc and the other of 600 cc engine capacity. Performing well in general, both models were ultimately rejected as unsuitable because of poor ground clearance and excessive weight.

In September 1939 Ariel's VA was tested for suitability against a War Department 16H Norton. This was followed in mid-1940 by a demonstration of the company's Model W/NG prototype, witnessed by officials for the War Office and the French Government. The testing of the model suitably impressed the French officials, the Ariel factory ledgers detailing a quantity supplied to their government during 1940. The British, however, only considered the W/NG suitable as an emergency purchase, should it become necessary.

In late 1939, following the outbreak of war, Ariel supplied a quantity of the 500 cc model VA to the War Office. This was presumably because the demand for service machines had dramatically increased following the outbreak of hostilities. Further orders arrived for other models produced by the company, and yet more following the Dunkirk evacuation to compensate for the huge losses of equipment. Thereafter the War Office settled with the W/NG model, as supplied by the company, for the remainder of the Second World War.

During the later stages of the war many of the early W/NG models supplied at the beginning of the war, along with smaller quantities of NH and VH models, were modified to bring them up to the same standard as the current models then being supplied. The principal modification involved fitting pannier and pillion equipment, although smaller modifications were also carried out.

Following the end of the Second World War, Ariel, along with other major manufacturers, saw the bulk of their motorcycles disposed of by the War Office as surplus to peacetime requirements, according to official policy. Many went to civilian dealerships for reconditioning to civilian specifications, while others were supplied to overseas governments, notably the Norwegians, for use by that country's post-war forces.

ARIEL MODEL VA3 557 CC SV SINGLE-CYLINDER – 1935 EVALUATION MODEL

Ariel's Model VA3 was procured as one of the seven manufacturers' models evaluated for military suitability during the tests of 1935. The model supplied was of standard civilian specification of the time, but with the addition of a service specified crankcase shield, a Dunlop sports rear tyre, and a carrying rack on top of the rear mudguard.

During the course of the tests, the MEE noted that although the cross-country

Official photograph of the 1935 Ariel VA3 test model. (The Tank Museum, 138/D6)

performance of the model was good, the machine was difficult to ride across specific obstacles such as logs. Defects noted were few and an interim inspection of the test model at 5,565 miles showed the only real wear to be at the top of the cylinder-bore and on the piston, indicating that it was top heavy.

Following the conclusion of the tests, the MEE expressed a liking for the model. Ultimately, however, the VA3 was not procured for service use as Ariel were intending to replace it with a new model.

ARIEL MODEL 4F (SQUARE-FOUR) 597 CC OVERHEAD-CAM FOUR-CYLINDER – 1936 TEST MODEL

Loaned to the War Office and tested by the MEE during October 1936, this was a completely standard civilian specification model. The particular machine concerned was supplied direct from Ariel and was considered for testing because, at the time, the War Office favoured the quietness and performance of twin- or multi-cylinder machines.

The results of the testing found the model to be extremely powerful and well able to negotiate difficult country within the limits of its ground clearance, although its considerable weight led to the conclusion that the type would be unsuitable for War Office use.

ARIEL MODEL 4G (SQUARE-FOUR) 997 CC OHV FOUR-CYLINDER – 1936 TEST MODEL

Supplied along with the 600 cc Model 4F Square-Four, on loan to the War Office for evaluation purposes, the larger 1000 cc Model 4G Square-Four was likewise evaluated by the MEE for military service suitability during October 1936.

Following the completion of the tests, the results were more or less identical to those of the 600 cc 4F model.

ARIEL MODEL VA 497 CC SV SINGLE-CYLINDER – 1939 PROTOTYPE

Just prior to the outbreak of war, Ariel offered the War Office its Model VA for testing as it was similar to the current BSA M20s and Norton 16Hs in service.

Performance tested against a standard War Department Norton 16H and one fitted with a spring frame, it performed well enough for a contract to be issued soon after.

ARIEL MODEL W/VA (LIGHTENED) 497 CC SV SINGLE-CYLINDER – 1939

Only one Model W/VA (XG10208) was produced, in request for a lighter machine, but how the lighter weight was achieved is not known.

Testing was carried out at Farnborough against a standard W/VA and standard Norton 16H, where the lighter model proved the easiest to handle.

The project was probably shelved because the War Office had decided by this stage on the W/NG.

ARIEL MODEL W/NG 349 CC OHV SINGLE-CYLINDER – 1940 PROTOTYPE

The forerunner of the company's standard wartime service Model W/NG, the prototype was based on Ariel's winning machine of the 1938 Scottish six-day trial. The prototype was prepared ready for demonstration to War Office and foreign officials by mid-1940, the result of the demonstration obviously impressing the French Government as orders followed.

The British testing of this on-loan machine (XG12179) in July 1940 showed up a number of faults. The machine's condition was described as merely fair on the customary strip-down and inspection, and it was noted as suitable only for emergency purchase. By the time the test had ended and the reports been finished in August 1940, however, a British order had already been issued.

ARIEL MODEL W/VA 497 CC SV SINGLE-CYLINDER – 1939–40

The Model W/VA was supplied by Ariel in limited quantities during the early part of the Second World War, probably because it held similar characteristics to the War Office Norton 16H and BSA M20 machines which had been in service since the outbreak of the war.

Basically a militarized civilian model, the W/VA model served principally with the War Department (Army) in a variety of second-line roles, which probably involved fitting a sidecar to a number of examples.

Small quantities were also supplied to the Air Ministry (RAF) and the Ministry of Agriculture, no doubt for use in conjunction with the efforts on the

Official photograph of an Ariel W/VA. (IWM, KID 5699)

home front by the Women's Land Army at various farming locations throughout the country.

ARIEL MODEL VH (RED HUNTER) 497 CC OHV SINGLE-CYLINDER – 1940

The 497 cc Red Hunter model supplied to the War Office following the Dunkirk evacuation of May 1940 was principally a civilian specification model, and the small quantity of machines supplied were either readily available for delivery or available for construction without delay from stocks of parts available. Accordingly, the batch supplied contained machines fitted with either the single- or the twin-port cylinder heads; the Ariel factory ledgers note the various VH models supplied to the War Office as either 'VH' or 'VH2', indicating these two versions.

The Model VH was Ariel's competition/sporting model of the time and all are believed to have served with the War Department (Army).

ARIEL MODEL NH (RED HUNTER) 347 CC OHV SINGLE-CYLINDER – 1940

Along with the larger 500 cc Model VH, the 350 cc Model NH was also a competition/sporting model of the Ariel range. It was purchased by the War Office along with the contract for the batch of VH models. All are believed to have served with the War Department (Army).

Ariel Model VG (De-Luxe) 497 cc OHV Single-Cylinder – 1940–1

The Model VG De-Luxe was a civilian specification machine supplied to the War Office at irregular intervals between April 1940 and January 1941. It is presumed that the type was supplied to satisfy the demands of the time or to employ stocks of completed machines or parts otherwise lying redundant; all are believed to have served with the War Department (Army).

Ariel Model NG (De-Luxe) 347 cc OHV Single-Cylinder – 1940

The Ariel NG De-Luxe model was the civilian specification lower capacity version of the 500 cc VG model. Purchased at the same time as the small batches of VH, NH and VG models, and presumably for the same reasons, all are believed to have served with the War Department (Army).

Ariel Model VB (De Luxe) 598 cc SV Single-Cylinder – 1940

This was a civilian specification model, and only two machines were supplied during August of 1940. Following this delivery, no further Model VB De-Luxes were supplied. Primarily because of their size and type of engine-unit fitted, it is presumed that these two machines were ultimately to have sidecars fitted at some stage of their service life.

Ariel Model W/NG 347 cc OHV Single-Cylinder – 1940–5

The Ariel W/NG model became the company's principal and, after 1941, the sole model supplied to the services. Between 1940 and 1945 some 40,000 plus W/NG models were produced for primarily the British War Department (Army), with smaller quantities also being supplied to both the Air Ministry (RAF) and the Admiralty Department (Navy), as well as several second-line formations, including some civil defence organizations, and orders from foreign governments. Indeed, the first service order for the W/NG model was placed by the French Government.

Based on a pre-war competition model, the production Model W/NG Ariel was subjected to various minor alterations and modifications over the course of its five year production run between 1940 and 1945. The first production quantities of W/NG models still retained civilian pattern front and rear number-plates, even if no number was carried on them, but these were no longer fitted after 1940. A top-feed floatchamber was also specified for the carburettor on most early models as opposed to the bottom feed of later production models. The two triangular tool-boxes were fitted on the offside and initially had the screw-knobs to secure the lids positioned in the centre-face of each box. This design was modified during 1941 for tool-boxes incorporating a revised pattern lid, the top fitting having a half-hinged lid and the bottom box the fastening knob repositioned to the more common location in the top upper corner of the lid.

All Model W/NGs produced up to the end of 1941 were still fitted with gear-change, kick-start and footrest rubbers, along with tank knee-grips and celluloid or rubber handlebar grips. All of these fittings had to be withdrawn from

Official photograph of a 1941 Ariel W/NG. (REME Museum)

production models from 1943 onwards owing to the rubber shortages arising because of the Japanese conquests in Burma and other areas of the Far East. To compensate, cast-steel patterned footrests were fitted to offer some element of grip to the rider, and standard military pattern canvas webbing handlebar grips were fitted in place of the rubber ones. Further modifications to the W/NG model included replacing the previously employed rubber-mounted handlebar with a solid clamp. (Service usage had shown instances of the handlebars actually turning in the rubber mounts during heavy cross-country use and so, in 1942, rubber-mounting was stopped at engine-number BH 23937.) That same year the universally introduced military pannier-frames, bags and new rear-carriers in which to accommodate the latter were also fitted. Pillion facilities were now specified as standard, and all these components were fitted to the model during the production stage. It should be noted that many earlier W/NG models were updated after 1942 by fitting the then current pannier and pillion fittings, with Ariel frequently supplying complete sets of equipment for such purposes. Later models were fitted with a pressed steel primary chaincase and engine timing-cover, in a drive to conserve supplies of aluminium alloy, and the removal of the steering-damper on the forks. In late 1944 the last batches of machines were produced with a revised lighting system, which incorporated a revised headlight and switch-panel position, plus Universal pattern Vokes air filter fitted to the top of the fuel tank as standard.

The W/NG model, was fairly popular with the services during the Second World War, and particularly so with troops on the front line, who found its performance, ground-clearance and competition ancestry a bonus in forward

Official photograph of a late wartime Ariel W/NG. (IWM, KID 5030)

rough terrain areas. The model retained its popularity for the remainder of the war and continued in service in forward and second-line areas in much the same way as before.

The type also served in limited numbers with both the Air Ministry (RAF) and the Admiralty Department (Navy), and probably with certain other bodies as well.

Surprisingly, the W/NG model is not at all common today when compared to surviving examples of other manufacturers' models; this is particularly unusual when the total production figures of the model are considered. It is known that many war surplus W/NGs were sold to other countries for use by their own forces following the end of the war and several ex-military W/NG models exist that were dealer-reconditioned to a civilian specification.

Aveling Barford

AVELING BARFORD EXPERIMENTAL LIGHTWEIGHT 125 CC SINGLE CYLINDER 2-STROKE – 1938

Aveling Barford built only one experimental prototype lightweight, which was a mini motorcycle weighing 154 lb. It had several unorthodox features, most notably its drilled angle iron sprung frame.

First delivered on 24.11.38, the machine was returned twice (first on 25.11.38 and then on 29.07.39) for modifications between trials. It was thoroughly tested in July 1939, where it completed 206 road miles and 151 cross-country. After testing, the riders criticized the cramped riding position (even though the motorcycle height was adjustable), which threw a lot of weight on to the riders' wrists, and

The 1938 Aveling Barford prototype mini-motorcycle. Note its very crude construction. (PRO, WO 194 (33) – 481)

the foot-brake was considered to be badly positioned. Generally it was considered to perform very well across country and on loose surfaces with its tracks fitted, and was also easy to handle, but the top road speed of 25 m.p.h. was considered too slow; as the test progressed, this decreased further still as the engine bearings wore, letting air into the crankcases of the machine's Villiers engine.

Although not considered suitable for use by the War Office, the general design was considered as a potential basis for a future War Department lightweight.

On a slightly sad note, the motorcycle appears not to have survived the war; it is listed in a November 1944 census record as being converted to an air compressor!

BMW

Two motorcycles were registered in 1940, but it is unclear which models they were. It is possible that they were either captured models or motorcycles straight out of a showroom, purchased in an attempt to evaluate quickly the opposition's equipment.

If captured they are likely to have been models R35, R75 or R12 (in combination or solo form) and if bought from a showroom, models R51, R66 and R71 are possibilities.

BMW R12s captured in the desert and being used by British troops. (E. Thorne)

A BMW R75 undergoing evaluation after being captured in the desert. Note the British registration on the petrol tank. (IWM, STT 6996N)

BSA

BSA was the largest motorcycle manufacturer in Britain at the outbreak of the Second World War, and perhaps naturally the largest supplier of motorcycles to the armed services, its involvement with the services having started during the First World War.

During 1929, three BSA S29 De-Luxe models were purchased from the company by the War Office for participation in the seven-make trials of the time, but the testing was cancelled prior to completion because of hasty decisions within the higher echelons of the War Office at the time. During the early 1930s the War Office began to favour multi-cylinder engines, believing them to be quieter than single-cylinder versions, and BSA supplied sizeable quantities of their 498 cc War Office V-twin model to both the War Office and the Air Ministry between 1933 and 1937, with minor changes to each contract.

By 1935, War Office opinion about machine suitability had changed yet again, and it now came out in favour of either 350 cc or 500 cc capacity single-cylinder machines of either SV or OHV configuration – twin-cylinder machines had proved to be no quieter after all. BSA was thus to submit its current W35–6 model for War Office evaluation, alongside products from six other principal motorcycle manufacturers of the time.

Following completion of the 1935 War Office trials, however, the W35–6 model failed to meet with War Office approval. In the following year, BSA submitted another of its products for testing – its first 496 cc SV single-cylinder motorcycle, the first M20. Completion of the testing this time, however, showed the machine's engine to have suffered unacceptable wear and it was thus declared unsuitable for War Office procurement.

Undefeated, BSA was to submit a further three improved versions for War Office evaluation during 1937 and two of these were subjected to the standard military 10,000 mile reliability trial. Following the completion of the trial the MEE considered the reliability of the model as only 'fair', although it did note the type as 'suitable for WD requirements'. Thereon commenced a near thirty-year love hate relationship between the British military and the BSA M20 model, an affair that was to continue in certain isolated instances until 1971.

In 1937 the War Department (Army) received a batch of BSA's B20 model for employment as military training machines. A second order followed that was delivered during early 1938.

Also in 1938 the first sizeable War Office order was placed with BSA for the M20 model, along with a small order for some of the company's 'Gold Star' competition machines as well.

In 1939 further quantities of M20 models were ordered, as well as quantities of military specification C10 lightweight models, principally intended for military training. Following the outbreak of war in September of that year orders for the M20 model continued, although following the collapse of France in mid-1940 BSA, along with most other manufacturers, was inundated with War Office demands for machines of all types and that year supplied quantities of M20s, M21s, C11s, C12s, B29s, M22s, M23s and M24s, many simply militarized civilian destined models.

By 1939 military thinking had concluded that any purpose-built military motorcycle had to be of a lightweight design, with a specified upper-weight limit, a reasonable performance and other stated qualities necessary for service use. So, following several prototypes in 1940 and one production batch in 1941, the W-B30 350 cc lightweight service model was suddenly cancelled by the War Office during late 1941, just as mass production was about to commence. As a result the service-rider was to be sentenced to the M20 model for the remainder of the war and beyond.

During 1944 a War Office standardization committee was established to assess the possibility of a new universal motorcycle for the services. Yet again military opinion changed, now back in favour of twin-cylinder machines. BSA offered a twin-cylinder SV machine of 500 cc capacity for War Office consideration. The proposed new requirement and the establishment of a standardization committee were the result of the Ministry of Supply becoming increasingly concerned about the numerous types of machines then employed throughout the services and the subsequently heavy demands for spares and repair facilities – a complicated situation to administer if nothing else.

Development of the twin-cylinder machine, however, was slow and lacked the urgency of earlier years, particularly as the end of the war was now in sight. It was not until well after the end of the Second World War, during the late 1940s, that the results of the 'twins' trials were available. The motorcycle eventually chosen was Triumph's 500 cc SV-twin TRW model. In many ways BSA was to have the last laugh, as their M20 model was to continue in service as the standard military model right up to the end of the 1950s, and then remain serving in limited numbers, notably overseas and with Territorial units, until the end of the following decade. In British military service, the M20 model actually outlived the TRW Triumph, a supposed replacement for the ancient BSA. The M20 further served alongside the 350 cc OHV unit-construction BSA W-B40 service model, which was introduced during the early 1960s and which served in limited numbers up to the mid-1980s. The last M20 model was not retired from military service until the beginning of the 1970s!

BSA Model S29 De-Luxe 499 cc SV Single-Cylinder – 1929

Three of BSA's Model S29 De-Luxes were purchased by the War Office for evaluation purposes for the seven-make trial of 1929 and were all of standard civilian specification of the time, although fitted with the then optional electric lighting.

The War Office trials, conducted by the MWEE, were never completed satisfactorily and the results never properly assessed nor collated. As the War Office was impatient to receive a replacement for their ageing Triumph Model H machines, it did not want to wait for the results of the trials, which were therefore cancelled, and it went ahead of its own accord, purchasing machines manufactured by Douglas.

BSA War Office Twin 498 cc OHV V-Twin (Experimental) – 1932

According to surviving official documentation, this motorcycle was not actually purchased by the War Office, but was loaned by BSA for evaluation purposes and remained the property of the company for the duration of the assessment period.

Catalogue picture of a 1929 BSA Model S29 de luxe, as bought for use in the 1929 trials. (BSA Cycles Ltd)

This motorcycle evolved as a result of the War Office's desire for quieter machines, at the time its opinion being that twin-cylinder machines were generally quieter than single-cylinder models.

The War Office Twin was tested against contemporary products from rival manufacturers, these being the Douglas L29 and the Matchless Silver Arrow. Following completion of the standard War Office 10,000 mile test, it proved to be the most reliable of the three machines. However, although ultimately recommended as a model suitable for military service, concern was expressed over the considerable wear to the pistons and cylinders of the machine.

BSA War Office Twin 498 cc OHV V-Twin – 1933–7

Following the largely successful testing of BSA's experimental War Office twin-cylinder machine during 1932, the company duly began to receive orders for production models of the type during the following year from the War Office, delivery of the first examples probably being made during late 1933.

As the model settled into military service it was obvious that the problem of piston and cylinder wear that had afflicted the experimental model of 1932 had not been fully resolved with the production machines. It was generally thought that lubrication problems in the cylinder areas were the root cause of the wear problem. BSA itself specified the use of a high quality lubricating oil for use in the machine. Once in service use, however, even in peacetime, machines were frequently lubricated by an inferior quality product, which the War Office had purchased in bulk and which was intended for general use in everything from tanks to stationary engines. During 1935 the MEE tested examples of the BSA War Office Twin using Wakefield Castrol XL and the results indicated that this or similar offered far better protection against wear than the standard War Office bulk M265 grade oil.

BSA War Office Twin. Note that this example has been converted to foot change, as were all later versions supplied to the War Office. (PRO, WO 194 (45) – 6937)

Various minor changes affected the model during the span of its production and supply to the War Office, the majority of these affecting different contracts as opposed to individual machines. Notable changes in 1935 included the installation of cast-iron pistons, a modified lube system, and air-hardened cylinders being fitted on some machines. Late machines probably all had pillion equipment fitted and certainly foot-change gearboxes.

It is interesting to note that on the outbreak of the Second World War in 1939, the War Office and the Air Ministry still had numbers of the Twins 'on the books' and some still in first-line use, particularly in situations where the Norton 16H and BSA M20 models had not yet been delivered as replacements.

BSA 249 CC OHV SINGLE-CYLINDER – 1936

This machine was tested and rejected on the same day, although the reasons for its rejection remain unknown. Information on this model's performance during testing unfortunately no longer exists, and neither is it certain which model was tested as BSA had three listed that year – the B–2, the B–18 Light De-luxe, and the B–3 De-luxe.

BSA B23 348 CC SV SINGLE CYLINDER – 1936

Tested over one day, this motorcycle was then returned presumably because it was deemed unsuitable.

Trials were also carried out with a BSA 249 cc OHV, a 500 cc OHV and a 348 cc OHV during the same day, and it would seem that these too were rejected by the War Office.

BSA B26 348 CC OHV SINGLE-CYLINDER – 1936

This machine was tested and returned on the same day as the three other models supplied by BSA. Archive details on this model's performance during testing unfortunately no longer exist.

BSA M22 496 CC OHV SINGLE-CYLINDER – 1936

This motorcycle was brought in along with three other BSA models for a one-day test, the outcome of which is unknown.

BSA WAR OFFICE TWIN (LIGHTENED) 498 CC OHV V-TWIN –1934

The problem of piston and cylinder wear on the production War Department Twin was not the only concern of the service authorities of the time. It had also been tentatively suggested that the standard production model was not lightweight, and considerably heavy to manoeuvre, particularly off-road. A lighter version, coupled with less power and thus easier to ride, was suggested, with a maximum speed of 50 m.p.h.

BSA set about reducing the weight of the machine by taking a standard model and fitting a lighter saddle, an Elektron gearbox shell, lighter flywheels, a smaller fuel tank and wheel rims and tyres of a smaller width while removing the steering-damper and the rear rack. It also lightened the crankcase shield, mildly retuned the engine and modified the top of the frame. However, after the

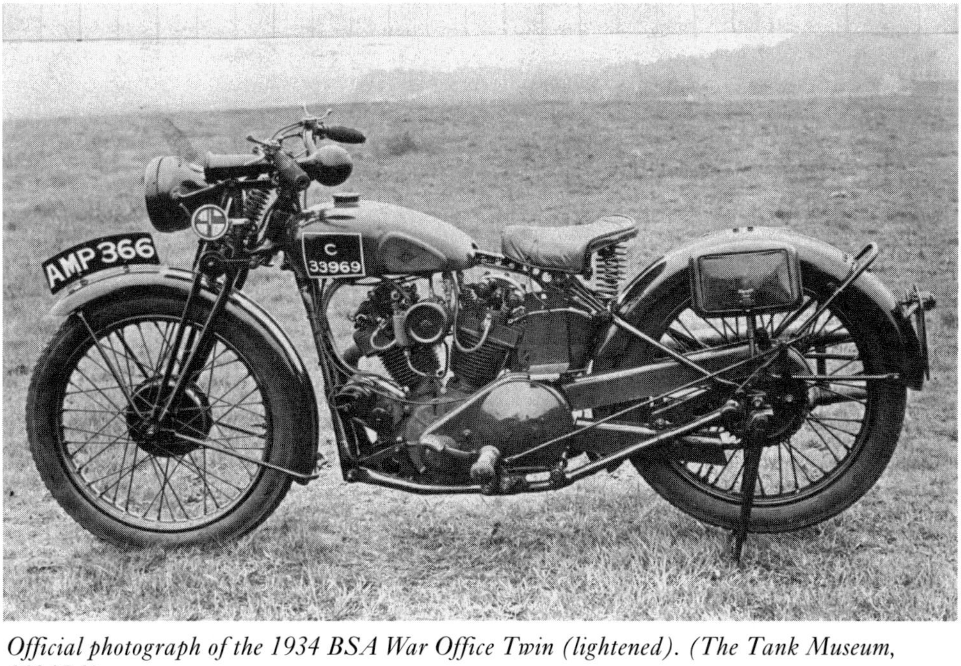

Official photograph of the 1934 BSA War Office Twin (lightened). (The Tank Museum, 162/B1)

modifications were completed the machine was a mere 22 lb lighter than the standard model.

Testing concluded that the weight saving was so small as not to matter and the detuning of the engine, coupled with the still heavy weight of the machine (380 lb), notably impaired the overall performance, particularly on cross-country and on fuel consumption (46 m.p.h. compared with the standard version's 53.4 m.p.h.). The end result was that no further action was taken in respect of lightening the War Office Twin, the project remaining a one-off, with the War Office now looking toward new designs of machine as an alternative to the BSA Twin.

It is also worth noting that the Army thought that the steering-damper was essential for cross-country use and it did not like the deletion of the rear rack for obvious reasons.

BSA Model W35–6 499 cc SV Single-Cylinder – 1935 Evaluation Model

In 1935 the War Office instigated a trial involving the motorcycle products from seven different manufacturers including BSA, with all manufacturers supplying 4-stroke single-cylinder machines of either SV or OHV engine configuration. BSA's model was its 499 cc single-cylinder SV Model W35–6, which was subsequently purchased.

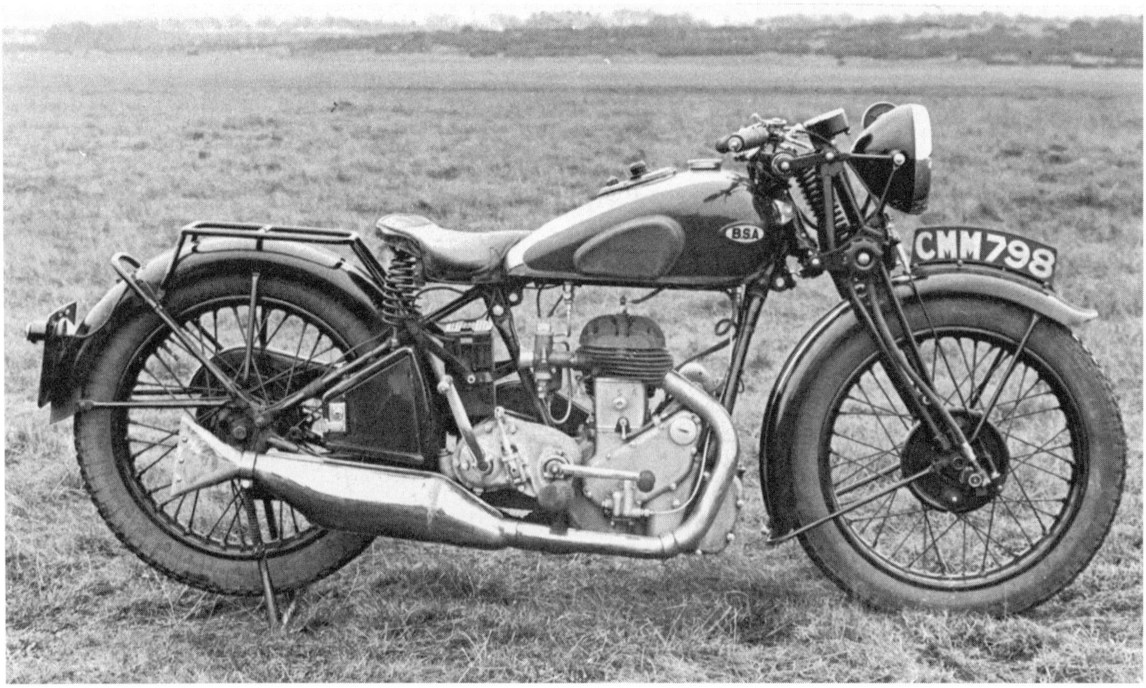

Official photograph of the 1935 BSA W35–6, used in the 1935 trials. (The Tank Museum, 138/F5)

The model was ultimately to fail the MEE 10,000 mile test with several faults noted throughout the course of the 8,000 miles the test example actually completed. At 339 miles the engine seized due to the piston sticking in the cylinder-bore through lack of lubrication due to loss of oil. A further problem occurred at 2,498 miles when the fuel tank started to leak. Other notable defects were a broken oil-gauge and a slight knock from the engine, plus the machine's brakes were considered to be rather poor in the wet. At 6,237 miles the test model was fitted with a new engine that was carefully run-in, but by the time 7,563 miles had been completed a cracked cylinder-barrel was noted between the cylinder-bore and the exhaust-port. Other modifications and alterations included converting the test model from a hand-change to a foot-change gearbox at 2,498 recorded test miles, modifying the lube system to overcome the seizure fault, and at some stage, fitting another frame.

BSA Model M20 496 cc SV Single-Cylinder – 1936 Evaluation Test Model

Following the failure of the company's W35–6 model during the 1935 trials, BSA submitted a new model for War Office evaluation during 1936 in a further bid to win another government contract.

The M20 test model was initially evaluated by the MEE at Farnborough, Hampshire, where it showed itself to be at least comparable to Norton's similar 16H model. In light of this, a full reliability trial of the type was initiated.

Completion of the trial was not as successful as had been hoped, although the model did improve on the performance of the previously tested W35–6 model by at the least completing the trial programme.

The old BSA curse of cylinder-bore and piston wear was again highlighted during the course of the test, a new cylinder, piston and other engine components having to be fitted at the 6,538 mile stage.

The result was that the MEE considered the reliability of the model as 'fair' and thus not entirely suitable for military service.

BSA Model M20 496 cc SV Single-Cylinder – 1937 (Improved Version)

Having noted the comments of the MEE about the W35–6 model of 1935 and the original M20 model of the following year, BSA supplied a further three M20 models to the War Office under contract 294/C.991 during 1937. These three had been fitted with improved components to offset the previously noted reliability and wear problems.

Two of the three examples purchased were delivered to the MEE for use in the standard War Office 10,000 mile reliability trial, while the third example was delivered to a normal service unit for general use and assessment.

The two examples tested showed improved reliability figures on completion of the trials, although they were still only considered 'fair' as opposed to 'good'. This said, however, the military authorities did note the model as suitable for their requirements. Thereafter, the military model M20, as it was known to literally thousands of British servicemen and others, was born.

Official photograph of the 1936 BSA M20 prototype (the first military version). Note the lack of an engine-head steady and 20 in rims instead of 19 in (as used on later versions). (IWM, KID 5608)

Modified prototype BSA M20. Note the added head steady and air filter. (IWM, KID 5738)

It should be noted that these pre-production M20 models differed to a considerable degree from the later, more commonly encountered wartime production version. Differences were to include mechanical as well as cycle components, although the model was not generally altered in design to the version familiar to many until midway through the 1939 production year.

BSA MODEL B20 249 CC SV SINGLE-CYLINDER – 1937–8 (H–B20 AND J–B20)

The BSA B20 model was primarily a civilian specification motorcycle that was purchased by the War Office principally for use as a learner-rider training machine and also for light communication duties.

The first contract was placed with BSA and delivered to the War Office during 1937, the machines supplied therefore built to the specification laid down by BSA for that year. The second, larger contract was placed and largely completed within the same year, the last deliveries being made to the War Office during early 1938. However, the second contract was placed after the commencement of production for the 1938 season, so these machines were constructed to the specification for the 1938 model, prefixed by the letter 'J' rather than the first contract's letter 'H'.

A final point to note is that the B20 model was purchased without prior testing and evaluation by the MEE as was standard practice.

Official photograph of a 1937 BSA B20. The 1938 version differed only in minor details. (IWM, KID 5655)

Official photograph of a 1938 BSA M24. Note the very non-military finish. (IWM, KID 5613)

BSA MODEL M24 (GOLD STAR) 496 CC OHV SINGLE-CYLINDER – 1938 (J–M24)

In a shrewd attempt to make its motorcycle products even more favourable with the War Office, BSA persuaded the War Office to purchase some of its 500 cc 'Gold Star' models for trials and competitions of both a national and international nature during 1938. A major competition win would provide the country, the War Office and BSA itself with considerable publicity. To gain further favour from the War Office BSA provided one of its own competition riders to coach the British Army teams.

Following War Office approval and the coaching of the Army trials teams by the BSA rider, the teams competed in all the leading events of the time, giving a particularly good performance at the 1938 International Six-Day Trial in Wales. It has been suggested that this success led to the War Office's first order for a large batch of M20 models, the request coming only days after the successes at the trials.

BSA MODEL C10 249 CC SV SINGLE-CYLINDER – 1939–40 (K–C10 AND W–C10)

The BSA C10 model supplied to the War Office was basically a standard civilian specification with a few minor alterations. These included the use of WM2 wheel rims so that the wider War Department tyre could be used, and the addition of an ignition warning-light and a small carrier on top of the rear mudguard.

A BSA C10 in service with the Royal Navy. (IWM, A2831)

The model was supplied under two contracts, with some 1,935 machines being provided in total. The initial pre-war contract was for 585 machines of the 'K' specification of 1939, while the second contract was for the 'W' type of 1940. As between the civilian and the military versions of the motorcycle, there were also slight differences between the 1939 and the 1940 models. These included the tool-box, the speedometer-drive, the engine-tappet cover, the rear light, the number-plate and the front fork-damping, which was repositioned.

The C10 model was purchased with the primary intention of providing a cheap, lightweight utility machine for training duties and light communication work – basically the same requirements for which its predecessor, the B20 model had been employed. The C10 models, however, were a distinct improvement on the B20s, having a foot-change gearbox for a start.

Unlike the B20 model, the BSA C10 was tested for suitability by the MEE, although this was of no real value since the first batch of the type had already been purchased and put into service prior to the testing. The model was compared with Royal Enfield's then similar offering, the 250 cc SV Model D, also purchased by the War Office in similar quantities and for a similar purpose. The official side considered the Royal Enfield Model D to have a slightly better performance than the BSA C10 model, although the BSA product was considered to be more dependable. Although neither type was considered to be outstandingly reliable, on inspection at the 5,000 mile point of testing neither displayed any real wear to the mechanical components, and both models were noted as suitable for the War Office, for training and light communication duties.

The C10 model was thus used by the War Office until at least 1942. Thereafter many were transferred to other government departments for the remainder of the war. As far as the training role of the C10 model was concerned, it was replaced by early production, larger capacity machines, themselves withdrawn from first-line service following replacement by newer or improved types.

BSA Model C12 348 cc SV Single-Cylinder – 1940 (W–C12)

The BSA C12 model of 1940 was the final model of the 'C' group of lightweight utilities, having a larger engine capacity (348 cc) than the 249 cc SV C10 model and the 249 cc OHV C11 model. Both the C10 and C11 models continued in production after the war in much the same basic mechanical format, although when the pre-unit construction C12 model reappeared during the 1950s it had an engine capacity of 249 cc and not 348 cc, as its predecessor had in 1940.

Perhaps rather strangely, the War Office did not pursue any contracts for the supply of the BSA C12 model despite the engine being comparable in performance with both the Royal Enfield Model C and the Triumph Model 3SW, both SV 350 cc machines and then in current production and use.

The model was not entirely rejected for service use, however. In September 1940 the Admiralty Department (Navy) received some sixteen examples of the type to order.

BSA Model M22 496 cc OHV Single-Cylinder – 1939 (K–M22)

According to the BSA factory ledgers, six M22 models were supplied to the War Office direct from the factory in September 1939. The contract number is not known and neither are the precise details relating to specification of the models supplied. It can be presumed, however, that the six examples supplied were civilian models, militarized as far as paintwork was concerned, and immediately available for delivery.

BSA Model M23 (Silver Sports) 496 cc OHV Single-Cylinder – 1939 (K–M23)

Due to the immediate demands for machines of all types following the outbreak of war, as well as the six Model M22s, a slightly larger quantity of the similar M23 'Silver Sports' was also supplied. According to the factory ledgers, nineteen examples of the 1939 specification M23 model were provided, probably standard civilian models finished in the usual military paint scheme.

BSA Model M24 (Gold Star) 496 cc OHV Single-Cylinder – 1939 (K–M24)

One of BSA's top of the range models, the 1939 specification M24 'Gold Star' model was again ready for immediate delivery from the factory's stock of completed machines, a total of eight being supplied directly to the War Office. It can be presumed that they were close to standard civilian specification and fitted with full road equipment, again being militarized only to the extent of the paintwork. It is probable that the supplied examples were used for general army duties, along with all the other hurriedly requisitioned models, rather than for competition use, despite the type being a powerful competition model.

BSA Model M21 591 cc SV Single-Cylinder – 1939 (K–M21)

These machines were the last of the 'M' group BSA models to be supplied to the War Office direct from the factory in October 1939, only a few weeks after the outbreak of war. As with the similar M22, M23 and M24 models, the type was a civilian specification model and available for immediate delivery, although only one machine was actually supplied, rather than the several examples of other types, all of which may have been 'impressed' into service.

BSA Model C11 249 cc OHV Single-Cylinder – 1940 (W–C11)

Some 530 C11s were supplied during early 1940 to the Office of the High Commission of India, London, presumably for service overseas. Although the machine was based on the 1940 civilian specification C11 model and shared many parts with its C10 stable-mate, the following alterations were incorporated into the government contract: a rear carrier above the mudguard; a tank-top mounted air filter (not the later military Vokes Universal type, however), indicating possible use in a hot, dusty climate; an additional tool-box; a standard mag-dyno unit in place of the usual coil and car type distributor components; a standard pattern saddle in place of the rubber Dunlop type; and different oil and petrol filler-caps, similar to those fitted to the M20 model but of a smaller size.

BSA Model B29 (Silver Sports) 348 cc OHV Single-Cylinder – 1940 (W–B29)

The BSA B29 model with its sporting performance and single-cylinder engine fitted with hairpin valve-springs was a new model introduced during late 1939 for the 1940 production range. Not originally intended for military service, few of the type had been sold to the civilian market of the time before a contract was issued by the War Office for immediate supply of the model.

Probably militarized only to the extent of its overall service paintwork, an estimated 167 examples were supplied to the War Office during the latter half of 1940. Smaller quantities of impressed machines from dealers' stocks may also have been made available.

BSA Model M21 591 cc SV Single-Cylinder – 1940 (W–M21)

The BSA M21 model supplied to the War Office held both the same demand date and the same contract number as the comparatively small quantity of B29 models also supplied. The demand date followed the evacuation of the British Army at Dunkirk and the loss of much equipment.

It is possible that these M21 models were originally destined for Holland, but had not been delivered before that country fell to the Germans. It is therefore not confirmed whether the machines were militarized civilian specification models or purpose-built military types.

The M21 model was not generally a faster machine than the M20 model. Although it had a larger capacity engine, this was designed primarily to provide a greater degree of flexibility for pulling a sidecar, in the nature of low-speed, high-gear engine torque, rather than additional speed. It is possible that several examples of the military supplied M21 model were ultimately to be fitted with sidecars for various purposes.

BSA Model WM21 600 cc SV Single-Cylinder SWD Combination – 1940

Tested in August 1940 against a standard Norton 'Big 4' and also an experimental 596 cc OHV Norton combination, this machine was found to perform better than the 'Big 4', but only comparable to the 596 cc combination. However, its top speed (46 m.p.h.) was considered too low for service use and its petrol consumption unacceptable. On the plus side, it was considered easier to handle than the two Nortons (largely because of its narrower track) and was less affected by the sidecar wheel's drag. Needless to say it was not recommended for service use and was considered to need redesigning.

Specification wise, it could carry three men and 1 cwt of equipment, weighed 5¾ cwt, and had 3.50–19 tyres; how the sidecar wheel drive worked is not known.

BSA Experimental Model 500 cc SV – 1940

Few details are known about this model, but it is probable that it was a lightweight M20 and it used an experimental frame (EX315). Other manufacturers at this time (such as Norton) were also looking at lightening their current War Department models as an alternative to the special lightweights currently under development.

BSA 348 cc Experimental Lightweight OHV Single-Cylinder – 1940 Prototype

BSA developed a 348 cc OHV single-cylinder experimental model during the early part of 1940 as a result of the War Office's considerable interest in a purpose-designed military lightweight machine with the performance of a standard 500 cc SV model.

The original War Office requirement was issued during 1939, but at this time BSA, along with Matchless, were not invited to supply a suitable model for evaluation against the three types tested from Norton, Triumph and Royal Enfield.

Tested by the War Office during the spring of 1940, after it had been developed and supplied under contract, the one example produced proved to be of satisfactory performance, comparing well with Triumph's 3TW. On this basis a second machine was actioned for further testing with a number of amendments incorporated.

It is of note that BSA based this experimental lightweight machine on their 1940 B29 'Silver Sports' model, although obviously with many modifications and changes, including weight reduction. This machine can generally be considered as the military-designed B30 prototype, a model with considerable potential yet no future, at least not with the military.

Official photograph of a pre-production BSA B30. (IWM, KID 5045)

BSA MODEL B30 348 CC OHV SINGLE-CYLINDER – 1940 PRE-PRODUCTION VERSION

Following the success of the pilot version, this second version, incorporating the amendments, had gained 25 lb in weight. After 5,000 miles of testing against an Ariel W/NG, the motorcycle was found to be in good condition, and its increase in weight was noted down as not seriously affecting its ease of handling. Subsequently, fifty machines were ordered to the same specification, although these were some 15 lb heavier because of restrictions on the amount of aluminium that could be used.

BSA MODEL B30 348 CC OHV SINGLE-CYLINDER – 1941 (W–B30) PRODUCTION MODELS

A production batch of fifty B30s was supplied under contract during the spring of 1941 and distributed among units and formations in order to further assess the type's suitability for military service. Although the majority were to be received by British Army units, it is interesting to note that three of the fifty examples were allocated to the United States, two to Canada and a further one to Associated Motor Cycles, who would fit teledraulic front forks.

The modifications incorporated in the fifty pre-production examples over the original 1940 prototypes included: a smaller front brake; a different headlight and stays, the former containing a dry-cell battery; a direct lighting system, the usual dynamo replaced by an alternator situated atop the magneto; the removal of the standard lead-acid battery and carrier; a repositioned field-stand; a different chainguard; a different fuel tank, which had no knee-grip rubbers; and many other details too numerous to list.

Official photograph of a production version of the BSA W-B30. (REME Museum)

The War Office were extremely pleased with the overall performance and suitability of the B30 model, placing a larger order with BSA for the supply of the first of supposedly many, under contract number 294/C.13290. Without prior warning, however, the War Office abruptly changed the contract's specification for the supply of 10,000 standard M20 SV models. The likely explanation would seem to be last minute concern by the War Office over the potential difficulties of calling yet another model into military service, together with all the necessary spares and servicing requirements.

BSA Model M20 496 cc SV Single-Cylinder – 1939–45 (K–M20 and W–M20)

Viewed as a near failure in the eyes of the War Office in 1936, this model was ultimately to evolve into perhaps the most illustrious and longest serving model in the history of British military motorcycling, not to mention becoming the most numerous type produced for the War Office itself.

The military model M20 was produced by BSA in several variations until 1942, when the type was largely standardized, undergoing only minor modifications thereafter until the end of the Second World War. The very earliest examples supplied, the K–M20 models from the 1939 production year, were generally a type constructed from a combination of standard and de-luxe model components with the addition of certain military specified fittings. (However, it is interesting to note that, principally from contract number 294/C.3655 onwards, the factory ledgers detail the type as 'de-luxe'.)

The military specified additional fittings included the large 8 in Lucas DU142 headlight, complete with the switchpanel and ammeter, a timing-gear cover incorporating a screw-in plug permitting access to the magneto drive-pinion nut, and 'winged' filler caps for both petrol and oil tanks. Other points of interest, concerning certain early W–M20 examples as well as the War Department K–M20 models, include the presence of a semi-rod operated front brake, a screw-in speedometer drive-box on the front wheel brake-plate face, a rather bulbous 3½ gallon fuel tank, and an alloy tappet cover carrying the BSA 'piled-arms' emblem, and the lack of a cylinder-head engine-steady bracket, pillion seat and footrests. Both front and rear number-plates were fitted as standard, and some models also had an oil-pressure button-indicator incorporated in the timing cover. The early military M20 models were fitted with a long field-stand on the rear nearside of the machine, attached to, and pivoted from, a lug brazed on to the upper nearside rear-frame tube (deleted on later models). When not in use this stand was secured horizontally along the rear nearside of the model by means of a spring-clip attached to a stud affixed to the central rear mudguard stay-cum-lifting handle (also deleted on later versions).

According to the factory ledgers, a number of the later K–M20 models within contract 294/C.3655 were originally destined for customers in Sweden, South Africa and India, despite the war having started, and that even after some six months of hostilities, BSA along with several other manufacturers were still selling their products to overseas governments and commissions including Holland, Ireland, India and South Africa as well as civilian dealers and distributors.

Official photograph of a 1939 BSA M20 ('K–M20'). (IWM, KID 5727)

From October 1939 detail changes were made to the W–M20, as the former K–M20 was now known. These included a new less bulbous 3 gallon fuel tank and girder-forks minus the hand-adjusted damper-knob, which was replaced by a simple locknut impossible to adjust while riding. The speedometer driver was relocated to the nearside of the front wheel, the valanced rear mudguard was removed, and finally Jaegar speedometers were fitted to some models.

During late 1940 certain numbers of civilian specification M20 models were purchased by the War Office direct from the BSA factory, mainly to de-luxe specification as applicable to the civilian market of the time, although a few standard examples were also supplied, probably militarized only to the extent of the colour scheme.

The 1941 model differed only slightly from the 1940 model, both front and rear number-plates being removed, and the alloy tappet cover replaced by a plain steel version.

Between 1941 and 1942 further changes to the M20 were made, including the reinstallation of the offside hand-adjusted damper-knob. Service experience of the model, particularly in North Africa where proper roads were few, had shown the need for readily-adjustable fork damping in order to offset wear and possible failure of the fork. The first damper-knobs were made of bakelite, and later of pressed steel. Other changes included the use of a 6 in Lucas DU42 headlight, complete with the hooded, slotted black-out shield, instead of the 8 in DU142 type, and the fitting of the universal War Department pattern L-WD-MCT1 tail-light. By early 1942 a new full-size rear carrier had been fitted to accommodate the newly introduced universal War Department pattern steel pannier-frames and bags, together with a pair of lower support-stays for the frames. Pillion equipment was also now standardized and a pillion seat and footrests were fitted to all production machines. To accommodate the new equipment it was necessary to alter the design and mounting position of the long nearside field-stand, which was now much longer than before. The securing clip was repositioned to sit just above and forward of the nearside rear wheel spindle nut, the stand sitting at an angle of approximately 45° as opposed to near horizontally as before.

Late 1942 saw the deletion of rubber fittings on all new machines, the replacement of the handlebar grips with universal War Department canvas items and the relocation of the horn to the nearside front engine-plate on many machines. Further modifications include the removal of the rib-centred rear mudguard in favour of a simplified plain item, although the front mudguard continued to retain the ribbed centre until the end of the war.

During the latter half of 1943 the girder-fork steering-damper was removed from all new machines, the crankcase sump-shield was redesigned to become a pressed steel item incorporating additional protection at the sides for both the engine and frame-rails, and the fuel tank was altered by having the rear offside corner removed to accommodate the substantial hose section leading from the tank-top mounted Universal War Department pattern Vokes air filter to the carburettor air intake. This last modification was carried out on a large proportion of machines destined for service in hot, dusty climates. By early 1945 the Vokes filter was fitted as standard to the fuel tank of all new models irrespective of where they were destined to serve, the filter being secured to the tank by mounting-strips attached to the previously redundant knee-grip locating

A mid-war BSA M20 in service in Algiers, early 1945. Its rider is Peter Sharp. (Peter Sharp)

holes on either side of the fuel tank. The last notable change to effect the model during the war occurred in early 1945, when the lighting system was altered by removing the ammeter and installing a simple push-button 'change-over' switch for the headlight, the main lighting switch now being of a different pattern, located on a simple bracket beneath the offside of the saddle.

The vast majority of BSA M20 models delivered were employed by the War Department (Army), although smaller quantities were also used by both the Admiralty (Navy) and the Air Ministry (RAF). It is interesting to note that the Air Ministry used quantities of the model fitted with a Swallow-manufactured sidecar, and that a great number of the smaller M20 model contracts throughout the Second World War specified sidecar-lugs for the frame, generally removed from all the larger contracts, which were specifically solo only.

Although intended as a general-purpose motorcycle for convoy escort and long-distance communications duties, due to the sheer number supplied the model was employed ultimately in every theatre of war and for virtually every purpose imaginable, whether suitable or not. It is perhaps for this reason that the model is the one best remembered by and familiar to most ex-servicemen and other individuals when military motorcycles are mentioned. The post-war service of the BSA M20 model further increases its renown, the type being retained in service as the standard War Department motorcycle throughout the national service period of the 1950s and onwards in limited numbers until the end of the next decade, this despite the fact that it was never totally suitable, and was most probably retained only because of the huge quantities of machines and parts available following the end of the war.

Admittedly, by the end of the Second World War the model's reliability was reasonably good, having served through six years of harsh conflict without any major failing. The M20's clutch had always been a problem, especially if contaminated by oil, and would drag or slip when hot, not to mention not fully releasing on occasions (even when new!) due to the limitations of the single-spring multi-plate design. The post-war service authorities were so concerned about the problem that a modification directive was eventually issued during 1958, permitting the installation of four small screws to the central spring-nut in an attempt to effect some adjustment to the non-adjustable design! Another M20 idiosyncrasy, never fully resolved, was a tendency for the machine to refuse to start when hot, largely due to the heat from the cylinder evaporating the fuel in the carburettor before it could enter the engine. The model was also prone to backfire through the carburettor causing a fire, and post-war regulations invariably specified the carriage of a fire extinguisher somewhere on the machine.

With so many examples produced, the BSA M20 is a common machine today, although few retain their correct original factory specification, especially the early wartime or pre-war examples. During the course of the Second World War and throughout the post-war period, virtually all M20s were rebuilt by the military at least once, if not several times. Engines were changed around under service-exchange schemes and rebuilt models were constructed from stocks of parts assembled from all years and contracts. In certain instances, the military authorities would fit a brand-new frame or engine-unit to a rebuilt machine and not stamp the item fitted with a number, further complicating dating such a machine today.

RAF M20 in service with a Radio Observation Unit in Sutherland, Scotland, during 1942. The rider is Reg Humphries. Jackson, his colleague, is seated on the rear carrier. They were the only two motorcyclists attached to the unit. (Reg Humphries)

Official photograph of the BSA Twin, as supplied at the end of the war. (REME Museum)

BSA 495 CC SV PARALLEL TWIN-CYLINDER – 1944–5 PROTOTYPE

This model was developed by the company towards the end of the Second World War as BSA's answer to the War Office's request for a standardized military motorcycle to replace most types then in use. Once again, thinking had changed and was now inclined towards a twin-cylinder machine of 500 cc capacity, retaining an SV configuration.

A sole example was built, fitted with telescopic forks, and submitted for evaluation. However, the War Office's testing programme was to become a long, drawn-out affair and interest in the project declined somewhat with the end of the war clearly approaching. Following the cessation of hostilities, and faced with the prospect of enormous stocks of now redundant machines and stark post-war economies, the programme was temporarily suspended. When interest recommenced during the late 1940s the War Office in the end favoured Triumph's TRW model.

Douglas

Douglas were the largest manufacturer and supplier of military motorcycles for the allied forces during the First World War, the company name being as familiar then as perhaps BSA's was to become in the next global conflict. However, during the interwar years the company's business with the War Office gradually diminished and by the outbreak of the Second World War the Douglas company had ceased supplying any motorcycles to the military, its role during the war concerned with other forms of mechanical and industrial production.

In 1929 a quantity of the company's 350 cc SV flat-twin Model L29 were hastily purchased by the War Office, which was too impatient to wait for the results of the seven-make trials currently being conducted by the MWEE and in which the L29 was involved. During 1931, a Model A31 was tested, but ultimately was not pursued as the MWEE stated a preference for the latest version of the existing L29 model, the L29/4, following comparative testing.

In 1934 Douglas submitted two examples of the company's 500 cc 'Blue Chief' model for War Office evaluation, one fitted with a 4-speed gearbox and the other a 3-speed. Following testing, the MEE concluded that the 4-speed version was no better than the 3-speed. Another 3-speed was purchased for further evaluation during 1935, but the model failed to pass approval for service.

Following this, Douglas had no further involvement with the War Office in respect of motorcycles until about 1944, when the Ministry of Supply requested the company to produce two prototype machines to the late war design specification for a proposed standard military motorcycle. However, neither of these prototypes met with approval, and Triumph secured the contract with its TRW model. Douglas had one final involvement with the War Office in the immediate post-war period, when the company supplied to contract seven machines of 125 cc engine capacity with post-war registration numbers of 20 CL 57 to 20 CL 62. Little more is known about these.

Official photograph of the first version of the 1929 Douglas L29. (PRO, WO 194 (45) – 5872)

DOUGLAS MODELS L29, L29/2, L29/3, L29/4 348 CC SV FLAT-TWIN – 1929–32

The Douglas Model L29 was procured initially as a hurried replacement for the War Office's fleet of by then ageing and obsolescent machines, the bulk of which were of Triumph origin. By 1929 officials at the War Office were too impatient for a suitable replacement motorcycle to wait for the MWEE to collate the results of the various machines on trial, and instead instigated a much shortened trial between the Douglas L29 and a Triumph Model NL3. The results showed in favour of the Douglas model, being lighter and easier to handle, and a first contract for supply of the type was placed.

Although the seven-make trial was concluded during late 1929, principally because of the actions of the War Office, testing continued on a reduced scale and the Douglas, AJS and Matchless machines were chosen for further evaluation. The MWEE report concluded that it had made no decisions as a result of these tests. Relevant or otherwise, the War Office was to purchase more Douglas machines, all Model L29 but with detail changes from contract to contract, hence designations L29/2, L29/3 and L29/4.

It is worth noting that Douglas listed the Model L29 for 1929 only, the 'L' designation standing for 'lightweight', even though it was only marginally different to a heavyweight model, the B29. The L29 was replaced the following year by the Model L3, which was a completely different machine and also a true lightweight. Evidently, after 1930 the L29 was built exclusively to War Office order.

An improved version of the Douglas L29, termed the L29/3. Among other detail changes, the footboards have been replaced by footrests. (PRO, WO 194 (45) – 6893)

The final version of the Douglas L29, termed the L29/4. Note the totally different frame, which now has a centre stand. (PRO, WO 194 (45) – 6891)

Official photograph of the 1931 Douglas A31 test model. (IWM, KID 5432)

DOUGLAS MODEL A31 348 CC SV FLAT-TWIN – 1931

The Model A31 was new to the Douglas range of machines for 1931 and an example was tested by the MWEE for suitability for service usage. Following a period of evaluation, the model was considered to have satisfactory performance despite a defective piston gudgeon-pin causing a breakdown at the 4,850 mile stage of testing. To further assess the type's suitability, it was retained at Farnborough for comparative trials against the new Model L29/4 from the company, which itself was claimed to be an improvement over the then current Model L29/3.

Compared to the Model L29/4, the Model A31 was a true lightweight machine, weight reduction having been achieved by the lightening of various components. The MWEE, however, considered that eventually such lightened components would have to be restored to their original weight if they were to withstand rigorous usage under typical service conditions. Principally on this basis, the Model A31 was discarded in favour of the new Model L29/4.

DOUGLAS EXPERIMENTAL MODEL – 1932

Although this particular motorcycle is listed as an experimental model of 1931, it was not actually delivered until 1932.

At the time of writing, it had not proved possible to establish which Douglas model underwent testing.

DOUGLAS MODEL 5Y2 'BLUE CHIEF' 500 CC SV FLAT-TWIN – 1934–5

Three of these models were to be evaluated by the MEE, with the first two examples being loaned by the Douglas company during 1934. Of these, one was fitted with a 3-speed gearbox and the other with a 4-speed version. Tested during

Official photograph of the 1935 Douglas 'Blue Chief' (military version), as finally purchased with a 3-speed gearbox. (The Tank Museum, 245/D1)

November 1934, both examples were considered to have a good off-road performance, but the MEE found that no advantage could be gained by the 4-speed model. Consequently, another 3-speed model was purchased during 1935 for further testing, during which it completed some 2,930 miles on roads. The MEE reported the model to have a generally unsatisfactory performance with a high consumption of both oil and petrol, and mechanical reliability leaving much to be desired. In light of this, further trials of the model were discontinued.

DOUGLAS MODEL DV60 602 CC SV TRANSVERSE FLAT-TWIN – 1944–5 PROTOTYPE

The only motorcycle produced by the Douglas company during the Second World War, the DV60 was built in response to the War Office request for a standardized model of military motorcycle. The prototype machine constructed upon the specifications laid down by the Ministry of Supply was termed the Model DV60 and was submitted to the MEE at Farnborough for evaluation prior to the end of the war.

Testing was slow, however, and eventually abandoned completely because of the approaching end of hostilities. The entire project was then temporarily shelved. The model was eventually to reappear in early post-war years with a new frame and other minor detail alterations in an attempt to secure the contract, but ultimately this was won by Triumph's TRW model, the Douglas product along with offerings from both BSA and Norton, fading into obscurity.

Official photograph of the Douglas DV60, which is labelled as 'No. 2'. (IWM, MVE 12851/1)

Excelsior

The Excelsior company, like several other comparatively small manufacturers of motorcycles, entered the Second World War engaged with other forms of government contract work rather than the supply of motorcycles. With the larger manufacturers able to produce and deliver machines on a grand scale, the engineering facilities of smaller companies were deemed better utilized on other aspects of much needed war work.

However, the mid-war years saw the Excelsior company once again involved with limited motorcycle manufacturing, which continued alongside all other forms of contract work at the time.

The motorcycles produced included the famous 'Welbike' for the airborne forces, plus a very small quantity of the company's 'Universal' model of 125 cc capacity.

PROTOTYPE 'WELBIKE' 98 CC SINGLE-CYLINDER 2-STROKE – 1942

It should be noted that the very first 'Welbike' prototype model was not actually an Excelsior, the company having had no involvement with the original concept or design.

Along with the Royal Enfield WD/RE 'Flying Flea' and the James ML, the 'Welbike' was originally designed to provide the developing British Airborne Forces with a form of cheap, lightweight, reliable and semi-expendable form of

Official photograph of a pre-production Excelsior 'Welbike', modified to tow the container in which it was dropped. (Crown Copyright/A&AEE Boscombe Down, NB 3383–3)

transport for limited front-line use following a parachute or glider-landing. With space and weight at a premium within an aircraft, the size and weight of a motorcycle were crucial. A small folding design that could be dropped by parachute from an aircraft into a drop-zone was considered the best option, the machine being contained within a modified standard equipment container for the purposes of the drop. Once on the ground, the machine had to be capable of being released from the container and brought into use with the minimum of delay.

This prototype machine was produced at the military research establishment at Welwyn in Hertfordshire by J.R.V. Dolphin. The initial model was rather crude and basic, fitted with a 98 cc Villiers 2-stroke engine. The name 'Welbike' was coined a short time later, the first part of the name relating to the town where the machine was created. Following its construction, the prototype was subjected to a certain degree of testing to establish suitability for its intended purpose. It proved to be incredibly tough for such a small machine, and although really harsh treatment bent and distorted the type, it would not actually break apart. Interestingly, the prototype 'Welbike' reflected only a few features of the small Aveling Barford machine on test a few years earlier (see p. 20).

EXCELSIOR 'WELBIKE' 98 CC SINGLE-CYLINDER 2-STROKE – 1942 PRE-PRODUCTION VERSION

Following completion, the prototype machine was delivered to the Excelsior motorcycle company's premises for further development. It was examined in detail and minor development modifications were carried out on paper. New jigs and fixtures were made for the type incorporating these modifications, which included improvements to the fuel tank, tyres, footrests and throttle. A handful of pre-production machines were constructed to further assess the machine's suitability for production and service. How many of these versions were built has not been established, although an estimation would be a minimum of six. Incredibly, at least one survives today in private ownership.

Official photograph of a Mark 1 Excelsior 'Welbike'. This was modified like the pre-production version, but with a revised attachment method. (Crown Copyright/A&AEE Boscombe Down, NB 3383–1)

All of these pre-production versions were subjected to extremely varied and rigorous testing. Experiments conducted around September 1942 included dropping the suitably packaged machine from an aircraft for it to land with the aid of a parachute. It is likely that at least a couple of these pre-production versions were destroyed or damaged during such testing, although this cannot be firmly established.

A further point that arose from the trials was that the type's Villiers junior de-luxe engine-unit needed some slight modification. As standard, it was found that the little 98 cc unit was struggling to attain full power across poor, soft terrain with a fully-laden soldier sitting astride. Accordingly, the engine-unit was 'retuned' to provide a marginally increased performance, and built with generous clearances to the working parts so that it could be driven at full power immediately on starting, without risk of seizing or damaging the power plant.

All the experimentation on the model was carried out by the Airborne Forces Experimental Establishment (AFEE) at Sherburn-in-Elmet, near Leeds, Yorkshire. Besides the drop tests, the motorcycle was tested for its towing ability, the idea being to ascertain whether the machine could tow its own dropping container, fitted with wheels but loaded to 350 lb. This it managed, but only on hard level surfaces.

EXCELSIOR 'WELBIKE' 98 CC SINGLE-CYLINDER 2-STROKE – 1942–5

On completion of the trials and development work on the pre-production versions of the model, production of the type commenced in earnest. A small, simple design, the 'Welbike' proved to be cheap and fast to produce. This is highlighted by the fact that the model was painted while still on the production line. Following the fitting of the engine but before the fitting of the wheels, saddle and handlebar grips, the machine would be hung on a rail in the paintshop and completely sprayed with the appropriate colour. The wheels, saddle and grips would then be added and the whole put into another area for test and delivery! The 'Welbike' was the smallest motorcycle to see service with the British military and quite likely the smallest military machine in comparison to the products of other nations as well. Initially, all production was allocated for issue to the expanding airborne forces, particularly for use in parachute assaults, although by late 1943 the type was also in use by assault troops, mainly Army Commandos and Royal Marines (on charge to the Admiralty), on beachheads such as Anzio, Normandy, etc. By 1944, and into 1945, the 'Welbike' was also being used by the RAF, particularly in the Far East, where the type was considered ideal solo-transport around an airfield. Several aircrews 'acquired' examples to stow aboard their aircraft for such times as and when required.

Three main production versions of the 'Welbike' were built, each subsequent version improving slightly on the previous model, although the modifications were usually very minor. Total wartime 'Welbike' production, excluding the pre-production versions, was some 3,923 examples, of which the first 1,183 examples were of Mark 1 design. The most noticeable difference between this version and later versions was the lack of a rear mudguard. The next contract was for 1,400 examples of a lightly modified design, these machines designated Mark 2, Series 1. The third and final 'Welbike' contract was for 1,340 machines, which were again slightly improved, and designated Mark 2, Series 2. Apart from the lack of a rear

Above left: The Mark 1 Excelsior 'Welbike' with a dynamo attached. This conversion was known as a Wel-charger and was a modification carried out by the Airborne Forces. To ride the motorcycle the driving chain had to be removed and the dynamo turned 90° clockwise. Note the added centre stand. (Airborne Forces Museum). Above right: A Mark 2 Excelsior 'Welbike' in use in Singapore. (REME Museum)

The Wel-charger with the dynamo disconnected for riding. (Airborne Forces Museum)

mudguard on the Mark 1, other differences between the early and late machines included the saddle-type fuel tanks, which on early versions had a vent-screw in the left-hand tank to enable the unobstructed filling of the tank, and the filler-cap itself being incorporated with the pump that was used to pressurize the fuel tanks prior to starting the machine. This was a time-consuming operation and on later versions a filler-cap was added to the left-hand tank and the vent-screw switched over to the right tank, thus avoiding the need to remove the fuel pump. Other modifications affected the mounting of the tanks and the positioning of the fixing straps to the frame. As previously mentioned, all Mark 2 models acquired a small rear mudguard as well as splash-shielding between the fuel tanks.

Contrary to popular belief, the 'Welbike' was perhaps not as widely utilized as had been intended. Ideas for the use of the model, tested and practised in training, frequently proved impractical when it came to actual operations. Having landed in a hostile, exposed area, many parachutists were more concerned with getting under cover as fast as possible and the idea of spending time, even if minimal, setting up a 'Welbike' for riding was often less attractive than getting out of the area on foot. Parachute operations also frequently separated men and equipment, sometimes by miles, and thus much was lost, often to enemy hands. Further, at night or in extremely soft, poor terrain, the little 'Welbike' with its small wheels and 98 cc engine, carrying a rider and equipment with a total weight of up to 300 lb, was simply not up to the job. Because of this, further tests were carried out on an improved container in May 1943, designed to take some of the load off the motorcycle. The Mark 1 versions saw the most usage and consequently the loss rate was highest among this version. Many of the later Mark 2, Series 2 models were never actually used and were disposed of after the war still in their original packing.

It is rumoured that eventually the majority of 'Welbikes' were disposed of overseas as, without some modification, the type was unsuitable for civilian use in the United Kingdom – among other features the machine lacked the necessary two brakes required by law. However, some at least were sold off within the United Kingdom, probably for 'running about on farms'.

A final twist to the 'Welbike' story was the redesigning of the model during the early post-war period by its original designer, J.R.V. Dolphin, who took his ideas to Brockhouse Engineering (trailer manufacturers during the Second World War), whereupon the Corgi was born. Today, one can occasionally see Corgis at military vehicle shows painted green and termed 'post-war parachutists' scooters'; or even on the odd occasion an actual 'Welbike'! As far as can be ascertained, the post-war Corgi was never used by the military and the authors know of no evidence to substantiate claims to the contrary.

EXCELSIOR 'UNIVERSAL' 125 CC SINGLE-CYLINDER 2-STROKE – 1942

Little is known about this particular machine's involvement with the military, although at least one example was supplied to the War Office under contract during early 1942 and there exists the possibility of further small quantities of the type also being supplied.

The 'Universal' model was fitted with a Villiers 9D engine-unit identical to that fitted to the similar James ML model. In fact, the Excelsior machine was similar to the ML in many other respects. It is likely that the type was originally acquired for assessment for suitability by the airborne forces, along with the James ML and the Royal Enfield WD/RE, as the machine's contract number is very close to the one issued to James for their ML model.

Francis Barnett

Like James, Norman and Excelsior, Francis Barnett was a manufacturer that used proprietry 2-stroke engines from Villiers of Wolverhampton. Although 2-stroke engines were generally not favoured by the War Office, the MWEE did start testing one in 1928, choosing Francis Barnett as the supplier of the motorcycle. This one-off was a specially modified Model 9 motorcycle, constructed to meet the requirements of the military. Testing was carried out at the MWEE, who were also testing a lightweight from Levis and a 3-wheeler from OEC; the results obtained were inconclusive.

The following year (1929) Francis Barnett was chosen to take part in the MWEE's seven-make trial. For this, it supplied three bored-out Empire Model No. 12 motorcycles, the only 2-stroke models participating. However, before all the testing was finished, the authorities went ahead with a rushed trial between a Douglas and a Triumph, before finally opting to buy the Douglas. Some six months later, when the trial finished in November 1929, the modified Model 12s were rejected (along with several other makes), largely because they were considered not powerful or robust enough to withstand service life.

Following this trial, the authorities abandoned 2-strokes in preference to 4-strokes for the next seven-make trial in 1935, and it was not until 1938 that they looked again at a 2-stroke motorcycle. However, in 1941 Francis Barnett did get an opportunity to supply another motorcycle, as a contract was issued for either one or several 150 cc 'Plovers', but why or for whom they were bought is not known at the time of writing.

FRANCIS BARNETT MILITARY LIGHTWEIGHT 172 CC SINGLE-CYLINDER 2-STROKE – 1928

This motorcycle was one of the first military motorcycles developed by the MWEE, the other being the OEC 3-wheeler.

Studying the photograph, the motorcycle appears to be based around a Model 9 Francis Barnett which had a 172 cc twin-port Villiers engine. Modifications carried out on the standard model were larger tyres, special clearance mudguards, and special gear ratios.

In 1928 it was tested against a Model M Levis and one of the OEC 3-wheelers, but the test results were regarded as 'inconclusive' and 'tended to show that lightness was of great importance in connection with the development of a cross-country motorcycle and the problem was to reconcile light weight with speed on the road and general robustness of construction'. Following this, no further development of this motorcycle is believed to have been carried out.

Official photograph of the 1928 Francis Barnett Lightweight, which was based on the company's Model 9 motorcycle. (PRO, WO 194 (45) – 5813)

FRANCIS BARNETT MODEL 12 (MODIFIED) 350 CC SINGLE-CYLINDER 2-STROKE – 1929

Three of these were bought for the 1929 seven-make trial, in which they were the only 2-strokes competing against mainly SV and OHV machines.

Although Francis Barnett's Model 12 was normally a 250 cc on the civilian market, these three had enlarged engines to take them out to 350 cc and this was achieved by upping the bore from 67 mm to 79 mm. Quite what else was changed over the standard machine is not known, as in the official War Office photograph, the motorcycle looks very standard.

Testing finished in late 1929, when the machine was rejected as unsuitable along with several other makes. It is probable that this was because of its lack of power across country (i.e. no bottom-end power), which was a continuing criticism of all 2-strokes at the time, and also because of its light construction which meant parts were easily damaged in severe use (cross-country riding).

FRANCIS BARNETT 'PLOVER' 150 CC SINGLE-CYLINDER 2-STROKE – 1941

Bought under contract, it is not sure if one or several of these machines were actually purchased, neither is it known whether the model chosen was a K40 or a K41.

Official photograph of the modified 1929 Francis Barnett Model 12, as used in the 1929 trials. The engine capacity was increased from its normal 250 cc size to 350 cc by boring it out from 67 mm to 79 mm. (PRO, WO 194 (45) – 5871)

Considering the date it was purchased, it is possible that the 'Plover' was being looked at for the role eventually filled by the Royal Enfield WD/RE and James ML models.

Gillet-Herstal

GILLET-HERSTAL 728 CC PARALLEL TWIN-CYLINDER 2-STROKE SWD COMBINATION – 1939

This Belgium-made combination was tested and demonstrated in mid-1939 along with a 'Big 4' Norton. Brought over to England by M. Gillet at Norton's request, it was demonstrated by a Belgium driver carrying two passengers. It proved to be a good performer on gravel and sand but suffered a bit in the mud, possibly through its own weight (9½ cwt, compared to the Norton's 6½ cwt).

During testing, it failed a few tests which the 'Big 4' passed, but generally there was little to choose between the two motorcycles, and neither was considered better than the other.

Technically the Gillet had a few advantages over the Norton, as it had a sidecar wheel brake (which made steep descents easier to control) and a reverse gear.

Gillet-Herstal Combination similar to that tested by the War Office in 1939. (Bart Vanderveen Collection)

Harley-Davidson

Along with the Indian motorcycle company, the American company Harley-Davidson was to supply a quantity of their combination and solo motorcycles to the British and commonwealth countries under the 'Lend-Lease' agreement of 1941. To date, the final quantity of Harley-Davidson motorcycles supplied to and used by the British forces is not established, although it is known that the Air Ministry (RAF) employed a quantity of the WLC solo model and that the War Office (Army) utilized a limited number of the larger capacity combination machines. The South African forces were also sent a large quantity of machines via the British Supply Council, with other commonwealth countries, principally Canada, supplied direct from Harley-Davidson. It is of note that most of the combination machines supplied had left-hand sidecars fitted, even though normal American practice was to fit a right-hand version. During 1941 a combination model, ELC, plus a solo WLC test model were supplied for evaluation purposes via the Canadian forces. Both versions were subjected to a form of suitability test but not the standard 10,000 mile reliability and endurance test, probably because a prompt decision was required.

When it is considered that the British had been looking at the suitability of new lightweight machines of some 260 lb in weight at this time, with examples having been supplied from BSA, Triumph, etc., and rejected for various reasons including their weight, cost, performance, poor fuel consumption, etc., it is therefore rather surprising that these low-slung, heavy, cumbersome machines with poor fuel consumption and cross-country capabilities and weighing, at the very least, some 550 lb (WLC solo), were considered at all for British military use. Indeed, at the time, the War Office were voicing criticism of the weight of their then current machines including the BSA M20, the Norton 16H and the Matchless G3, and these were at least some 150 lb lighter than the WLC. Other disadvantages of using American machines for the British military were the unfamiliar control layout, including a hand-operated gear-change (dropped in the mid-1930s by British manufacturers) and foot-operated clutch, all of which required time-consuming practice from the British riders. On the plus side, however, all the American machines were very comfortable to ride with large leather-topped saddles, wide handlebars and footboards for the feet. They were, by virtue of their design, weight and construction, incredibly robust and consequently reliable and extremely well suited to long-distance road use, in which most were ultimately employed.

At the end of the Second World War, virtually all surviving Harley-Davidson machines supplied to the British military were disposed of as surplus on to the public market. In the late 1940s a number of dealerships advertised in the press, offering both new and reconditioned Harley-Davidson Model U combinations for sale, as well as quantities of the smaller solo WLA/WLC version. However, Harley-Davidsons used by the RAF overseas, in places such as Singapore, are known to have remained in service until the late 1950s.

HARLEY-DAVIDSON MODEL WLC 750 CC SV V-TWIN – 1941–4

The first example of the Canadian specification WLC was received for evaluation testing in September 1941, and was delivered to a depot in Slough, Berkshire. This machine had almost certainly been acquired via the Canadian authorities and must have been accepted as it was soon to enter limited service with the British forces, principally with the RAF.

It is likely that the first WLC supplied for testing was to 1942 model specifications, as initial deliveries of the type may also have been. These early versions differed in a number of details to the 1943 (export) specification models, which were supplied later on. The most notable differences were the use of longer front-forks, the positioning of the headlamp and horn, the tail-lights and the lack of a rear luggage carrier. Apart from these features there are numerous other detail differences between the two models, and more differences still between these and the similar American military specification model, the WLA, which incidentally was never officially used by the British.

HARLEY-DAVIDSON MODEL ELC 1000 CC OHV V-TWIN COMBINATION – 1941

As with the smaller WLC model, an example of this large combination machine was delivered for evaluation by the War Office during late 1941, again presumably acquired via the Canadian authorities. Although information is unclear, the model appears not to have gained acceptance for British military use.

A 1943 Harley-Davidson WLC in service with 83 Group, 2nd Tactical Air Force, RAF, in Holland during late 1944. The rider is Reg Humphries. (Reg Humphries)

An early Harley-Davidson WLC at a brigade HQ. Similar models were initially supplied to the British. (The identity of the Canadian rider is not known.) (IWM, H28023)

A Harley-Davidson Model UA Combination, similar to the ones supplied to the War Office. (Bart Vanderveen Collection)

HARLEY-DAVIDSON MODEL UA/MODEL US 1200 CC SV V-TWIN COMBINATION – 1942–3

The Model UA and Model US were basically militarized versions of the company's civilian Model U machine. As with all other Harley-Davidsons, the Model UA and US were really only suitable for long-distance road use and therefore, in consideration of all other factors, only at their best in the hands of an experienced motorcyclist (as was the similar Indian Chief combination).

Most Lend-Lease UAs differed to the ones used by the US Army; they had valanced mudguards, a different silencer and a front wheel stand. Late models had sand pads added to the rear stand, both 16 in and 18 in wheels are known to have been fitted, and occasionally the sidecar bodies had doors fitted in them. All Model USs were delivered to South Africa.

Indian

Following the withdrawal of the British forces from France at Dunkirk in mid-1940, and the consequent loss of large quantities of much needed equipment, the British Government looked towards the then neutral United States and her industrial might for assistance. This request was to evolve into the 'Lend-Lease' agreement of 11 March 1941, which enabled the United States to supply Britain with a wide variety of industrial and humanitarian aid without invoking a change to the American constitution.

Among the enormous quantities of goods and equipment supplied by the United States to Britain were some 10,000 motorcycles of various types, supplied by both Harley-Davidson and Indian, although Indian were ultimately to supply the bulk of the equipment. The first Indian models to be delivered into the United Kingdom were the large 'Chief' combination machines, namely the Model 340 B, which was followed by large quantities of the smaller solo Model 741 B. Both models were to see service with 'free' forces within the United Kingdom (e.g. the Dutch, Polish, etc.), the Air Ministry (RAF), and with rear echelon troops within the British Army in the United Kingdom (such as the Corps of Military Police, etc.). The machines also saw limited use with civil defence and fire organizations, and commonwealth and governmental departments and ministries, some of the latter in some of the most remote and far-flung locations in the world.

Delivery of the major Indian model, the 741 B, was halted by mid-1943 as British motorcycle production had finally caught up with demand, and by 1944 even the British manufacturers were being instructed by the government to slow down production of machines because of stockpiling, supply outstripping demand and the course of the remainder of the war now being firmly in favour of the Allies. Along with examples of Harley-Davidsons, large quantities of surviving Indian machines, primarily 741 B models, were disposed of via civilian dealerships following the end of hostilities. These disposals principally concerned machines located within the United Kingdom; those that had been sent to numerous overseas locations were usually disposed of *in situ* or simply left there.

Only one other Indian machine was to be evaluated by the War Office for suitability during the Second World War, namely the Model 640, which the Canadian forces were using at the time. Although not established, the type was presumably rejected in favour of the smaller, lighter, and more economical Model 741 B.

A point of interest with all the Indian and Harley-Davidson models supplied was the typical American design of the rider's controls. With a hand-change gearbox, a left-hand operated throttle twistgrip and a foot-operated clutch among other peculiarities, the average British military rider was required to retrain his mind in the operation of the machine both prior to and when actually riding. This persistent state of unfamiliarity with the American types was perhaps one of the main factors that contributed to their unpopularity in the higher echelons of the War Office and their distribution among second-line formations and to some of the more remote outposts of the Empire. As with Harley-Davidson, however, all the machines were built to a high standard and were very sturdy and reliable, furthermore, they were infinitely more comfortable to ride than their British-built counterparts.

INDIAN MODEL 340 B 'CHIEF' 1200 CC SV V-TWIN COMBINATION – 1940–1

These large and powerful combinations were originally ordered by the French Government, but following the fall of France during mid-1940 it seems that the models not yet delivered were reallocated to the British War Office to be used at a time when such machines were urgently required after Dunkirk.

Official photograph of an early version of the Indian Model 340B Combination. (REME Museum)

All the combinations supplied were fitted with right-hand sidecars rather than left-hand, as was usual in the United Kingdom. A number of them were allocated to the free Polish forces, at the time located in Scotland. Many of these machines were to have the overall basic light olive-drab paint finish supplemented by random overpainting of a wavy, curved camouflage pattern in a darker shade of green or brown, similar to an aircraft.

Several subsequent contracts were placed with Indian for further supplies of the Model 340 B, with minor differences in the specification of the early and later versions. Early models (French specification) were fitted with a pillion saddle, legshields, a spare wheel carried on top of the sidecar body, a civilian pattern air cleaner (rather than the later model's military pattern oil-bath type cleaner), plus a civilian pattern rear light rather than the later twin-light arrangement. It also seems that some later specification Model 340 Bs were subjected to a tyre size reduction from 450.18 to 400.18, among other detail changes.

When tested in the summer of 1940 by the War Office, it was concluded that the Model 340 B held a good performance from the engine. However, the type suffered from poor ground clearance and, compared with the British Norton Model No. 1 'Big 4' combination, the lack of sidecar wheel drive, plus the immense weight of the machine, rendered it useless for cross-country work. The brakes were also regarded as poor, making the model unsafe for general road work unless it was controlled by specially selected riders, who possessed considerable motorcycling experience. The overall summary concluded that the type was unsuitable for War Office usage except on the road, and only then in experienced hands. That said, the demands of the early war years and the conditions of the Lend-Lease agreement left the British authorities with little alternative at the time other than to accept the model into limited service, suitable or otherwise.

It is of note that some of these machines were disposed of as early as 1943, when numbers of the type were transferred from the military into the hands of the Mid-Lothian Post Office, presumably to be used for delivering parcels, a task to which it was well suited.

INDIAN MODEL 640 B 750 CC SV V-TWIN – 1940

Two examples of the 750 cc V-twin Indian Model 640 B were subjected to evaluation by the War Office during 1940. They were supplied at a similar time to the two comparable Harley-Davidson models, also subjected to evaluation, and it is presumed that the testing was conducted prior to the possible purchase of a quantity of the type.

Very little is known concerning the testing of these machines. As with the Harley-Davidson models tested, it can be assumed that the machines supplied were of Canadian military specification.

Official photograph of a late version of the Indian Model 340B Combination. (REME Museum)

INDIAN MODEL 741 B 500 CC SV V-TWIN – 1941–3

The Indian Model 741 B machine was by far the company's most prolific model of the Second World War. In comparison to most typical American machines, the Model 741 B had a considerably smaller engine capacity, although it still retained most of the features and characteristics of its larger stablemates, including bulkiness and weight, which unfortunately only served to restrict further the moderate performance of the 500 cc SV V-twin engine.

Virtually from its inception, the Model 741 B was produced by Indian specifically for export purposes under the terms of the Lend-Lease agreement, and was delivered worldwide to just about every allied country, outpost and organization, in quantities ranging from one solitary example to a few thousand. The type was originally supplied fully assembled and ready for immediate use, although later supplies arrived in crates, only partially assembled for ease of transit and storage. Some of the early examples of the Model 741 B to arrive in the United Kingdom had to have their wiring and electrical layout substantially modified by the military authorities in order to comply with the strict black-out regulations then in force. On 17 December 1941 Indian issued a set of instructions to accompany a standardized kit of parts necessary to complete the modification work. The changes also required the removal of the lower rear light, but interestingly, photographic evidence suggests that this was not always carried out, the light itself possibly being disconnected rather than removed completely. Other common modifications to the model, though not affecting all machines, included the extending of the foot-brake face, and the removal of the tool-box, saddle-bags and crash-bars, the latter usually painted white if left fitted. Other minor alterations were also implemented. As with Harley-Davidson, there were changes in details between early and late specification machines including a change of air cleaner from a round to a rectangular pattern, the bolt-on headlight mounting on early versions becoming part of the forks, the primary chaincases still affording access to where the pre-war magneto drive went on some early versions, and rubber-covered footboards changing to ones of perforated steel. Also, incorrect information which appeared in early manuals was corrected in later editions.

Although initially supplied at a time when machines were much needed, the War Office, together with many servicemen and women generally regarded the Model 741 B with suspicion and distain, principally because of the type's poor overall performance and the unconventional (at least to the British) layout and operation of the machine's controls, which made it initially difficult to ride. One contract set out to alleviate this by ordering fifty machines with Norton handlebars and controls, although whether the clutch and gearchange were altered is unknown.

However, the authorities were unable to simply reject the model, the nearest alternative being to allocate the type to second-line units, formations, other services (such as the RAF) and to commonwealth forces. Other quantities of the type were 'disposed' of by allocating them to every possible overseas outpost, department, ministry or embassy where, following the end of the war, they were quietly forgotten about.

When contracts for the 741 B ceased in 1943 the United States was left with surplus stocks of machines that had been awaiting despatch overseas, and in

Official photograph of an Indian 741B at Farnborough, May 1942. (REME Museum)

which the American military authorities themselves now had little interest. In 1944 they disposed of the machines, selling them off to the public at substantially discounted costs. This caused the Indian company extreme concern, as the discounted price was far cheaper than it could afford to sell, or even manufacture at. This matter was only one of a number of unfortunate incidents that effectively culminated in the death of the Indian company a few years later. In the United Kingdom many of the machines previously issued to the Army were transferred to various civilian and governmental organizations during 1943 and 1944. Following the end of the war virtually all Model 741 B machines in service within the United Kingdom were disposed of through dealerships, for refurbishment and sale on to the civilian market, including stocks of brand-new machines still packed in their shipping crates.

INDIAN MODEL 344 'CHIEF' 1200 CC SV V-TWIN COMBINATION – 1944

Essentially the same machine as the earlier Model 340 B, the 1944 specification model 344 'Chief' combination incorporated a number of modifications over the earlier version. By this time the combination had been superceded by the 'Jeep' light utility car for at least the last two years, and it is believed that these later 1944 Model 344s were ordered for a specific, unestablished purpose and for issue to the military in India.

In comparison to the earlier Model 340 B, this later version had the sidecar fitted to the left side of the machine and had standard American military lighting as fitted to the 741 B.

James

In the years before the Second World War the James Cycle Company Ltd, of Greet, Birmingham, was one of the numerous moderately sized motorcycle manufacturers of the period offering a comprehensive range of machines, from small lightweight utilities through to large capacity 4-strokes. The depression and recession years of the 1930s, however, had considerable affect on the firm, as it did most motorcycle manufacturers. Although James managed to survive and witnessed the outbreak of the Second World War it was, by this time, mainly producing various utility-type machines powered by a variety of proprietary engines manufactured by Villiers. With war underway, the company's engineering and production facilities were redirected towards manufacturing other products for the war effort, notably aircraft components and munitions.

It was not until 1942, some three years after the outbreak of war, that James became involved in motorcycle production again. At the time the British Airborne forces, comprising parachutists, glider-borne troops and all other conceivable assault and supporting elements, were expanding rapidly, becoming a fully-operational force capable of leading the assault on the axis forces. Equipment for use by the Airborne forces was a priority and procurement and development of such happened without delay. One requirement for the Airborne and assault formations was a reliable, lightweight motorcycle that would take up minimum space en route to battle, could be delivered and brought into action easily, was capable of being manhandled over impassable obstacles by one man, and yet was cheap enough to be abandoned should the need arise.

Following a similar course to that of Royal Enfield's WD/RE model, the 'Flying Flea', a small quantity of 1939 civilian specification 150 cc James K15/K16 machines (the exact model is unconfirmed) was procured for evaluation purposes by the War Office. As further testing was conducted with the lighter 125 cc K17 model, it is presumed that these 150 cc models were simply too heavy for Airborne use. The K17 made a reasonable impression with the authorities and the model was developed further into the prototype example of what was to become the ubiquitous James ML (military lightweight) model. Further testing led to the procurement of twelve more modified prototypes for evaluation purposes, the results of which were incorporated into the final production version of the ML model. With the company's ML model now approved by the War Office and in production, James spent the final years of the Second World War producing this model along with other types of work for the war effort. The end of the war saw the loss of service contracts for a time but the wartime success and reputation of the ML model secured the company's success in the years immediately following the war.

Catalogue pictures of James Models K15 and K16. Similar versions were bought for testing. (James Cycle Co. Ltd)

JAMES MODEL K15 OR K16 150 CC SINGLE-CYLINDER 2-STROKE – 1942

Ten examples of this model were procured under contract by the War Office for evaluation purposes to assess its suitability for possible use by the developing Airborne and assault formations. The exact model is unconfirmed. The machines were all built to 1939 specification and it is presumed that they were supplied from unsold stock, or alternatively built up from stocks of spares held at the factory since the outbreak of war.

Little is known of the results of the testing or the fate of the machines concerned. It is presumed, however, that the model was ultimately rejected by the War Office because of its weight.

JAMES MODEL K17 125 CC SINGLE-CYLINDER 2-STROKE – 1942

It is presumed that the K17 model was supplied to the War Office for evaluation purposes at the same time as the larger K15 or K16 models, and quite probably caused these two models to be rejected. Two examples of the K17 were supplied, again presumably either from unsold stock or built up from spares held by the factory, and again to 1939 specification.

As for the K15/K16, little is known of the test results but it seems clear that the K17 model performed well enough as James went on to produce a machine based on the K17 model that was to become the ML model prototype machine.

Catalogue pictures of James Model K17. The War Office bought similar models for testing. (James Cycle Co. Ltd)

JAMES MODEL ML 125 CC SINGLE-CYLINDER 2-STROKE – 1942–3 PROTOTYPE

Development of the K17 model resulted in a prototype machine supplied for War Office testing during late 1942/early 1943. This machine bore a passing resemblance to the K17 model and was designated the model 'ML' (Military Lightweight). It was available for testing at around the same time as the Royal Enfield WD/RE model (prototype) and performed reasonably well for the intended role. Further modifications were suggested, which led to a further twelve modified examples of the type being delivered. All were sent to various Airborne and assault formations throughout the military and performed well, with only minor modifications suggested for incorporation into the main production versions, one change being a shorter rear mudguard.

JAMES MODEL ML 125 CC SINGLE-CYLINDER 2-STROKE – 1943–5

The production version of the ML model began to be delivered to the British Army during March 1943, about the same time as the equivalent Royal Enfield WD/RE model. All models were initially allocated solely to Airborne and assault formations in training, with some later going to the Admiralty.

Ultimately, the James ML model was to see more wartime service with assault and other ground formations than with Airborne units, the Royal Enfield WD/RE model taking precedence here. Most period photographs of the ML model in action show the type in the hands of assault or Commando personnel. Indeed, the ML acquired notoriety as a 'mechanical sheep-dog' on the Normandy beach-heads during the D-Day landings of June 1944, rounding-up and directing columns of troops on the sands and dunes. It is likely that this is where its nickname the 'Clockwork Mouse' was coined.

Compared with the rival WD/RE model, the James ML was at least 26 lb heavier, much of the weight probably arising from the use of heavy brass castings and components on the model's Villiers 9D engine-unit, principally the exhaust-ports and the heavy magneto flywheel assembly. Although not an excessive additional weight under normal conditions, 26 lb was considered critical when packing an aircraft, loading a glider, or dropping by parachute.

Another disadvantage of the ML model was the fact that no purpose-designed drop-cage had been produced to enable it to be dropped by parachute, as the WD/RE could.

However, the James company was evidently pleased to be producing motorcycles again, even if just one particular model, and certainly made sure that everybody could identify its product. In particular, the company capitalized upon its past reputation, using the word 'famous' in its advertising campaign, as well as the fact that its ML model with front-line formations was spearheading the war against Germany at the time. In many ways the company had a right to be proud of its ML model, as it was generally considered to be much more reliable than the rival WD/RE both mechanically and in durability, the lighter weight of the WD/RE resulting in marginally greater fragility in both respects.

With the end of the war in 1945, the bulk of the surviving ML models were either disposed of to dealers, or returned to the factory for rebuilding to civilian specification before being released on to the market along with similar new civilian examples of the model. With new machines impossible to find and fuel still rationed, a cheap ex-military ML model was ideal for transport purposes as it could return at least 100 m.p.g.

A Canadian paratrooper on a James ML. This photograph was used in James's advertisements although, for the purpose of the advert, the James name was added to the petrol tank, above the Army registration number. (The National Motor Museum, 14880/8)

Levis

Levis was one of England's leading 2-stroke manufacturers before the Second World War, although it did fit 4-stroke engines to its motorcycles as well.

The company's first involvement with the War Office came in late 1928 when the MWEE were carrying out comparison tests of lightweight and heavier motorcycles.

The model initially bought for this test was the 250 cc Model M, which had a 3-port engine. Weeks later two further models were bought, this time Levis's 6-port models, which were then despatched to Egypt for evaluation. In July 1929 the reports of the testing in Egypt showed that the 6-port had performed well against the OEC 3-wheeler and the Triumph NL3, and indeed was considered to be the best machine.

Based on this, more 6-port models were ordered in August and another batch again in 1930. Ultimately, however, they were dismissed as most officials favoured 4-strokes, and no more 2-strokes were bought until nearer the outbreak of war. Strangely enough, Levis did receive a wartime order for some 350 cc machines which ended up being cancelled two months later; it is not known whether any were delivered.

LEVIS MODEL M 250 CC SINGLE-CYLINDER 2-STROKE – 1928

Bought with the idea that a lightweight motorcycle would perform well and meet Military requirements, this motorcycle was purchased for comparison testing with other types of motorcycles, one of which was the OEC 3-wheeler.

Testing was carried out by the MWEE at Farnborough, and although the model's lightness proved an asset, its speed on the road and general robustness were not to their liking.

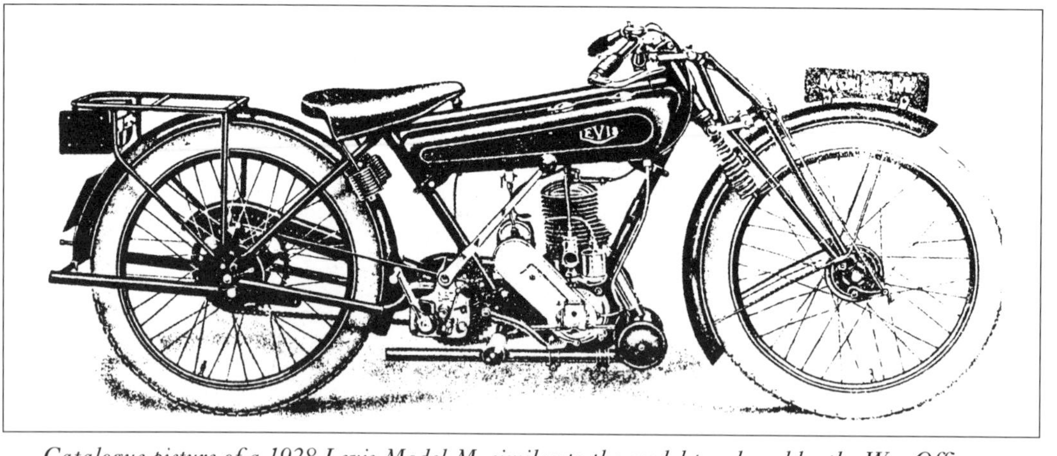

Catalogue picture of a 1928 Levis Model M, similar to the model purchased by the War Office. (Levis Motor Cycles)

LEVIS 6-PORT 250 CC SINGLE-CYLINDER 2-STROKE – 1928–30

This model was supplied presumably to overcome the criticisms of the Model M. They were sent straight to Egypt for testing with other manufacturers' models, namely Triumph's NL3 and OEC's 3-wheeler.

The results of the reports from July 1929 concluded that the Levis was the best machine, and much better than the previous Model M. Following on from this two more orders were received, one in 1929 and the other in 1930.

Interestingly the 1929 Egypt reports made no note of engine seizures under sustained load, although this was to occur on some machines in the cold UK!

Further testing in Egypt in 1930/1 showed that the 6-port had sufficient power for normal cross-country work, although it was underpowered for cross-country hill climbing, and that it was a good performer on roads. Ultimately, although the 6-port appeared promising, it was still considered unreliable (due to seizures) and not robust enough for service, probably a rather prejudiced idea as Ministry officials really preferred 4-strokes.

LEVIS 350 CC – 1941

A demand for 2,000 motorcycles was issued to Levis, only to be cancelled just over two months later. Whether any actually got built or delivered, and even which model they were, is not known at the time of writing.

Official photograph of a Levis 6-port. (PRO, WO 194 (45) – 5412)

Matchless

Matchless was the third largest of the major manufacturers to supply military motorcycles during the Second World War with their well-known G3 and G3/L models. The G3/L in particular became perhaps one of the most popular and sought-after machines during the war, principally because of the fitting of the then new teledraulic front forks which, in military usage, were a considerable improvement and advantage over the girder-fork designs of the period.

During the First World War, Matchless had been a small, almost insignificant supplier of motorcycles for military use and it was not until 1929 that the company became involved with service models again when three examples of the company's 350 cc SV Model T/4 machines were purchased for evaluation purposes in the seven-make trials of that year. However, prior to completion of the 1929 trials, War Office impatience for a new military model led to the hurried purchase of Douglas Model L29 machines, thus when the reports from the trials became available during November 1929 they were, to a degree, rather pointless.

The 1929 trials reports did, however, designate several motorcycles as unsuitable for military service. The Matchless product, along with the AJS and Douglas models, were retained for further testing, having shown some potential. Ultimately, no further Model T/4 machines were purchased for evaluation, although in the following year, 1930, a 400 cc narrow-angle V-twin engined 'Silver Arrow' model was purchased, largely because opinion at the War Office was changing, twin-cylinder motorcycles now considered quieter then single-cylinder machines.

Following evaluation, a small quantity of the 'Silver Arrow' models were purchased for service use in 1931, although the reports received by the War Office from the Armoured Fighting Vehicles (Signals), Southern Command, stated that the machine was unsuitable.

The company next became involved with the military in 1935, when their Model 36/G3 machine showed promise in performance tests, although its overall reliability, did not procure as much confidence.

Also in 1936 a 250 cc G7 was tested and a number were purchased (before the test results were available) for use in instructional purposes. The results finally described the model as only fair, and no further motorcycles of this type were purchased.

None the less, the Model 36/G3 proved itself enough for the War Office to place an order for a quantity of 110 examples and following the testing of a specific machine, serial number C 353544, during late 1937 the type managed to acquire a good report from the MEE. The Model G3, with various modifications, continued to be purchased by the War Office until 1942, the pre-war quantities supplied being varied and small in comparison to the bulk of the type delivered following the outbreak of war in September 1939.

Although Matchless was supplying military motorcycles to War Office order during late 1939 and early 1940, the company, along with most other motorcycle manufacturers, was still producing limited quantities of machines for the civilian markets, including overseas customers. However, this state of affairs was dramatically altered in mid–1940, when the War Office purchased or requisitioned virtually every remotely suitable civilian motorcycle, awaiting despatch or completion at the manufacturers or for sale in showrooms, to replace the quantities of military motorcycles lost following the Dunkirk evacuation. Matchless supplied from factory stock limited quantities of their civilian specification G80, G90, G5 and G3 models accordingly.

In 1940 Matchless also participated in the War Office lightweight motorcycle project, supplying the MEE with, initially, experimental 250 cc and, later, 350 cc machines. The 250 cc version proved unsuitable because the engine capacity was too small to provide necessary performance, while the 350 cc model was ultimately more successful and the forerunner of the 41/G3/L model of the following year, which was arguably the most popular of the wartime British military models.

The G3/L model, introduced during late 1941, was to remain in volume production until 1945, the quantity actually produced being the third largest behind BSA with its Model M20 and Norton with its Model 16H. Matchless production from 1942 until the end of the war was entirely devoted to the G3/L model, with minor detail changes and improvements from contract to contract.

MATCHLESS MODEL T/4 350 CC SV SINGLE-CYLINDER – 1929

Selected by the War Office for evaluation purposes in the seven-make trials of 1929, the Matchless Model T/4 was eventually to complete the testing. However, prior to completion of the trials and collation of the results of the various machines on test, the War Office, impatient for a new military motorcycle, purchased Douglas machines after a short comparison with the Triumph product then on test.

Official photograph of a 1929 Matchless T/4, used in the 1929 trials. (PRO, WO 194 (45) – 5878)

Following completion of the trials, which must have now seemed rather pointless, machines from Matchless, AJS and Douglas were deemed successful. However, further frustration was caused as the military authorities could not decide which machine would be most suitable. As War Office preference now lay with twin-cylinder machines, which it considered to be quieter than single-cylinder versions, no further Model T/4s were purchased.

MATCHLESS 'SILVER ARROW' 400 CC SV V-TWIN – 1930–1

The War Office's change of preference in the early 1930s for supposedly quieter twin-cylinder machines was a particularly important consideration for military machinery, and Matchless supplied it with an example of their 'Silver Arrow' V-twin engined model for evaluation against the current Model L29 Douglas machine.

Testing, however, showed the Matchless product to be rather unreliable. Following the completion of a somewhat troublesome 12,200 miles, the example was replaced with an improved 1931 specification example, which incorporated various improvements over the defects that had been noted. After the completion of 1,650 miles, the later model proved satisfactory to the MWEE, although certain minor repairs and adjustments had been necessary.

Further evaluation of the model was carried out by the Armoured Fighting Vehicles (Signals), Southern Command, who, following an extended trial of the type, concluded that 'certain features would prevent this make and type of motorcycle being suitable for signal duties'. Nothing specific was quoted although it is reasonable to assume that the inter-connected brakes on the model were cause

A 1931 Matchless 'Silver Arrow' on manoeuvres on Salisbury Plain. (The National Motor Museum, C16433A)

for concern. Of the thirty-seven examples of the type purchased during 1931, thirty were issued to the Cavalry Armoured Car Company for trials to determine their general suitability for normal service duties. (Fifteen of these were fitted with air cleaners.) Presumably, the model was found to be unsuitable as no further examples were ordered.

MATCHLESS 'CLUBMAN' 347 CC OHV SINGLE-CYLINDER MODEL 36/G3 – 1935 EVALUATION MODEL

During 1935 Matchless was to supply the War Office with an example of their Model 36/G3 'Clubman' for evaluation and the example delivered was subjected to the standard MEE 10,000 mile reliability test in the seven-make trials of that year.

Throughout the evaluation period, the model suffered minor problems (which were to be expected) and other, more notable faults including soft hairpin valve-springs (which Matchless offered to replace with stronger coil springs), collapsed rear wheel bearings, a badly worn gearbox (replaced at completion of 8,832 miles) and sprockets.

Many of the faults had arisen because the model was basically a standard commercial type, slightly modified for military testing but still ill-prepared for the extremely demanding MEE testing procedures. The minor modifications incorporated were different tyres, and the addition of a rear carrier, a low-level exhaust and, quite possibly, a lower bottom gear ratio.

Official photograph of the 1935 Matchless G3 evaluation model, as used in the 1935 trials. (The Tank Museum, 151/A2)

It is worth noting that this example of the well-known Matchless Model G3 was considerably different to the later military Model G3 of the early war years. Among detail differences were the Duplex cradle frame, the cylinder head with hairpin valve-springs, a centre stand (rather than a rear stand), the foot-brake pedal and the wheels.

MATCHLESS MODEL G3 347 CC OHV SINGLE-CYLINDER – 1936–9

Despite the problems noted about the G3 evaluation model of 1935, the War Office was evidentally not detracted and subsequently ordered small quantities of the Model G3 under contract between 1936 and 1939 prior to the model undergoing redesign for the 1940 season.

Those machines supplied before the war continued to have the Duplex cradle frame and generally the same specification as the original test model of 1935, although certain annual changes to detail were incorporated as improvements were introduced, including a change to 14 mm spark-plugs, a new crankcase, the enclosure of the valve-springs and changes to the fuel tank. Some models were also fitted with air cleaners.

A further MEE evaluation of the model during 1937 noted improved levels of reliability and wear over the original trial model of 1935.

MATCHLESS MODEL G7 246 CC SV SINGLE-CYLINDER – 1936

During late 1936 Matchless was to supply the War Office with a quantity of its Model G7 250 cc SVs. These were all built to a standard 1937 civilian

Official photograph of a 1938 Matchless G3, as bought to contract C2073. (REME Museum)

Official photograph of a 1936 Matchless G7. (PRO, WO 194 (45) - - - - -)

specification, with the type being destined for training purposes primarily with the Royal Corps of Signals.

Introduced into service without the usual MEE evaluation procedure, one example was eventually subjected to the standard 10,000 mile test at Farnborough, Hampshire. Following the completion of 10,333 miles, 801 of which were cross-country, the reliability of the model was described as only fair. Notable faults included considerable wear on the cylinder-bore and the loss of grease from the wheel bearings. In summary, it was suggested that a more reliable and robust motorcycle should be found for training purposes, and no further Model G7 machines were purchased.

MATCHLESS MODEL G80 'CLUBMAN' 500 CC OHV SINGLE-CYLINDER – 1940

Twelve examples of the 1940 civilian specification Model G80 were purchased by the War Office under contract during mid-1940 following the Dunkirk losses.

The machines supplied were standard civilian models, held at the factory and awaiting either completion or delivery to the commercial markets. When purchased by the authorities they were presumably finished in standard service colour schemes of the period.

MATCHLESS MODEL G90 'SUPER CLUBMAN' 500 CC OHV SINGLE-CYLINDER – 1940

As with the twelve examples of Model G80 machines supplied during mid-1940, a solitary example of the 'Super Clubman' version was available, held at the factory and ready except for the appropriate paintwork.

MATCHLESS MODEL G5 'TOURIST' 500 CC SV SINGLE-CYLINDER – 1940

Along with the G80 models and the solitary G90 model, two examples of the company's G5 'Tourist' model were supplied from factory stock during mid-1940, again to 1940 specification.

MATCHLESS MODEL G3 347 CC OHV SINGLE-CYLINDER – 1940 CIVILIAN SPECIFICATION

One solitary civilian specification G3 model was supplied from factory stock along with the G80, G90 and G5 models. The civilian specification model was rather an oddity as, by then, the military model G3 machines were rolling off the production line in large numbers.

MATCHLESS EXPERIMENTAL LIGHTWEIGHT 245 CC OHV SINGLE-CYLINDER – 1940 PROTOTYPE (CONTRACT C.6674)

Evaluated during the spring of 1940, this particular machine was loosely based around the company's existing civilian specification Model G2M.

The model had been developed in response to the War Office's requirement for a purpose-built lightweight military motorcycle. The reduction in weight had been achieved by using parts either manufactured lighter than standard or made from special lightweight alloys (in the case of castings). Other weight reductions were made, including the substitution of the standard heavy battery for lighting with a direct lighting system using an alternating generator for charging purposes.

Following the testing of the model it was considered good for a 250 cc machine, although requiring considerable revving of the engine to keep the type going across country, which had the disadvantage of higher engine wear as well as an unwelcome increase in noise.

Testing was carried out against the Norton 350 cc SV lightweight and the BSA 348 cc OHV lightweight, where it was to perform better than the Norton (Matchless had claimed it would perform better than a 350 cc SV) and comparable to the BSA, although it did not pull as well unless on full throttle. However, the testers were pleased with its fuel consumption.

MATCHLESS EXPERIMENTAL LIGHTWEIGHT 245 CC OHV SINGLE-CYLINDER – 1940 PRE-PRODUCTION VERSION (CONTRACT C.8019)

This version was tested against the original model and the lightweight 350 cc SV Royal Enfield over 5,000 miles, during which the performance of the engine did deteriorate.

The conclusion on this model was that it should not be recommended for War Office use, as it considered that too much strain was placed on the 250 cc engine, which needed more overhauls and adjustments than desirable, and that 340 cc should be the minimum for War Office motorcycles.

MATCHLESS MODEL 40 G3/L EXPERIMENTAL LIGHTWEIGHT 347 CC OHV SINGLE-CYLINDER – 1940

During 1940 the War Office was clearly determined to reduce the weight of military motorcycles then in service, and several manufacturers, including Matchless, were developing and supplying prospective machines for evaluation. Matchless had taken note of the criticisms that its Model G3 was a rather heavy machine, particularly off-road, and thus set about pruning at least 56 lb from the existing Model G3, the experiences gained from its experimental 250 cc model proving useful in this venture.

The resulting model was the machine destined to become the well-known Model G3/L, the 'L' supposedly standing for 'lightweight', which was generally applicable to the prototype model but rather less-so to later production variants. In addition to the considerable weight saving, the model was fitted with the then revolutionary teledraulic front forks, which were based upon pre-war forks of German design. They proved a vast improvement over the previous girder-fork design, still fitted to other motorcycles of the period, chiefly in terms of comfort and increased up and down travel when in use off-road.

At least two examples of the prototype lightweight Model G3/L are thought to have been built, but despite being a successful design, War Office orders for quantities of the type did not appear straight away. The principal difficulty was the decision by the War Office to adopt one specific motorcycle for universal military service to replace the multitude of different types then in use.

Following considerable testing it was almost certain that Triumph's lightweight model 3TW would be chosen as the standardized War Office motorcycle, and had it not been for the German Air Force, this would probably have been the case. During November 1940 the city of Coventry was subjected to severe air raids with the city centre virtually razed to the ground. Among the many buildings destroyed were the Priory Street works of the Triumph Motorcycle Company, and drawings, parts, plans and machines relating to the company's Model 3TW military lightweight twin were lost. Little could be salvaged from the rubble, and so the market was open once again for a lightweight machine to replace the unlucky Model 3TW. Matchless were able to offer their proven prototype Model G3/L to take up the position left empty by the elimination of the Triumph product.

MATCHLESS MODEL G3WO 347 CC OHV SINGLE-CYLINDER – 1940–2

Matchless had initiated several changes and improvements to its products for the 1940 season, which were introduced during late 1939; such changes affected the company's War Office specification Model G3, principally the fitting of the company's revised frame design incorporating a single front-down-tube. Other changes included the fitting of a cylinder head from the similar AJS 350 cc model, which used coil-type valve-springs instead of the hairpin variety, a marginally redesigned cylinder barrel, incorporating the cutaway of some of the finning, and the fitting of a second tool-box above the existing one.

Some 18,500 examples of the Model G3WO were to be supplied to the military between late 1939 and early 1942 (before the type was withdrawn in favour of the

A 1941 Matchless G3 in the desert, as viewed from Edward Thorne's tent. (E. Thorne)

new model G3/L) with minor detail differences between contracts. One of the changes was the phasing-out of the tank-top instrument panel, which had been fitted to early examples prior to the issuing of contract number C.7183. However, 256 examples of the machines in contract number C.8078 still had the panel fitted, presumably to use up stocks of otherwise redundant components.

Interestingly enough, despite production of Model G3/L commencing during late 1941, the model G3WO continued to be built alongside the new machine, presumably because War Office contracts for the type remained valid until early 1942. Certain Model G3WO machines produced in the last contract, during early 1942, were altered slightly to accept revised components from the new G3/L model, which included crankpins and brake-shoes, probably because stocks of standard Model G3WO components had run out. Indeed, the last fifty Model G3WO machines produced became something of a hybrid, being fitted with, among other components, the engine and teledraulic front forks of the new Model G3/L.

Certain other detail differences between early and late production G3WO models included the fitting of a four-position headlight switch in place of the earlier three-position type, standard military specification speedometers superceding the earlier model, which had been fitted with a trip facility, and, on specifically fuel tank panel models, the substitution of the standard battery with a NiFe version.

Although officially replaced by the Model G3/L during 1942, the Model G3WO remained in War Office service until the end of hostilities, odd examples still being seen during the early 1950s, although the type was generally withdrawn from front-line duties by the end of 1943.

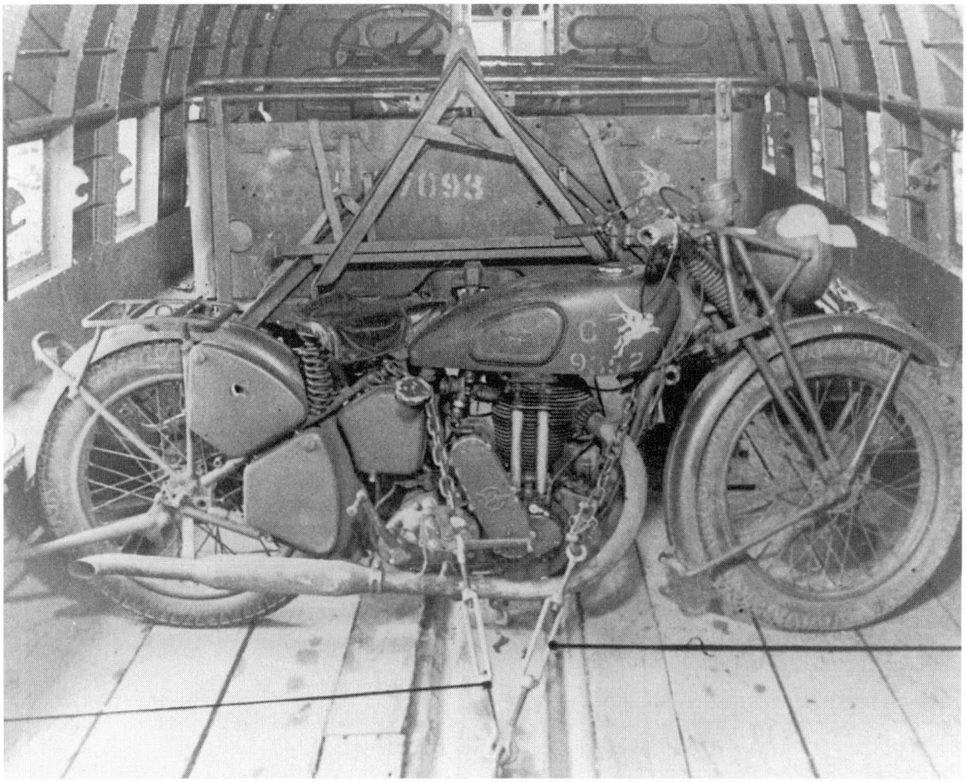

A Matchless G3 in aerial use, strapped down behind a Jeep inside a Dakota. Note the bullet hole in the upper tool-box lid!(Airborne Forces Museum)

Unpopular when employed off-road because of its weight, the Model G3WO was, however, favoured for general road usage, principally because it possessed a good degree of performance and was not, in fact, too far removed from the pre-war civilian 'Clubman' sporting model .

MATCHLESS MODEL 41 G3/L 347 CC OHV SINGLE-CYLINDER – 1941–5

The well-known Model G3/L motorcycle of the Second World War was the production model of the prototype lightweight Model G3, developed and tested during 1940. Once entered into military service it soon attained popularity among the majority of service users, principally because of the new teledraulic front forks. The G3/L, although mildly detuned compared with the earlier Model G3WO, was also still capable of a decent performance both on- and off-road in comparison to other service models and thus was a machine much sought after by those issued with less sporting mounts.

Despite the prototype lightweight having been tested during 1940, the first production Model G3/L machines were not available until the latter half of 1941 and it was not until mid-1942 that the type appeared in any considerable

Official photograph of a 1941 Matchless G3L. Note the ribbed front mudguard and lack of a front wheel stand. (Airborne Forces Museum)

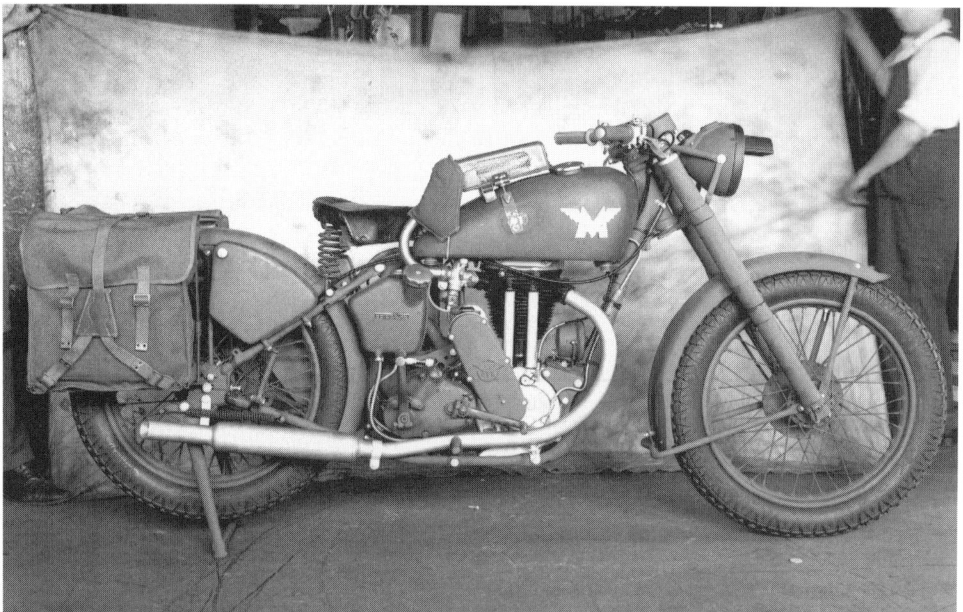

A 1942 Matchless G3L fitted with a Vokes filter. For some reason the pillion seat has been removed. (IWM, KID 5775)

numbers. The first Model G3/L machines delivered bore scant resemblance to the original prototype lightweight of 1940. This was mainly because of alterations made necessary by mass production, and also the incorporation of certain other components for service standardization and use. Such changes increased the overall weight of the model over that of its prototype. Initially, ribbed front and rear mudguards, the large Matchless metal fuel tank emblems, and rubber handlebar grips and combination type control levers were fitted. Other points of note included the fitting of only one fuel tap, (which meant draining the tank before its removal) and the lack of a front stand, which rendered the front wheel difficult to remove. Also, the universal pannier-frames were not fitted on the early G3/L machines as they had not yet been introduced into service.

Once entered into service, the Model G3/L was mildly developed as improvements were sought and changes were made to consecutive contracts issued for the type. Metal badges on the fuel tanks were replaced by transfers, rubber handlebar grips by canvas grips, and ribbed mudguards by plain ones. The engine valve-timing was improved and the teledraulic front fork yoke and handlebar lug altered to provide improved strengthening. Control levers were initially either of Bowden combination pattern or Amal single components, with the machine's crankcase often marked with an A or B to signify which type were fitted. (These were later substituted by 'standardized' universal components.) Pannier-frames were fitted to virtually all machines produced from late 1942 onwards. Twin fuel taps and a front stand were also introduced about this time.

The wartime demands upon all manufacturers also affected Model G3/L production to a certain degree, for a short time the light-alloy engine-timing cover being produced from cast iron. During 1942 a shortage of electrical lighting components from Lucas led to some 5,000 Model G3/L machines being fitted with component parts of Miller manufacture, although the magneto was to remain of Lucas manufacture throughout. Although by and large the type remained fairly consistent throughout the remainder of the war, many other detail changes were made which affected the Model G3/L. The last examples produced had Universal Vokes air filters factory-fitted to the top of the fuel tank, a task which involved having to reintroduce the knee-grip fastening holes to mount the filter.

G3/Ls were retained by the services for use in the post-war period along with the BSA Model M20. The last examples of the type were disposed of during the 1960s when replaced by the BSA W-B40. Although held in high regard by those issued with one for riding, the Model G3/L was less popular with workshop personnel, largely because the sheer compactness of the model in the original design (to both increase ground clearance and reduce weight) led to time-consuming maintenance schedules, already hindered because almost all components were difficult to get hold of. Virtually all engine maintenance required the fuel tank to be removed, and to simply take out the oil filter required the saddle to be taken off. Even worse, in order to remove the machine's dynamo, the entire primary chaincase and clutch had to be taken out, and the teledraulic front forks frequently caused overhaul difficulties to military personnel familiar only with girder-forks.

None the less, the Model G3/L attained a good reputation for itself throughout the war and is well remembered.

An experimental Matchless with rear suspension. Note the AJS style engine with forward magneto and the large head and barrel which may mean that this motorcycle was a 500 cc. (The National Motor Museum, C16412A)

MATCHLESS OHV SINGLE-CYLINDER – 1944 (REAR-SPRUNG PROTOTYPE)

The Model G3/L, praised for its teledraulic front forks, still retained the conventional rigid rear frame and the possibility of some form of rear suspension system had been suggested on a number of occasions. During 1944 Matchless produced a prototype model to evaluate the suitability of this system and produced a specific machine that was loosely based on the existing Model G3/L, although generally constructed using several different parts from the Associated Motor Cycles (AMC) range. The machine had a Model G3/L front frame and similar teledraulic front forks with brake assembly. The engine fitted was of the pre-war AJS variety with the magneto mounted forward of the engine, necessitating the fitting of a different timing cover to that of the Model G3/L Matchless. A new rear frame was constructed and fitted with the new suspension arrangement, which was similar in appearance to a smaller version of the frontal teledraulic fork legs. Other details included the fitting of a centre stand and pillion footrests that actually rose and fell with the movement of the rear suspension.

Moto-Chenille

MOTO-CHENILLE 'MERCIER' 350 CC OHV SINGLE-CYLINDER – 1939

This was very much an experimental motorcycle, and as such very unorthodox. It had a 4-wheel track-laying bogie in place of the front wheel and its engine and gearbox mounted on the handlebars.

When it was ridden, the testers considered it slow, noisy, unwieldy, very uncomfortable and requiring considerable skill even to ride it; consequently it was rejected.

It was of Swiss origin (although powered by a British 350 cc OHV JAP) and was also tested by the French Government. Pictures of this motorcycle sometimes show it with an armoured front, but it is thought the motorcycle tested by the British did not have this.

Demonstrated in mid–1939 by its designer, it proved to be useless at hill climbing and showered its rider with stones and mud. No road testing was conducted due to licencing restrictions and this may have been a blessing in disguise, as it was considered unsafe on the wet roads of the testing ground when it cornered at speed.

The military regarded it as having no value to them; its low petrol consumption of 24 m.p.g. and its weight of 375 lb would certainly not have been acceptable.

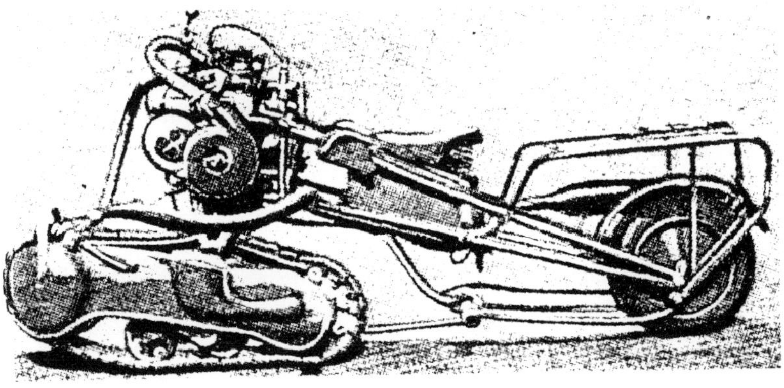

A Moto-Chenille Mercier similar to the one tested by the War Office. The version tested did not have the front shield fitted. (Bart Vanderveen Collection)

Catalogue picture of a 1929 New Hudson Model 83, similar to the version bought by the War Office. (New Hudson Ltd)

New Hudson

NEW HUDSON MODEL 83E 350 CC SV SINGLE-CYLINDER – 1929

A manufacturer from the 'vintage' motorcycling era, New Hudson supplied three of its models to the War Office for evaluation purposes, under contract, during mid-1929. These were assessed with the products of several other companies, who were hoping to secure government contracts. The three models from New Hudson were 350 cc SV Model 83Es, which were supplied as standard except possibly for the finish, which was probably of service colour, and the use of non-bright components. It is not clear whether these models were fitted with the factory specified 'long-lever' or the 'quadrant-type' gear-change; both were listed as options in the company's 1929 sales brochure.

Evaluated during the 1929 trials, the New Hudson models were noted as being too heavy and were ultimately rejected as unsuitable for service use. Following this, New Hudson took no further part in the supply of motorcycles for War Office use. Only one example is believed to exist now, reputedly in Sweden.

New Imperial

Another motorcycle manufacturer from the 'vintage' era, New Imperial supplied one of their current models for War Office evaluation during the 1935 series of trials. Ordered and supplied under contract, the machine was a standard type New Imperial Model 40 OHV 346 cc, possibly of 1936 specification.

In its advertisements New Imperial emphasized the Model 40's unit construction, praising the virtues of the helical gear-wheels on the unit's primary-drive as 'silent in operation, unbreakable and wear-proof'. This claim may well have been applicable to the average civilian user, but was found not to be the case with the War Office. Following 7,000 miles of rigorous War Office testing, inspection of the engine revealed that it was noticeably worn. The evaluation report submitted considered the reconditioning of the unit to be of 'doubtful value' because an excessive amount of repair work was required. Needless to say, the War Office rejected the Model 40 as unsuitable for service use.

Four years later, during 1939, the New Imperial Company saw ownership pass into the hands of Triumph and only limited manufacture of the company's models continued, production ceasing altogether on 2 September 1939, the eve of Britain's entry into the Second World War. All of the company's remaining tooling, machinery, completed machines and spares were then transferred to Triumph's factory in Coventry.

Following this, it was not expected that any further New Imperial motorcycles would be constructed, as most of the surviving remnants of the company had been placed in storage for the duration of the war. However, following the Dunkirk evacuation in May 1940 and the subsequent loss of huge amounts of equipment, Triumph, along with the majority of other motorcycle manufacturers, was inundated with large orders from the War Office for machines. In an attempt to meet the demand, Triumph offered the War Office a small quantity of New Imperial motorcycles, as well as recommencing production of its own models. Thirty-three New Imperial machines were therefore bought under contract and delivered to the War Office at Stirling, in Scotland. The exact details of these models, built by Triumph from parts held in stock, are unclear although it is known that all were of 496 cc OHV unit construction, and most likely conformed to the specification of New Imperial's Model 76 or 76DL (de-luxe). Finish of the motorcycles would have been in the standard service colour of 1940, and it is not known whether the machines carried the New Imperial insignia or that of Triumph.

Following completion of this odd contract, no more New Imperial machines were constructed or supplied to the War Office, and the name disappeared.

NEW IMPERIAL MODEL 40 350 CC OHV SINGLE-CYLINDER – 1935

Supplied in civilian trim for the 1935 seven-make trial in the latter part of the year, this machine was rejected because of considerable wear on its engine and other components. Only 7,000 miles of the usual 10,000 were completed.

In some respects New Imperial was ahead of its time as its motorcycles were designed using 'unit construction', a trend not generally adopted by the British motorcycle industry until the early 1960s.

NEW IMPERIAL MODEL 76 500 CC OHV SINGLE-CYLINDER – 1940

These motorcycles were supplied when the company was under the ownership of Triumph, and were most likely built up from spare parts held at Triumph's factory in Coventry.

Whether the machines were the Model 76 or the 76DL (de-luxe) is not known, and it can only also be assumed that standard cradle frames were used rather than New Imperial's pre-war spring frame.

Official photograph of the 1935 New Imperial Model 40, as used in the 1935 trials. (The Tank Museum, 138/E1)

Catalogue picture of New Imperials likely to have been offered to the War Office by Triumph in 1940. (New Imperial/Triumph Eng Co Ltd)

Norman

A small manufacturer, Norman used proprietary engines of Villiers manufacture in its motorcycles. With small premises and limited production capability, only two models were produced by the company at the time, the 125 cc 'Lightweight' and the 98 cc 'Motobyk'.

For reasons that remain unclear, two contracts were issued to the company mid-war, around the same time that James and Royal Enfield were producing their 125 cc models to War Office contract. However, it is unlikely that any of Norman's machines were used by the military services as this would have added to the existing problem of the authorities having too many models for which to cater adequately. Instead, these motorcycles were most probably issued to reserve occupation personnel, ARPs and other Civil Defence organizations.

NORMAN 'THE LIGHTWEIGHT' 125 CC SINGLE-CYLINDER 2-STROKE – 1943

This motorcycle used the Villiers 9D engine, as employed by James in its Model ML, although it is unclear whether it had an Amal carburettor, or a Villiers (as preferred by the military). Whether these machines were manufactured from a large stock of parts held by the company or production had to be resumed is not known.

Norton

Norton was one of the principal British motorcycle manufacturers for the armed services and other government organizations; production totals by the end of the war were second only to BSA. Further quantities were supplied for use by the Commonwealth services, largely the Canadians, with some of these machines occasionally being passed back to the British at later dates.

The first Norton motorcycles were suppled for military evaluation in 1932, these being a 16H, a Model 18 and a Model 19. Following these tests, another Model 16H 490 cc SV was purchased for the seven-make trial in 1935 and subjected to evaluation by the MEE. It proved acceptable for military service providing that certain modifications were implemented. From late 1936 onwards annual contracts were placed with the company for quantities of the model. Demand continued prior to, and throughout the course of the Second World War, with the occasional contract calling for combinations. The machine was produced for ten years, the longest length of time the War Office ever kept to buying one model of motorcycle.

The 16H was used in numerous roles, and was perhaps the foremost British military motorcycle until early 1941, when models from other manufacturers began to appear in quantity. Many front-line units then swapped to these newer models, the Norton machines being relegated to second-line or training formations.

Following the end of the Second World War the Model 16H continued in use with the armed services, although in considerably reduced quantities. It remained in service in very limited numbers right up to the late 1950s.

Norton's other principal motorcycle supplied to the services was the Model No. 1 combination, commonly termed the 'Big 4', which employed a non-permanently-engaged sidecar wheel drive. The model was originally designed to provide an all-terrain light vehicle for advance formation battlefield duties and general reconnaissance. Supplied up to the mid-war period, the unit was eventually rendered obsolete by the introduction of the American-produced Jeep, supplied to the War Department under Lend-Lease terms.

Other motorcycles supplied to the services included a number of experimental lightweight models, as well as other solo and combination prototypes for evaluation. The first of these experimental types, a lightened 16H, was supplied to the services as early as 1936, only a year after its introduction to the War Office. It was tested and then rejected on cost.

In 1937/8 Norton started development on its SWD prototype 16H for the War Office, which ultimately evolved into the well-known 'Big 4' outfit.

Some 350 cc OHV motorcycles appeared in 1938, followed a year later by a special lightweight 350 cc SV and two spring frame motorcycles of 500 cc (one SV, one OHV), all of which were well tested and subsequently rejected, as was a second attempt at a lightened 16H.

By 1940 the War Office needed a more powerful version of its 'Big 4' combination, so a 596 cc OHV powered outfit was supplied and tested; although its performance was better, it was not very reliable. After this failure Norton started working on a V-twin powered outfit to achieve the new specification of a higher road speed of 55 m.p.h., which was felt necessary, but this project was killed off by the arrival of the Jeep from the USA.

In 1944 Norton also offered a new SV parallel-twin in an attempt to win the contract eventually awarded to Triumph's TRW, after a long drawn-out test period.

Pre-war, Norton were often involved with development work with the authorities. Silencers and seats were two of the ideas explored, and the Pannier bag racks fitted to all makes of Second World War motorcycles were in fact a Norton design.

NORTON MODEL 16H 500 CC SV SINGLE-CYLINDER – 1932

This motorcycle was loaned by Norton Motors for tests along with a Model 18 and a Model 19.

Of the three models tested, it obviously stuck in the minds of the War Office testers, as it was later selected as the model from Norton's range for the seven-make trial of 1935.

Results of the test are unknown.

NORTON MODEL 18 500 CC OHV SINGLE-CYLINDER – 1932

Like the 1932 16H and Model 19, this machine was on loan from Norton Motors for the same period of time. How it fared during testing is unknown as the results no longer appear to exist.

Norton Model 19 596 cc OHV Single-Cylinder – 1932

The Model 19 was supplied for testing along with a 16H and Model 18 in 1932, but only on an on-loan basis for the duration of testing. As with the Model 18, the test results no longer appear to exist.

Norton Model 16H 500 cc SV Single-Cylinder – 1935

Delivered as a standard hand-change model, this machine was altered to foot change during testing, fitted with a different set of handlebars and given an 18-tooth engine sprocket as opposed to the previous 19-tooth version. The machine was delivered and tested in late 1935, so it is possible that the motorcycle was of 1936 specification.

After all the MEE tests of 1935, the 16H proved to be the best 500 cc motorcycle and was therefore approved for service, even though it suffered some notable wear on the cylinder-bore, a burnt exhaust, a broken headlamp bracket, a split rear mudguard and a broken petrol tank mounting bolt, to name but a few defects.

Norton Model 16H 500 cc SV Single-Cylinder – 1936–45

Following Norton's success in the 1935 tests, orders for 16Hs were issued every year until the end of the war, the occasional order being for combinations.

The first batch ordered were built with the requested modifications arising from the test model, the most obvious one being the installation of a foot-change gearbox replacing the original hand-change type. Some later 1936 motorcycles

Official photograph of the 1935 Norton 16H, as used in the 1935 trails. (The Tank Museum, 138/F4)

Official photograph of a 1936 Norton 16H. Note the alterations over the 1935 model. (IWM, KID 5666)

had an air cleaner fitted to the right of the rear wheel for use in dusty conditions overseas, and it also appears that none of these early 16Hs had speedometers fitted.

From 1937 onwards the air cleaner was not fitted until the Universal Vokes appeared, although it did not become a standard fitment until quite late in the War.

The next real visual change to the 16H came in 1938 when a crankcase shield was added. Two types are known to have been fitted, one devised by the MEE and the other by the India Office, which was the larger of the two.

More changes occurred in the early war years when pillion equipment and pannier bag racks were added. Other changes around this time included the repositioning of the speedometer, the removal of the number-plates, the change to tubular footrests (rubbers removed) and canvas handlebar grips, and the installation of a new headlamp (the Lucas DU42).

It is worth noting that in 1940, just prior to the fitment of pannier bag racks etc., Norton briefly fitted a pair of tool-boxes, as a pair of 'saddle bags', over the rear wheel, and this was used on at least one contract.

Norton's 16H was supplied to all the services, as well as to the Canadian Government. A proportion were fitted with sidecars, these coming from several manufacturers such as Swallow. Other notes of interest were the use of 1 in diameter handlebars (all the other manufacturers used ⅞ in, with the exception of the Matchless G3 model), and interchangeable wheels.

Official photograph of a 1938 Norton 16H. (IWM, KID 5621)

A 1942 Norton 16H in use in the desert. (REME Museum)

NORTON MODEL 16H (LIGHTENED) 500 CC SV SINGLE-CYLINDER – 1936

This was a test only model taken to Farnborough in October 1936. It was a standard production 16H, made 28lb lighter by the use of light alloys.

Its performance was equal to that of the standard production model, but the MEE considered its additional cost was not justifiable.

NORTON MODEL 50 350 CC OHV SINGLE-CYLINDER– 1938

Little is known about these models other than that in surviving documents for this contract the motorcycles are labelled as 'Gold Stars', a name more associated with BSA.

It can only be assumed that these must have been some form of competition model, bought for use by an Army team.

NORTON MODEL 16H 500 CC SV SINGLE-CYLINDER SWD COMBINATION – 1938

Based around a trials competition outfit, this motorcycle was fitted with one of two possible systems for its SWD. It either had gears within the rear wheel and sidecar wheel or a Baughan Motor Cycles SWD system.

It is more likely that the Baughan system was used as Dennis Mansell (Norton's works rider) had had this fitted to his 1935 works Norton by Baughans.

The Baughan system was simple yet very effective and relatively reliable. It consisted of a direct shaft drive from the rear wheel spindle through a simple dog clutch and two leather discs that acted as universal joints.

Trials carried out by the MEE showed that the SWD considerably improved cross-country performance, which was better than that of the 7 h.p. Austin car.

NORTON MODEL 16H 500 CC SV SINGLE-CYLINDER – 1938

This was a civilian specification motorcycle which was tested to see how good the engine improvements and modifications were and to determine whether they could be considered for the military 16H. (The most notable change was the use of fully enclosed valve-springs.)

The MEE noted that although the machine was 12 lb heavier, its performance was comparable with that of the existing War Office machines and they considered it suitable for War Office use. However, these 16H models were never to be bought as the War Office stuck to the 1937 specification engine to the end.

NORTON 'BIG 4' (MODEL NO. 1) 633 CC SV SINGLE-CYLINDER SWD COMBINATION – 1938/41

Following the success of the 16H pilot model, a machine was developed with a 633 cc engine to enhance its performance, an improved shaft drive (presumably by now Hardy-Spicer joints were used), and a sidecar suitable for carrying a Bren gun and ammunition.

Crew for the 'Big 4' was increased to three (there had been no pillion on the

A 1941 Norton 'Big 4' Combination in use with the Free French. (REME Museum)

16H pilot model) and further trials were carried out at the MEE and at Studland Bay. The machine's cross-country performance was now considered excellent and with its various handles provided for lifting, it was possible for its crew to take the vehicle over very difficult country.

After this test, the remainder of the first contract was fulfilled with these motorcycles being issued to troops for trials.

Trials continued and the MEE noted that the defects in the design of the original pilot model, notably the SWD, had been overcome. Dunlop Sports type tyres were also found to give better performance than the Universal Tyre and its performance was well maintained over the 10,000 mile trial. It was noted as suitable for War Office use, presumably late in 1938.

As with the 16H, the wheels of the 'Big 4' were interchangeable, but it used 18 in rims and had 4.00–18 tyres (the 16H used 3.25–19).

Lend-Lease Jeeps from the USA eventually killed off the 'Big 4'. Later they were released on to the civilian market having had the SWD system cut off. This was done to prevent accidents; once the drive was engaged, the machine had no steering capability and it was feared that people would fail to disengage it once on tarmac.

It has been noted that some 'Big 4s' used by the RAF did not have the SWD system fitted and reasons for this can only be presumed.

Surprising though it seems, the British Airborne did use a few of these outfits, up to mid-1942 for glider-borne troops, but these were probably replaced by stripped-down Jeeps as they became available.

In time the 'Big 4' was totally phased out and replaced by the Jeep. It ceased to be used as a front-line vehicle probably from about early 1943, somewhat earlier than its more complicated German equivalents, the Zundapp KS750 and the BMW R75. These lasted until 1944, when they were dropped on cost grounds and not because they had been proved inferior by a 4x4 car.

NORTON MODEL 18 500 CC OHV SINGLE-CYLINDER (WITH SPRING FRAME) – 1939

This was the first of the two spring frame models offered for testing against an orthodox 16H in August 1939.

Testers noted that the spring frame gave increased comfort for the rider, reducing the level of strain, but they thought that the sprung rear wheel limited the ultimate performance of the motorcycle.

The test results concluded that it was impossible to differentiate between the orthodox 16H's frame and the spring frame motorcycle, because of the different engines and gear ratios used. It was therefore requested that a 16H engined version be produced, for a better evaluation.

NORTON MODEL 16H 500 CC SV SINGLE-CYLINDER (WITH SPRING FRAME) – 1939

Following the testing of the first spring frame model, this machine was submitted for testing at the MEE. It too had a sprung rear wheel and a plunger type front spring instead of the normal coil spring. It was 22 lb heavier than an orthodox 16H.

Interestingly, when the motorcycle was tested in December 1939 the testers considered that it did not perform as well as an orthodox 16H across country, but it was far more comfortable for long-distance work across country.

Also the MEE considered that it gave a slightly inferior performance over loose surfaces as the rear wheel tended to ride over the top instead of digging into the hard sub-soil, with the rider unable to use his weight to get a grip. On roads, however, the comfort was increased and at very high speeds steering was improved. The MEE concluded that these advantages made up for the loss in performance, but the extra weight was a decided disadvantage.

NORTON EXPERIMENTAL LIGHTWEIGHT 350 CC SV SINGLE-CYLINDER – 1939

This first model was built to the War Office's specification for a new lightweight motorcycle with an engine of 350 cc or greater, and a weight of 250 lb or less.

Norton's 348 cc SV single-cylinder offering just tipped the scales at 278 lb and was the heaviest of the first batch of three lightweights tested in late 1939. The other two prototypes were Royal Enfield's 350 cc SV (276 lb) and Triumph's 350 cc OHV parallel twin (263 lb).

Tested over the usual 10,000 miles the 348 cc machine was found to handle easier than a standard 16H, but the motorcycle was not very reliable and its frame got badly damaged during the test.

For reasons unknown, at one stage of testing the motorcycle was sent to Universal Aircraft Ltd, of Mitcham, Surrey.

NORTON EXPERIMENTAL LIGHTWEIGHT 350 CC SV SINGLE-CYLINDER – 1940

Following the 1939 version, two more similar motorcycles were supplied. This time the exotic materials used to build the first lightweight were dispensed with to make production cheaper, and consequently the overall weight went up slightly.

After rigorous testing the machine was still deemed to be unreliable and therefore not suitable for War Office use. It appears that the only two lightweights the authorities showed any interest in were BSA's WB30 and Triumph's 3TW, which were the best of the lightweights. Both were OHVs, not the now out of favour SV singles, which testers were beginning to suggest were disposed of.

NORTON MODEL 18 500 CC OHV SINGLE-CYLINDER – 1940

Either seven or twelve of these 500 cc OHV single-cylinder models were bought, at a time when the war was reaching its height and losses from Dunkirk had to be replaced. As the machines were bought immediately it is assumed that they were either built from stock at the factory or were already assembled and awaiting delivery to dealers.

NORTON EXPERIMENTAL LIGHTWEIGHT 500 CC SV SINGLE-CYLINDER – 1940

This model was presumably offered in response to the criticisms of the 350 cc lightweight's poor reliability, as it was fitted with a 16H engine, proven reliable after many years of service with the War Office.

With the 16H engine fitted, the lightweight weighed in at 304 lb and gave a very satisfactory performance. It was deemed superior to both the standard 16H and the 350 cc lightweight, but it still proved unreliable and was not approved by the War Office.

NORTON MODEL 19 596 CC OHV SINGLE-CYLINDER SWD COMBINATION – 1940

This combination was produced in response to the need for a more powerful version of the 'Big 4'.

Tested in mid-1940, it lost compression twice in 1,496 miles, the problem being caused by the exhaust valves overheating and not seating. Although the machine did perform better than the standard 'Big 4', its petrol consumption was worse.

NORTON 1096 CC SV V-TWIN COMBINATION – 1940–1

This SWD combination was built as a proposed replacement for the 'Big 4' in

A Norton 500 cc SV Twin at some stage during its testing. Note the lack of pillion footrests, even though a dual seat is fitted. (IWM, MVE 27490/8)

response to the War Office's request for a new model which had to have a top speed of 55 m.p.h. on the road. Power came from a JAP V-twin engine as Norton did not produce any engines larger than the 633 cc of the 'Big 4'.

Similar models were also being developed by Triumph and Sunbeam, until the arrival of the Jeep killed them all off.

NORTON 500 CC SV PARALLEL TWIN – 1944 PROTOTYPE

Built as a result of the Standardization Committee's search for a new standard motorcycle for War Office service, which had to be either a 500 cc SV twin or a 350 cc OHV twin, this model was tested against several other motorcycles from Douglas, Triumph, BSA and Royal Enfield. It was not chosen, the Triumph TRW coming out as the eventual winner.

OEC

OEC was a small manufacturer perhaps better described as a 'custom' manufacturer because of the wide range of options it offered in the choice of frames, engines and front forks in the construction of all its motorcycles.

Possibly OEC's first involvement with the War Office in the supply of motorcycles for the British Armed Forces was in the late 1920s, when the RAF ordered and took delivery of a number of 342 cc Villiers 2-stroke powered motorcycles. Whether these were ordered over a number of years in several quantities under several contracts, or as a one-off purchase is not known at the time of writing.

Also at about this time, in 1928, OEC became involved in the further development of the Army's 3-wheeled motorcycle concept, when it was asked to supply three machines, similar in design but different in weight.

The first, supplied in early 1928, was powered by a 490 cc JAP engine, and was followed later in the year by two Blackburne powered versions of 2¾ h.p. and 3½ h.p. Testing of all three was carried out at Aldershot and later in Egypt and India, although it had been discontinued in the UK certainly by late 1929 or even 1930.

Most of the documented testing in the UK, interestingly, seems to have been centred around the 3½ h.p. version, whose Duplex steering was proving unsatisfactory and was subsequently altered to pillar type. Although this provided better control, it was still difficult when compared to a 2-wheeled machine.

OEC literature called the 3-wheeler a 'Caterpillar Tractor' as the two small rear wheels could have a track fitted over them to turn the motorcycle into a half-track, thus improving its ability on loose surfaces or soft ground. (The track was usually carried on the rear mudguard when not in use.) These motorcycles could be converted to 2-wheelers by substituting the twin rear wheels for another single wheel, and also adapted to carry pillion passengers if required.

OEC's final involvement with the military was in 1929, when it supplied three 3½ h.p. Blackburne powered 2-wheeled solos for the seven-make trial of that year, during which the model was rejected, not even making the second round of testing.

OEC 342 CC SINGLE-CYLINDER 2-STROKE – LATE 1920S

This model was powered by a Villiers single-cylinder 2-stroke engine. Although it is known that the RAF were the only recipients of the machine, it has yet to be established just what quantities were delivered. Few other details on the model seem to exist.

OEC 3-WHEELER 490 CC SV SINGLE-CYLINDER – 1928

This 3-wheeler was delivered for trial in early 1928 along with two versions of slightly different design and also different engine capacities. Its first trial was finished by March 1928, and it was compared with the Army's earlier Triumph-based version.

A slightly surprising move by the War Office, considering the usual military secrecy, was to allow this motorcycle to be tested by the motorcycle press in mid-March of the same year. Shortly afterwards magazines such *Motor Cycling* and *The Motor Cycle* printed articles for friend or foe alike to read. Needless to say, this did not happen again until the war began, when results of Army motorcycle tests were again allowed to be published, presumably as an aid to recruitment, or even as a form of propaganda.

This version, unlike the other two, had a JAP SV engine, which leaned backwards in the frame, and an exhaust which ran down the left-hand side of the motorcycle. (On the 2¾ h.p. and 3½ h.p. versions, the exhaust ran down the right-hand side.)

The machine weighed a gigantic 453 lb, approximately 100 lb heavier than the

Official photograph of the 1928 OEC 490 cc 3-wheeler. Note how the engine is canted back in frame, unlike the smaller versions. (PRO, WO 194 (45) – 5353)

3½ h.p. version, on which all test reports seem to centre. The extreme weight of the former machine may explain why testing on it was so short lived, and why it was discarded so soon.

OEC 3-WHEELER 350 CC SV SINGLE-CYLINDER – 1928

This version, weighing around 354 lb and powered by a Blackburne SV engine, appears to have been the main test model, and testing continued at the MWEE until July 1929, with some testing also taking place in Egypt and India.

During testing the original Duplex steering was altered to pillar type as it was proving unsatisfactory for cross-country work. This change provided better control but, as with all the 3-wheelers, it was still not as easy to control as a 2-wheeler and the rider was quickly exhausted. The MWEE's general conclusions were that the machine's cross-country performance was not sufficient to warrant the extra complications entailed, and that the extra weight over a 2-wheeled motorcycle (approximately 95 lb) was not desirable.

OEC 3-WHEELER 250 CC SV SINGLE-CYLINDER – 1928

This version is the one used in the OEC catalogue pictures. Although it was very similar to the 350 cc version it had a number of lighter components on it, most notably the wheels and tyres, which reduced its weight to 310 lb.

How it compared to the other two 3-wheelers has not been established at time of writing.

Official photograph of the 1928 OEC 350 cc 3-wheeler. Note the two additional spiked stands that were not fitted on the 490 cc version. (PRO, WO 194 (45) – 5311)

Official photograph of the 1928 OEC 250 cc 3-wheeler. It was this version that was shown in the OEC brochures of the time, where it was referred to as a tractor. (PRO, WO 194 (45) – 5313)

Official photograph of a 1929 OEC model that was used in the 1929 trials. Note the large clearance between the rear wheel and the mudguard. This was needed to allow the fitment of the leather belt over the rear tyre to improve the machine's off-road abilities. When not in use it was stored on top of the rear mudguard. (IWM, KID 5589/HU63633)

OEC 2-WHEELER 350 CC SV SINGLE-CYLINDER – 1929

Three of these machines were bought for the 1929 seven-make trial but after initial testing the model was not chosen for further testing.

Power was provided by a Blackburne SV engine, although not the same version as on the 3-wheeler, and it came equipped with a rear tyre belt for off-road use, as did all the 3-wheelers.

Panther

Under its previous name of Phelon & Moore (P&M), the company was well-known for its association with the Royal Flying Corps during the First World War, and then the RAF from 1918 with its 3½ h.p. machines.

From 1925 the name Panther started appearing on the RAF's new combinations, and on its solo machines later on. With the arrival of these new machines, the old 3½ h.p. P&Ms were slowly phased out, with the last leaving service around the late 1920s.

The Panther model was to stay in service until the mid-1930s, when it was replaced to some degree by BSA's War Office Twin. Although the arrival of this machine apparently caused the end of Panther's association with the RAF (and also with the War Office), it appears that some Model 100s were bought around 1938–9.

PANTHER COMBINATIONS AND SOLOS, OHV SINGLE-CYLINDER – 1925–3?

These OHV motorcycles were to replace 3½ h.p. SV P&Ms that were in use with the RAF. First appearing in 1925, they lasted until the 1930s, when newer models from other manufacturers began to replace them and effectively ended the bond between Panther and the RAF. The model that specifically caused this was BSA's War Office Twin, which was introduced in the early 1930s.

A few interesting features about these motorcycles were their interchangeable wheels, stands for all the wheels (including the sidecar) and massive butterfly nut type oil-filler dipsticks, which could be removed without the use of a tool.

PANTHER MODEL 100 598 CC OHV SINGLE-CYLINDER – 1938–9

Possibly 100 of these machines were ordered, although at the time of writing it is not sure whether they were delivered.

Details of the model are scarce and only an official photograph in the Imperial War Museum's department of photographs confirms its existence as a War Office motorcycle.

One unusual feature was the separate dynamo and magneto set-up, which was quite different to the normal 1939 arrangement shown in catalogue brochures.

Official photograph of the Panther Model 100, as investigated by the Ministry of Supply. (IWM, MH 11972)

Royal Enfield

The Enfield Cycle Company Limited, commonly known as Royal Enfield, of Redditch in the Midlands was a major supplier of motorcycles to the services during the Second World War, along with other products produced for the government. The War Department (Army) was by far the major user of Royal Enfield motorcycles, although both the Air Ministry (RAF) and Admiralty Department (Royal Navy), together with several elements of the Civil Defence services, also made use of certain quantities of machines.

This, however, was not the case prior to the outbreak of the Second World War. During October 1935 the War Office purchased two Royal Enfield motorcycles as part of its evaluation programme. The particular models chosen were the Model C 350 cc SV single-cylinder and the small capacity Model B 250 cc SV single-cylinder. Neither model coped with the rigorous War Office testing programme, both suffering considerable mechanical problems within the specified 10,000 mile assessment limit and both subsequently rejected by the War Office for their poor reliability and endurance in comparison to the other makes evaluated at the time.

It was not until April 1940 that Royal Enfield supplied any more motorcycles for War Office evaluation. Then two 350 cc SV single-cylinder machines, manufactured from special lightweight steels and aluminium alloys in order to reduce the overall weight to the War Office's specified limit of 250 lb or less, were delivered, tested and later rejected, on the grounds that they were neither reliable nor robust enough to withstand the rigours of military use.

Earlier, in May 1939, Royal Enfield had received a sizeable order from the Department of Air Defence (embracing several organizations) for the supply of 600 motorcycles, these being Model D 250 cc SV machines a type not previously evaluated by the military. The Department of Air Defence required these motorcycles for general message relaying between dispersed units and the low performance Model D was considered both suitable and available at a time of increasing demand. Two months later, a further 900 Model D machines were ordered by the Ministry of Supply for military use in the training programme of personnel as part of the build-up to war.

Following the outbreak of war, Royal Enfield received further orders for motorcycles, which were generally of the 1940 civilian model range finished, as appropriate, for the military. After the evacuation at Dunkirk and the loss of virtually all equipment, most major motorcycle manufacturers were inundated with huge orders from the War Office for machines, further contracts being placed well in advance of the completion of existing ones. Supply rather than suitability was paramount in the initial stages; once the situation had settled a little, the War Office specified the supply of one standard type of machine in order to avoid potential problems caused by having a wide range of different machines. The type that was specified from Royal Enfield was the 1940 specification Model C 350 cc SV single-cylinder machine (much improved from the earlier offering of 1935), supplied and finished to War Office standard.

From 1942 onwards, the WD/C was superseded by the WD/CO, production of the WD/C ceasing during early 1942. During the course of the Second World War Royal Enfield also supplied the War Office with almost 8,000 lightweight 125 cc 2-stroke WD/RE motorcycles. Again, this existing pre-war design was

Official photograph of the 1935 Royal Enfield Model B, tested at the same time as the 1935 seven-make trials (but not as a part of them). (The Tank Museum, 138/E5)

evaluated for potential service use and, with developments, ultimately adopted primarily for use by Airborne formations and other assault troops in-line with the instigation and rapid expansion of the British Airborne arm after 1940.

In 1944, wartime production demands taking precedence, Royal Enfield (along with certain other manufacturers) did manage to undertake limited development work towards a new standardized model intended for military use as a replacement for many of the various types then in service. The particular machine it offered the War Office was a rather odd-looking 350 cc SV twin-cylinder model, which was eventually rejected after due assessment.

ROYAL ENFIELD MODEL B 250 CC SV SINGLE-CYLINDER – 1935

Only one civilian specification model was supplied to the War Office for military evaluation alongside the 1935 series of trials. This model was evaluated for general road use only by the War Office but its poor reliability and endurance led to its rejection for service use. Problems encountered in its 10,000 mile test were a broken inlet valve, a bent exhaust valve, a broken mag-dyno, loosening of the tank-top instrument panel, a broken chainguard, a twisted frame as well as other minor faults.

ROYAL ENFIELD MODEL C 346 CC SV SINGLE-CYLINDER – 1935 CIVILIAN SPECIFICATION

As with the 250 cc Model B, only one 346 cc Model C was supplied to the War Office for evaluation in the 1935 trials; it too was a civilian specification model.

Official photograph of the 1935 Royal Enfield Model C, as tested in the 1935 trials. (The Tank Museum, 138/F1)

This model was evaluated for general service use which included rigorous off-road testing as well as normal road use. It was subsequently rejected for service use because of its poor robustness and reliability. Problems encountered in its 10,000 mile test were faulty timing gears, overheating, the piston crown breaking off (twice), stripped teeth on the mag-dyno driving gear, partial seizure, a blown head gasket (requiring a replacement to be fitted), a broken mudguard stay and a broken primary chain.

ROYAL ENFIELD EXPERIMENTAL LIGHTWEIGHT 350 CC SV SINGLE-CYLINDER – 1940

Royal Enfield built two experimental lightweight 350 cc SV machines for evaluation by the War Office in response to the requirement for a general-purpose motorcycle that could be produced for service use, of a capacity of 350 cc or less and a maximum weight of 250 lb or less. Royal Enfield was not alone in producing such a model and was competing against similar offerings from other major motorcycle manufacturers. Produced in the spring of 1940, the engine design of the machines was based around the 250 cc SV Model D and, in common with their competitors, both were constructed of special steels and also of lightweight aluminium in order to keep the weight to a minimum.

Although the performance of both machines proved to be satisfactory, the Ministry of Supply held reservations about the models' robustness and reliability for service use. Consequently, none were ordered and the contracts went to BSA for its Model WB30 and to Triumph for its twin-cylinder Model 3TW.

The War Office serial numbers for these two motorcycles are not known,

Royal Enfield's Experimental 350 cc Military Lightweight of 1940. (Royal Enfield Owners' Club)

although they were both supplied under contract number C.6718 and were initially delivered to the War Office at Feltham, Middlesex. Incidentally, it is worth noting that the original lighting set was changed to the same type as that fitted on the Triumph 3TW.

ROYAL ENFIELD MODEL WD/D 248 CC SV SINGLE-CYLINDER – 1939–40

The Royal Enfield 248 cc SV Model D was an established pre-war design and was the first model in the Royal Enfield range of machines to be supplied in quantity to the War Office. The first large order for 600 Model D machines was placed by the Ministry of Supply in May 1939, during the preparations for war, for delivery to the Department of Air Defence and were intended for light communications duties between the various locations of the many elements of this organization. These machines were essentially civilian specification models finished in the appropriate service colours. The machines supplied after the outbreak of war, generally in early 1940, were basically the same but lacked the valanced rear portion of the front mudguard.

As time was at a premium, the model was considered suitable and ordered even though it had not been previously evaluated by the War Office. Further bulk orders followed for quantities of 900, 350 and 300 machines, along with several smaller orders.

In late 1939 and early 1940 small quantities of civilian Model D motorcycles were pressed into military service, overpainted in the appropriate colours. These were generally obtained from civilian stocks awaiting despatch at the factory or on sale in dealers' showrooms.

The Model D was employed mainly by the Army and its role was nearly always

Royal Enfield's Model WD/D, as supplied in 1939 and 1940. (Royal Enfield Owners' Club)

either for training purposes or for light communications duties. It was used to some considerable extent by female ATS (Auxiliary Territorial Service) personnel, for whom the Model D was both suitable and popular. Production of the Model D was halted during early 1941 and no further machines were made.

ROYAL ENFIELD MODEL CO 346 CC OHV SINGLE-CYLINDER – 1941

These motorcycles were accepted by the Royal Navy prior to their adoption by the War Office as Royal Enfield's main offering for the remainder of the war.

Pictures of these motorcycles (along with a rider from the Royal Navy) were used by Royal Enfield in advertisements to promote its products in the then current *The Motor Cycle* and *Motor Cycling* magazines of 1941.

Perhaps surprising, there are many differences between the later WD/CO and this model, which is much more similar to the WD/L and the WD/J2.

ROYAL ENFIELD MODEL KX COMBINATION 1140 CC SV V-TWIN – 1941

From the contract date it can only be assumed that these motorcycles were built up from pre-war stocks of parts still in the factory and that they were part of Royal Enfield's clear-out of old models, before the company switched over production entirely to WD/COs.

It is not known how the models were used, or whether they had passenger or box sidecars fitted.

Royal Enfield's Model CO, as bought by the Royal Navy in 1941. Note the differences with the WD/G and the later WD/CO. (The National Motor Museum, C15337A)

ROYAL ENFIELD MODEL L 570 CC SV SINGLE-CYLINDER – 1940

This motorcycle was loaned by the factory for testing in early 1940, when its suitability was compared with a standard WD 16H.

Although it was heavier than the 16H, testing showed that its petrol consumption was in fact better, and during its 1,000 mile test no mechanical failures occurred and it was considered to have stood up well to the test. Only two criticisms were noted, those being its ground clearance and the lack of a sump guard.

Interestingly, the test notes show this motorcycle as a 500 cc, although the Model L was usually 570 cc.

ROYAL ENFIELD MODEL WD/L 570 CC SV SINGLE-CYLINDER – 1940–1

Not originally intended for use by the War Office, this model was readily available for production and delivery, and was supplied during a time of urgent demand. Two orders were placed in 1940, with the last delivery being completed during early 1941. No further machines were built or supplied after this date.

Although the WD/L was initially supplied to the War Department (Army), it is of note that subsequently many were transferred over to the Admiralty Department (Royal Navy) for general shore-base duties, with a proportion going to the Air Ministry (RAF) as well. The WD/L continued in limited use with all three services until the end of the war with the few survivors being sold off as war surplus almost immediately.

A 1940 Royal Enfield WD/L. (Royal Enfield Owners' Club)

ROYAL ENFIELD MODEL KX 1140 CC SV V-TWIN COMBINATION WITH SWD – 1941

Only one machine was produced in response to the brief need for a more powerful version of Norton's 'Big 4'.

Powered by Royal Enfield's own SV V-twin, the model was short lived, along with similar models from Sunbeam, BSA and Norton, because of the arrival of the Lend-Lease Jeep from America.

ROYAL ENFIELD MODEL WD/J2 499 CC OHV TWIN-PORT SINGLE-CYLINDER – 1941

This machine was Royal Enfield's 499 cc OHV model single-cylinder motorcycle fitted with a twin exhaust-port head, of which the Air Ministry ordered a small quantity during mid–1941 under a single contract, number C.10103.

The WD/J2 was similar in appearance and construction to the WD/G, with near-identical fittings including tool-boxes and a large air cleaner box for the carburettor.

Interestingly, Royal Enfield publicity advertisements of the period always seem to show the WD/J2 on an airfield setting, complete with RAF rider.

ROYAL ENFIELD MODEL WD/G 346 CC OHV SINGLE-CYLINDER – 1940–1

Along with the WD/L, the WD/G was essentially a pre-war civilian version that was supplied to the War Office because it was readily available, along with tooling and parts, following the loss of equipment at Dunkirk.

The WD/G supplied was generally to a high performance 'sporting'

A 1941 Royal Enfield WD/J2, as used by the RAF. (The Enfield Cycle Co.)

specification, the engine in some machines fitted with a cylinder head and barrel of aluminium, which gave a high compression ratio and subsequent increase in top speed and overall performance.

Although the WD/G was seen to be the ideal replacement for the WD/C, two motorcycles from contract number C.9311 were tested for their suitability. The first did not live up to expectations and was considered to have a generally unsatisfactory performance, although it had handled well on the road. Modifications were suggested and carried out for the second motorcycle, consisting of wider gear ratios, a higher compression piston and a larger carburettor. Following 2,500 miles of testing in early 1941, the model was considered suitable for War Office use, but there was still concern over fuel consumption and it was also recommended that future motorcycles have their saddles raised by 1 in and that a rear stand be specified as opposed to the centre stand currently fitted. The same testers also recommended that the current SV WD/Cs be fitted with OHV engines (this was noted on 28.5.41).

A 1940 Royal Enfield WD/G. (Royal Enfield Owners' Club)

It is quite probable that many of the WD/G machines remaining in use later in the war, following the introduction of the similar model WD/CO, lost much of their original identity during workshop overhauls and rebuild programmes. In such instances, replacement components fitted would most likely have been WD/CO fittings and, in the case of an engine overhaul, the original unit was replaced by a reconditioned standard WD/CO powerplant.

ROYAL ENFIELD MODEL WD/RE 126 CC SINGLE-CYLINDER 2-STROKE – 1942–5

The WD/RE was procured by the War Office primarily as a lightweight, expendable means of transport for use by the developing Airborne elements of the armed services. The requirement was for a machine of adequate performance, reliable and robust enough for use off-road, of lightweight construction enabling it to be dropped by parachute or carried within aircraft or gliders, and capable of being manhandled by the rider over minor obstacles. The intended role of such a motorcycle was to provide an efficient means of relaying messages and signals with the minimum possible delay over relatively short distances between dispersed Airborne and assault formations, particularly in situations where radio communications were difficult or non existent.

Following the birth of the British Airborne arm in early 1942, the War Office procured under contract twenty WD/RE motorcycles from Royal Enfield for evaluation. The company had the basic model readily available, having introduced it on to the civilian market during 1939 as a general-utility, all-purpose lightweight. The models supplied for evaluation were essentially civilian model 1940 machines without modification, and had the pre-war frame design, a foot-brake on the right, an Amal carburettor, a low-mounted tool-box and a single-box exhaust system.

The evaluation of the machines was generally successful, although

Royal Enfield's 1942 WD/RE, as first supplied. Note the differences to the later WD/REs, including the exhaust system and headlamp and the addition of a speedometer. (Royal Enfield Owners' Club)

A much modified early WD/RE in the first version of its proposed dropping cradle in late 1942. (Royal Enfield Owners' Club)

An early WD/RE in the second version of its dropping cradle. Interestingly, the report from which this photograph comes describes the motorcycle as a DKW. (Crown Copyright/A&AEE Boscombe Down, NB 3383–2)

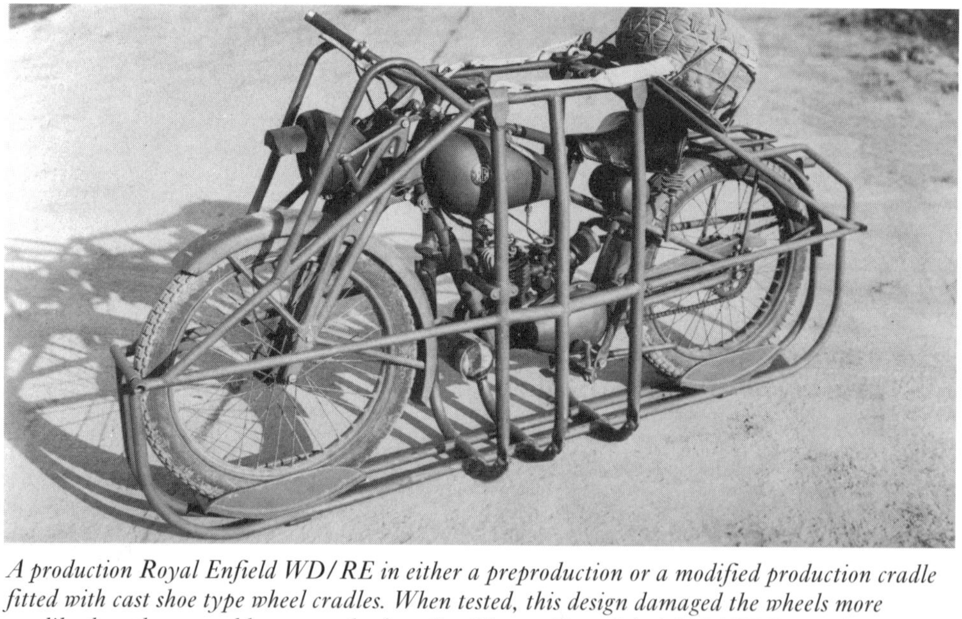

A production Royal Enfield WD/RE in either a preproduction or a modified production cradle fitted with cast shoe type wheel cradles. When tested, this design damaged the wheels more readily than the normal bar type wheel cradle. (Crown Copyright/A&AEE Boscombe Down, NB 3383–6)

A production Royal Enfield WD/RE in an Enfield-built production cradle. (Crown Copyright/A&AEE Boscombe Down, NB 3383–5)

A Royal Enfield WD/RE on No. 6 bomb rack of a Douglas Dakota. (Crown Copyright/A&AEE Boscombe Down, NB 3383–4)

modifications would be necessary before total acceptance by the War Office. The modifications included installing a twin-box exhaust system to help suppress noise, replacing the Amal component with a Villiers carburettor (hence the 'V' prefix on the engine), repositioning the tool-box to below the saddle as the existing space had now been taken up by the carburettor and air cleaner assembly, installing a folding kick-start, folding footrests and folding handlebars to ensure compactness when packed, and modifying the frame, principally so that the saddle could be raised to a height of 29 in. A revised, standardized Miller lighting system was incorporated into the design, a 35- instead of a 34-tooth rear wheel sprocket was fitted, a sealed vent was added to the filler-cap to avoid fuel spillage when the machine was packed in its drop carrier and the foot-brake was relocated to the left side of the motorcycle.

Following the modifications, the first large contracts for the WD/RE were placed during early 1943, with deliveries commencing forthwith.

In early and mid–1942 two different protective cradles for the machine were developed by the AFEE to fulfil the War Office's requirement that the machine could be safely dropped by parachute into a landing zone along with troops.

All versions of the cradle had to withstand being dropped from the bomb racks of aircraft such as the Halifax, Dakota, Lancaster and Albermarle and be opened quickly on landing, with minimal damage to the motorcycle.

Subsequent testing of the first cradle showed it to be insufficiently rigid and protective. The second prototype was tested in September 1942, and proved infinitely better. This was then modified, incorporating heavier tubing and increased bracing, and, in December of the same year, handed over to Royal Enfield as a pattern for preparing the finalized version. These went into production at the Enfield Cycle Company, Calton Hill, Edinburgh, to be introduced in 1943.

It should be mentioned that not all WD/RE motorcycles were dropped into the battle area by parachute. In reality, only a small percentage would have arrived by this method along with the initial assault formation. A far greater percentage arrived in troop-carrying gliders whereby up to four machines, with riders, could land in one group, usually in one piece and in a specific area. When delivered by glider, the motorcycles were not carried within the protective frames, and were secured by harness straps that attached to the interior of the fuselage of the glider.

A percentage of WD/RE machines were also employed for use outside the Airborne arm, principally by assault formations engaged in coastal landings during 1943 and 1944, when the machines were carried ashore from landing-craft and used for communication duties on beach-heads.

During the early post-war years, many surviving models were disposed of as war surplus, even though the type remained in limited service use until the end of the 1940s. Many were purchased by dealers and subsequently rebuilt as civilian models for sale to the public in the cheap utility class, and much sought after at the time.

ROYAL ENFIELD MODEL WD/C 346 CC SV SINGLE-CYLINDER – 1940–2

The 346 cc SV WD/C Royal Enfield became the company's main production model for the War Office for almost two years between 1940 and early 1942.

Official photograph of Royal Enfield's 1940 WD/C. (REME Museum)

During the production period, the type was subject to numerous changes and improvements. There were specification changes for nearly every contract issued, although most of these modifications were to the cycle parts and fittings rather than mechanical components.

Early WD/Cs had bolt-together fork legs, aluminium brake plates, rubber-mounted handlebars (of which some had mounting points for the levers attached), a lock on the rectangular tool-box, number-plates, a small rear carrier and a top-fed float chamber; they did not have filters on the timing-chest cover, pannier bag racks or pillion facilities.

As time went on changes had to be made to suit new requirements; the aluminium brake plates were replaced by steel ones (due to shortage of aluminium and the needs of the Aircraft Industry), racks and pillion facilities were eventually added, a rigid fixing for the handlebars was introduced to prevent them rotating, and a filter added to the engine-timing cover to improve the life of the big-end. Other minor changes were made to the design of the forks, tool-box knobs, and grass leg, among other things.

It should be mentioned that, contrary to popular belief, the WD/C was not identical to the later model OHV WD/CO (engines apart). It was virtually a completely different motorcycle, and very little was interchangeable between the two. (Engine crankcases, gear-boxes and frames were totally different.)

Although production of the WD/C ceased during late 1941/early 1942 (deliveries to the War Office terminating during early 1942), the model continued in service until the end of the war, chiefly with the Army and a number with the RAF. Most were used for light communications and convoy escort duty roles for most of their service, use of the type gradually diminishing during late 1944. Following the end of the war in Europe in May 1945, the WD/C Royal Enfield was among the first types of War Office machinery to be sold off to a transport-hungry public, with advertisements for the type 'Ex-WD Reconditioned As New' appearing in the motorcycle press as early as 1946.

Having been rebuilt from stocks of both new and reconditioned parts, these post-war 'new' Model C motorcycles were frequently fitted with an odd assortment of parts not specified for the type when originally constructed for the War Office. Examples of such include late-type WD/CO girder-forks with side-mounted check springs and raised speedometer bracket. A further point is that many of the ex-military engines fitted into these post-war rebuilt WD/C machines are still marked as military units and usually carry the contract number on the cases. However, it will often be found that the engine number is a post-war re-stamp on top of the original number, carried out so that the engine number matches the frame into which the unit was fitted when rebuilt.

ROYAL ENFIELD MODEL WD/CO AND WD/CO/B 346 CC OHV SINGLE-CYLINDER – 1942–5

The Royal Enfield 346 cc OHV WD/CO was introduced into War Office service during early 1942 as a direct replacement for the current WD/C 346 cc SV, which had been criticized throughout its service life for a general lack of overall performance.

During the four years of production the WD/CO, like the earlier WD/C, was subject to several noticeable changes and modifications. Some of these were the result of improvements while others were introduced because of the need to economize.

Early machines did not have the side-mounted check springs fitted to the forks as on all later models. Steering-dampers were fitted, only to be removed in later years along with the footrest, handlebar grip, kick-start and gear-

A Royal Enfield WD/CO/B, as supplied to one contract only. (Royal Enfield Owners' Club)

change rubbers, because of supply problems caused by the war in the Far East.

Later models had canvas handlebar grips, only two tool-boxes (the rectangular one was removed after the first contract), a new chainguard tail section, and a totally different frame. It is worth mentioning that there were in fact three styles of frames, of which the first two were similar, with different rear sections, but the third was vastly different.

One other major change, which was only temporary in 1942, was the installation of a Burman gearbox in place of the Albion type normally used for contract number C.13870. Machines so fitted were termed WD/CO/B.

Other changes to the WD/CO were minor, embracing horns, handlebar control levers and fittings, exhaust brackets, petrol-pipes, chainguards, etc. Machines produced from late 1944 onwards were generally factory-fitted with tank-top mounted Universal type Vokes air filters; those produced from early 1945 onwards were almost certainly fitted with the late war specification Lucas lighting equipment.

Between 1942 and 1945 the WD/CO served with elements of all three armed services, with a proportion also seeing service with certain Civil Defence Units. In comparison to the earlier WD/C, the WD/CO was employed in a wider range of uses, principally road communications and convoy escort duties. It did not see considerable usage in forward areas as perhaps originally intended, being generally rated below the Matchless G3/L and Ariel W/NG for performance and off-road suitability chiefly because of the poor ground clearance of the frame. Furthermore, the crankcase bottom was exposed to a degree and not protected by either a shield or frame-member as on other makes – important considerations for off-road use.

As with the WD/C, WD/CO machines were sold off following the end of the war, the first quantities arriving on the civilian market during early 1946 having been either factory rebuilt or dealer reconditioned in the majority of cases. Again, mismatched components of various dates were frequently fitted and engines and frames restamped to match each other.

ROYAL ENFIELD 350 CC SV PARALLEL TWIN – 1944 PROTOTYPE

This was Royal Enfield's response to the military request for a new standardized motorcycle for post-war service.

Although it had many features which were favourable from a wear point of view (totally enclosed primary and secondary chaincases), it was not pursued as 350 cc OHV twins or 500 cc SV twins were considered to be the minimum requirement.

Rudge Whitworth

Rudge Whitworth supplied examples of its products for evaluation by the War Office during the mid–1930s. Government contracts were eagerly sought by all manufacturers as they provided a profitable bulk order, together with good publicity material – the Government, it was generally assumed, only used the best of anything.

During the latter half of 1936 the War Office ordered under contract two motorcycles from Rudge Whitworth for evaluation purposes which were delivered to the MEE at Farnborough, Hampshire. The two models supplied were to standard civilian specification, although the Army removed the linked front and rear brake arrangement in order to bring the model into line with other manufacturers' models being assessed at the same time. One of the models supplied was the 250 cc OHV 'Rapid' model, while the other was the well-known 500 cc OHV 'Ulster' model. After testing, however, both models were rejected.

Not to be defeated, and inspired to a degree by the partial success of its 250 cc 'Rapid' model in comparison to other manufacturers' products tested at the time, Rudge Whitworth concentrated on developing a model specifically for service use which incorporated the successes and recommendations from the War Office tests. The new model was loosely based on its 250 cc 'Rapid', and was called the 'Service' model. The company supplied an initial batch of twelve of these new models under contract during the latter half of 1938, all delivered to the War Office at Chilwell, Nottinghamshire.

According to War Office records, no further Rudge Whitworth machines were supplied following this delivery and information relating to the fate of the type is now almost non-existent.

It is known, however, that production of motorcycles at Rudge ceased on 18 December 1939, although Autocycles were still being made for some time into 1940. The fate of the twelve models delivered prior to the outbreak of war is not entirely known, but one has been restored by a Rudge enthusiast.

A final note of interest is that in pre-war years, the Army display team (White Helmets) used a number of Rudge motorcycles in their act, and it may well have been because of this that Rudges were originally tested by the MEE.

RUDGE 'RAPID' 247 CC OHV SINGLE-CYLINDER – 1936

Initially loaned to Farnborough for testing in July 1936, this standard commercial model was to have some unspecified modifications carried out to it after its eventual purchase.

After the usual 10,000 mile test, of which nearly 2,500 miles were across country, the 'Rapid' was only described as 'fair' in terms of reliability, even though its performance was generally good.

Its main problem was its gearbox, which persistently failed, and largely because of this it was not recommended as a suitable alternative to the standard War Office motorcycle.

RUDGE 'ULSTER' 500 CC OHV SINGLE-CYLINDER – 1936

Delivered to Farnborough at the same time as the 250 cc 'Rapid', the 'Ulster' was also initially on loan and purchased later following modifications.

Prior to the modifications to the gear-change position and brake pedal (which were deemed necessary to bring it in line with other service models) and the lowering of the first gear from 13.9 to 1 to 16 to 1, the machine's performance was described as promising, no doubt partly down to its 4-valve head.

Official photograph of the modified 1936 Rudge 'Rapid' test model. (PRO, WO 194 (45) – 7897)

Following all these modifications, the usual 10,000 mile reliability trial was conducted, of which 2,620 miles were across country. Afterwards the motorcycle was described as only 'fair' in terms of reliability, requiring a considerable number of replacement parts (mainly valve-gear components which suffered unacceptable wear). Needless to say, the 'Ulster' was turned down.

RUDGE 'SERVICE' 247 CC OHV SINGLE-CYLINDER – 1938

Following the partial success with its 'Rapid' model, Rudge set about producing a purpose-made model for the War Office, loosely based on the successful machine.

To overcome the main criticism of the 'Rapid' (its gearbox), Rudge used its 'Ulster's gearbox, clutch (which then necessitated the use of a new chaincase), and rear wheel. Other notable changes included the use of a Lucas mag-dyno, a rear stand, uncoupled brakes, a right-side gear-change/left-side footbrake, and a prop-stand.

Twelve of these new 'Service' models were purchased under contract and issued to units for extended trials in late 1938.

Finally, it is thought that Rudge were given the go-ahead to build another 200 'Service' models which are reported to have been built, delivered, and later destroyed in an air raid. However, what is more likely is that Rudge, as a minor

Official photograph of a 1938 Rudge Service model. (PRO, WO 194 (45) – – – – –)

motorcycle manufacturer, was dropped when war broke out, as it could not supply the number of machines that would be needed, as larger manufacturers could. Also, the Hayes Middlesex factory, where the 'Service' models were to be built, made radars and these were probably regarded as more important than a few motorcycles.

Stewart-Ehrlich

A prototype manufacturer, Stewart-Ehrlich offered the Ministry of Supply a proposed model, a 250 cc split-single 2-stroke of unit construction, only for it to be turned down. Undeterred, it then offered a 350 cc split-single 2-stroke, this now coupled to a Burman gearbox. This time the MEE did conduct a day's trial on the model on 15 October 1941. Although no further testing was conducted some development was continued as this model later evolved into one of the post-war EMC motorcycles.

Sunbeam

Sunbeam originally supplied equipment during the First World War, and produced Ambulance-kitted combinations. Later the company tried several times to sell its models to the War Office, but it seems that each attempt was stopped because of a change of ownership.

In the late 1920s a Model 6 motorcycle was known to have been bought and it was about this time that the current owners, Marston, sold the name to ICI. (Whether Model 6s were also bought and supplied after the change of ownership is unknown.)

The next proposed Sunbeam was the 1936 'Lion', which was specifically altered for the War Office during testing only to have its reliability trial stopped because of yet another change of ownership in 1937.

The final time a Sunbeam-badged military motorcycle appeared was during the war. This motorcycle was a Matchless-engined V-twin combination with SWD, which was specially developed as a proposed replacement model for the Norton 'Big 4'. Once again there was a change of ownership, to BSA, but this time it was probably not the cause of the cancellation of the current motorcycle. The far more likely reason this time was the arrival of the Willys-Overland Jeep, after which development work on SWD models was stopped by all manufacturers.

SUNBEAM MODEL 6 492 CC SV SINGLE-CYLINDER - 1927

Details about this model are scarce and the only fact known to the authors is that the machine is now owned by a member of the Sunbeam Marston Register.

Whether the Model 6 was bought in limited quantities over a number of years or as a one-off in 1927 is not known.

SUNBEAM 'LION' 500 CC SV SINGLE-CYLINDER – 1936

This was a 500 cc SV model (similar to the War Office's new Norton 16H) and had been specifically altered hopefully to meet the requirements of the War Office.

Official photograph of the 1936 Sunbeam Lion, taken at Farnborough in the winter of that year. (PRO, WO 194 (45) – – – – –)

Initially, this model was only loaned for testing at Farnborough, which started in October 1936. However, after its initial performance testing, which proved promising, it was bought. Certain modifications were carried out, most notably installing a lower first gear.

Following this, the MEE's obligatory reliability trial was commenced. This was never finished, however, as the company was bought out by AMC, which already had a successful military model of its own, the G3, and did not want a second. All testing stopped and the 'Lion' was quietly forgotten.

SUNBEAM PROTOTYPE 1000 CC OHV V-TWIN COMBINATION (WITH SWD) – 1941

This was AMC's Sunbeam-badged offering to replace the Norton 'Big 4', but it was short lived because of the arrival of the Willys-Overland ¼ ton 4x4 Jeep from America.

Essentially the model was a Matchless MX2 V-twin powered combination, built to achieve the requested 55 m.p.h. road speed (the Norton 'Big 4' was always regarded as slow) and fitted with heavy teledraulic forks and a 'transfer' box for forward or reverse gear selection.

Reputedly, an order for a batch was given but never fulfilled, and sadly the prototype no longer exists.

The 1941 Sunbeam-badged Combination, as proposed to replace the Norton 'Big 4' by Associated Motor Cycles. (The National Motor Museum, C16422A)

Triumph

Triumph was a well-known name following the Armistice in 1918, its Model H machines having been employed in large quantities during the First World War, second only to the Douglas company in total numbers supplied. The Triumph models had earned a good reputation in service, which they retained in both public and military opinion throughout the years following the war. During the 1920s the Model H machines in War Office service were partially replaced by the company's Model P and both types continued in service for the remainder of that decade.

Keen to retain government contracts, Triumph itself offered a replacement model for its Model P, the Model NL3. Although the NL3 was not one of the contenders in the seven-make trials of 1929, the War Office none the less conducted a comparison trial between it and the Douglas L29. Even though the War Office concluded that it was a considerable improvement over the Model P, the NL3 was not selected for further evaluation and the type was withdrawn.

During the late 1920s/early 1930s Triumph also supplied two other models, the 494 cc Model N and the 549 cc Model ND, but these were bought in only small batches. It is not known whether the MWEE tested either model.

A Triumph 1925 specification Model P was also used during the 1920s as the basis for an experimental 3-wheeler all-terrain machine. The sole example was constructed by the Royal Army Service Corps. Produced and evaluated during 1926, the model was found to require certain changes in order to improve performance, and the project was passed over to OEC for further development under War Office supervision.

The next seven-make trial was held by the War Office in 1935, and Triumph offered its Model 3/1 for assessment. Later that year, the company underwent considerable reorganization and a change of name from Triumph Company Limited to Triumph Engineering Company Limited. Changes within the company included the revision of all products and the Model 3/1 was dropped from the range. Its replacement was the Model 3S, a similar 350 cc SV machine, which was supplied to the War Office for evaluation during 1936. It was consequently noted as being suitable for use by the War Office.

During 1939 the War Office requested Triumph, along with Norton and Royal Enfield, to supply a lightweight machine conforming to specific military requirements. Several prototype models were produced, the first incorporating special alloys to reduce its weight, although the final model dispensed with such features to off-set high costs. These prototypes evolved into the military 3TW model, a 350 cc OHV valve parallel twin-cylinder machine. The model so impressed the War Office that it decided to adopt the type as the standard military motorcycle for the duration of the war, the model replacing the multitude of others then in service. However, plans were cancelled overnight when the German Air Force blitzed Coventry, decimating the Triumph factory along with most of the city centre.

Despite the fact that it was virtually wiped out, Triumph did manage to continue with limited production in what remained standing of its Coventry works, and in temporary premises at the Cape of Good Hope, Warwick. It concentrated primarily on military SV 3SW and some 5SW models. It was not until 1942 that Triumph was able to resume full-scale motorcycle production at its new premises at Meridan. The only model built from then on was the 350 cc OHV 3HW. The proposed 3TW model was not resurrected, most probably because tooling for the model had been destroyed during the bombing.

During the latter half of the Second World War, Triumph developed another experimental model in response to War Office thinking. The model produced was a 500 cc SV twin-cylinder machine termed the 5TW and fitted with telescopic front forks. Produced during 1942, the model was not fully assessed by the War Office until the end of the war, and formed the basis of the post-war military TRW model.

TRIUMPH MODEL P 494 CC SV SINGLE-CYLINDER – 1925–7

The Triumph Model P was purchased by the War Office as a partial replacement for the ageing Triumph Model H, which had seen active service during the First World War. The Model H was not completely withdrawn, however, the type continuing in use well into the 1920s alongside the Model P.

The total quantity of Model P machines supplied to the War Office is unclear, although it is known that the type was supplied in both solo and combination versions. Ultimately, the Model P was replaced by other motorcycles and the combination versions by light cars.

TRIUMPH EXPERIMENTAL 3-WHEELED MOTORCYCLE 494 CC SV SINGLE-CYLINDER – 1926

This machine was the forerunner of the 3-wheeler machines later developed by OEC and was not actually constructed by Triumph itself. The machine was a civilian Model P, converted by the Royal Army Service Corps in the workshops of P Company.

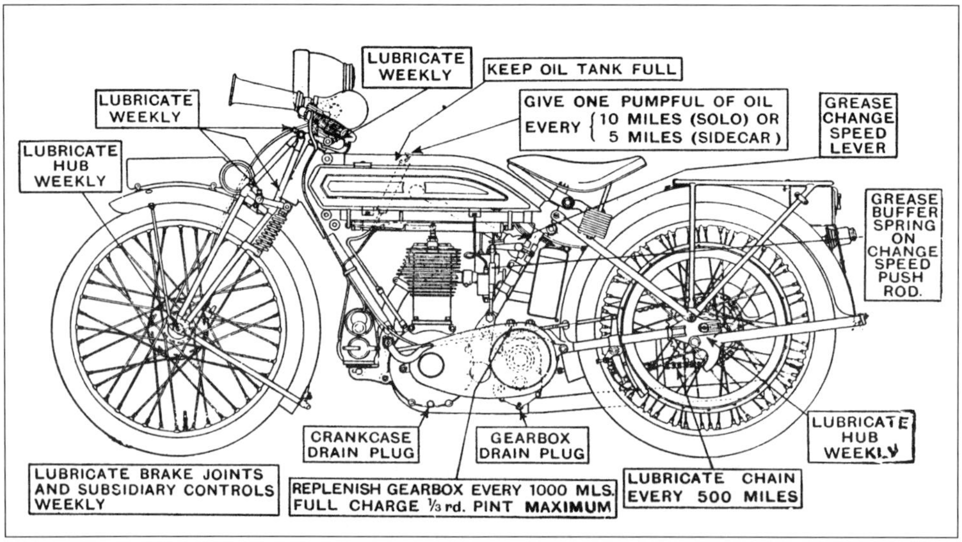

Military lubrication chart for the Triumph Model P. (Triumph Co Ltd)

Official photograph of the 1926 Triumph-based 3-wheeler, as built by the Royal Army Service Corps. (PRO, WO 194 (45) – 5318)

The idea of a 3-wheeled machine evolved as a result of the success of the Army's new 6-wheeled lorries. The drive to the rear wheel was by chain with a linking belt between both rear wheels. For improved grip in certain off-road conditions a track could be fitted over the rear wheels thus turning it into a half-track motorcycle.

Testing of the completed machine was conducted by Captain Bennet at Aldershot, the machine proving to be very good over soft ground and reasonably good over rough surfaces and tarmac. Although having many features in its favour, the machine did have certain problems, including both weight and ground clearance. A further problem was a tendency for the rear-most wheel to lift clear off the ground when there was a surge of power.

An improved machine was suggested, although this version did not reach fruition, the entire project being passed on to the OEC company for further development.

TRIUMPH MODEL N DE-LUXE 494 CC SV SINGLE-CYLINDER – 1928–9

Resembling the Model P machine at first glance, the Model N De-Luxe did have several differences. One of the main differences was a mechanically operated oil-pump in place of the Model P's hand-operated item, although the latter was in fact retained as an auxiliary item. Other differences included a heavier frame and different forks. The exact quantity of machines supplied to the War Office is not

Official photograph of one of the Triumph Model Ns, as purchased in the 1920s. (IWM, KID 5323)

Official photograph of a Triumph Model N Combination, as in service in the 1920s. (PRO, WO 194 (45) – 5316)

clear, nor has any evidence been found to indicate whether the type was ever evaluated by the MWEE prior to purchase.

TRIUMPH MODEL NL3 494 CC SV SINGLE-CYLINDER – 1929

This particular model was a saddle-tank version of the Model N, fitted with a 494 cc SV single-cylinder engine and of de-luxe specification. The type was produced for the 1929 model year only and shared many component parts with Triumph's Model NSD.

The Model NL was offered by Triumph in three optional guises. The base machine was the Model NL1, which was very utilitarian, without lighting or horn. The Model NL2 was fitted with a horn and Lucas acetylene lights, while the final optional version, the Model NL3, was fitted with a Lucas mag-dyno unit, electric lighting and a bulb-horn. The military authorities opted for the NL3 model, despite it being the most expensive.

Not a participant in the seven-make trial of 1929, the model was tested by the military in comparison with a 2¾ h.p. Douglas machine. The War Office, however, were impatient to receive a suitable new model for use and before all the trial results were collated they opted for the Douglas machines. The trials did not stop completely, however, the Model NL3 later being tested in Egypt against the OEC 3-wheeled machine and the Levis company's '6-port' product. Ultimately, the

Official photograph of a Triumph Model NL3, as in service in the late 1920s. (PRO, WO 194 (45) – 5549)

War Office were to favour the Levis product, although the Model NL3 Triumph was noted as being the best machine produced by the company for military evaluation to date.

TRIUMPH MODEL ND 549 CC SV SINGLE-CYLINDER – 1933–4

Following the Model NL3, the next Triumph machine to see military usage was the Model ND. This machine had a 'sloper' engine configuration with a full sheet-metal enclosure over the crankcase and gearbox.

Only three small contracts for the supply of the model are known of and it has not been established whether the type was evaluated for suitability prior to purchase. It is probable that the machines supplied to the War Office were fitted with a small rear carrier along with conventional handlebars, as opposed to Triumph's alternative 'clean' type then on offer.

TRIUMPH MODEL 3/1 343 CC SV SINGLE-CYLINDER – 1935

The Triumph Model 3/1 was one of the machines selected by the War Office for evaluation for suitability for military use in the seven-make trials of 1935. However, by the end of the year the model was withdrawn from testing, having been withdrawn from the Triumph range after the company was reorganized.

Official photograph of a Triumph Model ND, as in service in the early 1930s. (Bart Vanderveen Collection)

Official photograph of the 1935 Triumph Model 3/1, as used in the 1935 trials. (The Tank Museum, 138/E4)

At the start of the trials, the Model 3/1 was fitted with a hand-change gearbox which, after 2,415 test miles, was converted to a foot-change. Throughout the evaluation (between November 1935 and January 1936) the model suffered several problems, including persistent mag-dyno failures involving sheared armatures and stripped magneto driving wheels (on four occasions). Testing was halted by the time 4,530 miles had been completed.

Summarily, and despite the mag-dyno problems, the military assessed the performance of the machine as fair, with a good cross-country achievement.

TRIUMPH MODEL 3S 343 CC SV SINGLE-CYLINDER – 1936

The replacement model for the Model 3/1 following the reorganization of the company, the 1936 Model 3S was offered to the War Office for military evaluation and delivered to the MEE at Farnborough in December of the same year, with testing continuing into 1937.

Similar in design to its predecessor, the Model 3S incorporated a new, strengthened frame and a new gearbox design. Other details of note included revised forks, wheels and fuel tank, among other items.

The War Office trials concluded that the type's performance was at least comparable to the earlier Model 3/1, despite suffering from excessive cylinder wear in the engine, which was partially remedied by the fitting of a new barrel and liner. Overall, the machine was noted as fair in both reliability and condition and was summarily noted as being suitable for War Office use.

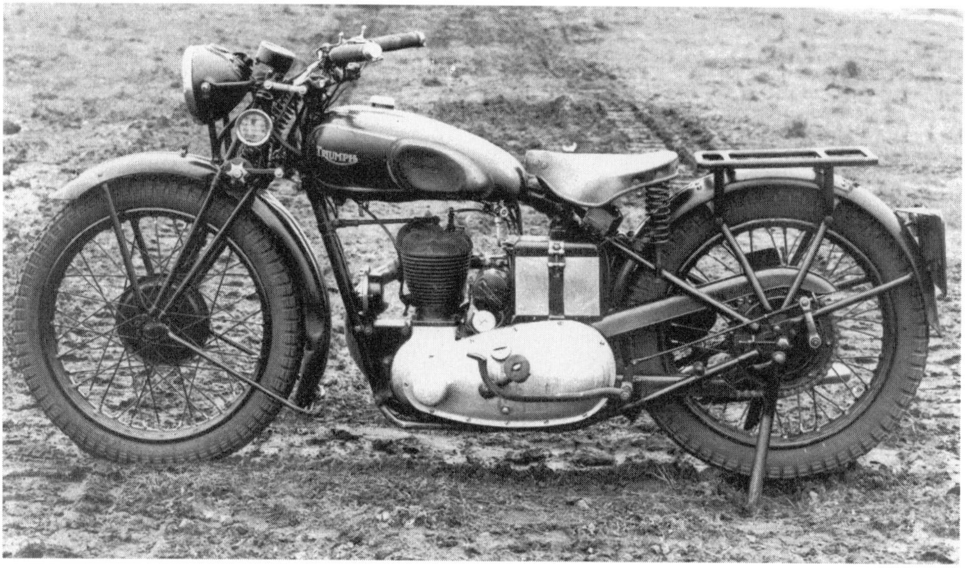

Official photograph of the 1936 Triumph Model 3S that was to replace the Model 3/1 in testing. (PRO, WO 194 (45) – – – – –)

TRIUMPH MODEL 3SW 343 CC SV SINGLE-CYLINDER – 1938–41

Between 1938 and 1941 some 10,000 Model 3SWs were supplied to the War Office, although the final machines built may have been destroyed before completion or despatch from Triumph's Coventry premises during the bombing of the city in November 1940. Limited production of the 3SW continued in temporary premises at Warwick following the bombing and the move into new premises at Meridan during 1942 saw the 3SW withdrawn in favour of the similar OHV Model 3HW, which was produced for the remainder of the war.

The military Model 3SW was based largely upon the civilian specification 3SE model (the E suffix standing for 'economy'), a utilitarian version of the standard civilian 3S. However, there were a number of differences on the military version including a low-compression engine, wide ratios in the gearbox, different handlebar controls, and a rear carrier and rigid-mounted handlebars. During its service, the Model 3SW underwent few changes. The most prominent alteration was the removal of the rear number-plate during late 1940, which coincided with the fitting of the Universal-pattern military tail/convoy light. Hooded black-out masks became a standard fitting from early 1941 onwards, and many of the later machines produced had an additional tool-box fitted on the off-side of the machine between the mudguard stays. Certain batches of machines also had some de-luxe items fitted such as 8 in headlights and rod-operated brakes, presumably to use up stocks of parts.

The War Office was the main user of the Model 3SW, although limited numbers were also used by both the Admiralty Department and the Air Ministry. Judging from surviving photographs of the type in service, it appears to have been used frequently by women, although the type has also been noted in use for

Official photograph of a 1938 Triumph 3SW. (REME Museum)

normal despatch duties in the Middle East during 1940. Despite production of the Model 3SW ceasing during 1941, the type remained in service until the end of the Second World War, principally in training and second-line roles. Following the end of hostilities in 1945 the model was quickly disposed of, many of the survivors being rebuilt to civilian specification during the late 1940s.

TRIUMPH MODEL 3TW LIGHTWEIGHT-PROTOTYPE 349 CC OHV PARALLEL TWIN – 1939 (SERIAL NO. C.3937042)

The prototype Model 3TW was produced in response to the War Office's specification for a lightweight machine of 250 lb or less, of 4-stroke engine design and having the performance of a 500 cc SV machine. Triumph developed and offered their 350 cc OHV parallel twin-cylinder Model 3TW for War Office evaluation and approval. It performed well enough to be proposed much later as the standard British military motorcycle for the duration of the war, the design to be produced by all other manufacturers.

In order to keep the weight of the machine within the limit specified by the military, liberal use was made of alloy steels and aluminium in the design, and direct lighting was fitted to further reduce the weight incurred by standard lighting systems, which incidentally did not work well enough until 30 m.p.h. in top was reached. The 10,000 mile testing showed the engine performance to be exceptional, although at a cost of rather excessive wear to the engine components and a gearbox failure at 1,693 miles. It was thought, however, that such wear could be cured by modifying the design somewhat and suggestions were passed on to Triumph. The machine also had other peculiar design features including the gearbox being in unison with the engine (an idea possibly adopted following Triumph's purchase of the New Imperial Company?), a removable U-section for the top frame tube to which the fuel tank was attached and an alternator powering the direct lighting. Finally the frame was welded together as opposed to the traditional brazing method. Tyres were 3.00 x 21 front and 3.25 x 19 rear.

TRIUMPH MODEL 3TW LIGHTWEIGHT-PROTOTYPE 349 CC OHV PARALLEL TWIN – 1940 (SECOND VERSION)

Following the original Model 3TW, a second prototype example was supplied for evaluation during 1940. This model was essentially the same as the 1939 version but with a slightly less exotic specification listing for the materials used.

The original's alloy head and barrel were substituted for components made from cast iron, along with several other lightweight alloy components. The reason for the change was principally one of cost, but also because of the urgent demand for lightweight alloys from the aircraft industry, which took precedence over motorcycle manufacture. The substitution of iron and steel components increased the overall weight of the machine by some 12 lb, although on testing, performance was still found to be satisfactory and largely unaffected by the increase. The engine wear problem was also largely resolved. Although this model and the original prototype had been considered to be rather 'sporty' in performance, the engine needed to be de-tuned to provide more bottom-end power, to enable the machine to be more suitable for novices to ride.

During testing (3,115 road miles and 2,519 cross-country) the gearbox fractured, so the Elektron casing was replaced by an aluminium version. Although other minor faults occurred elsewhere on the motorcycle, it was a considerable improvement over the first machine. However, more modifications were still requested for the next prototype, besides the de-tuning of the engine. These were a higher riding position and wider footrests, a lower front fork spring rate and dry plate Ferodo inserts for the clutch. During November 1940 the machine was also sent to Matchless to have tele-forks fitted.

A second model (the third 3TW) was then modified (heavier flywheels, new camshaft with less dwell, modified carb slide) to give the required engine characteristics and a higher riding position with wider footrests. After testing this motorcycle was considered superior to any other motorcycle submitted, although its fuel consumption did need improving.

It is probable that, from this model on, the alternator was moved from its position on the engine-timing cover, to outside of the engine sprocket in an effort to overcome the criticism of poor low-speed lighting found on the first model.

Fifty of this model were then ordered in mid-October, but this appears to have been amended shortly afterwards to two for verification with forty-eight to be delivered later on.

TRIUMPH MODEL 3TW PRE-PRODUCTION VERSION 349 CC OHV PARALLEL TWIN – 1940 CONTRACT C.8020

This version of the 3TW model was the intended version for mass production and incorporated only minor modifications over the previous two contracts.

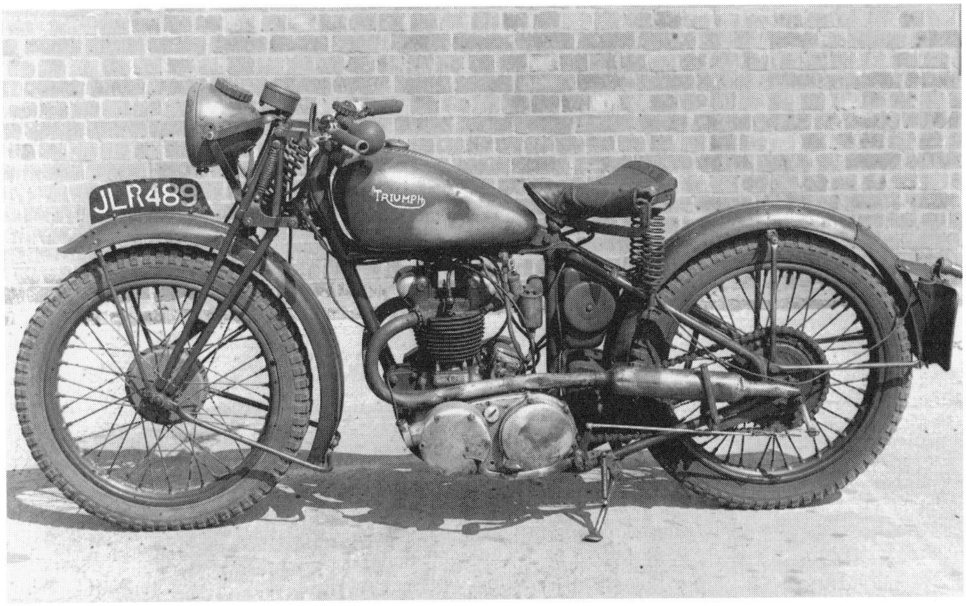

A rather battered Triumph 3TW prototype, missing a number of components. (IWM, MVE 16384/2)

These two motorcycles were essentially the same as the third 3TW and were bought purely to verify the results of that motorcycle. Following these results, an order was placed for forty-eight (later amended to fifty) full production models for issue to various units.

Triumph Model 3TW Production Version 349 cc OHV Parallel Twin – 1940 Contract C.8331

Once the pre-production version of the Model 3TW had received military approval, and various minor modifications had been completed, Triumph began to prepare for full-scale mass production of the 3TW model. Production of the first batch of fifty machines was underway at the Coventry factory when the premises were bombed in 1940. All machines were as good as destroyed along with plans, tooling for the model and spares. The company was able to salvage only a few examples of the 3TW from the ruins of the works, although, with production facilities destroyed, these were of little use. Following the bombing, the demand for other machines remained and Triumph concentrated its efforts on producing its 3SW and 5SW models from the limited facilities available for the time being.

Study of the production 3TW version indicates that the minor modifications to the pre-production and prototype models included the installation of a black-out shield to the headlight, the removal of the number-plates, and the addition of a revised rear carrier, lightweight Universal pannier-frames, pillion-carrying facilities, and 3.25 x 19 tyres front and rear.

A sole surviving example of the Model 3TW from contract C.8331 can be seen at the National Motor Museum at Beaulieu; no other survivors of the type are known to exist today.

TRIUMPH MODEL 5T (SPEED TWIN) 498 CC OHV PARALLEL-TWIN – 1939

Only two examples of Triumph's renowned speed twin model are known to have been offically purchased by the War Office during December 1939, although it is known that further examples of the type were impressed into service from factory stocks at the same time, as were examples of the similar 'Tiger 100' machine.

With both machines being purchased during late 1939, it is likely that they were to 1940 specification complete with the larger 4 gallon fuel tank in place of the previous year's 3¼ gallon tank.

Considering the performance potential of the model, it was probably only employed in service by experienced motorcyclists. The ultimate fate of the two models officially supplied is not known. The impressed civilian versions are known to have served in instances up to 1941.

TRIUMPH MODEL 5SW 493 CC SV SINGLE-CYLINDER – 1940–1

Triumph's 5S model was introduced to its range just prior to the outbreak of the Second World War, although the type was not considered for service by the War Office because both Norton and BSA were supplying the 500 cc machines required at the time.

Following the losses of equipment during the fall of France, the model was accepted for service and Triumph was able to supply some 1,500 models under two contracts placed.

The Model 5S was supplied to the same specification as the military Model 3SW and was thus termed the 5SW. It was identical to the Model 3SW in virtually all respects, the only difference being the increased engine capacity, which required the use of different pistons, flywheels, crankcases, cylinder head and barrel. At a time when machines were urgently required the 5SW was readily available and could be produced using Model 3SW components and stocks of 5S engine components, which were to hand in the works.

The 5SW model was quite popular with those to whom it was issued, principally because it was the size and weight of a 350 cc machine but had the performance of a 500 cc machine.

TRIUMPH MODEL 3H 343 CC OHV SINGLE-CYLINDER – 1940

According to the surviving records, only 140 examples of the OHV 3H model were officially supplied to the War Office in response to its requirement for machines following the losses inflicted during the fall of France.

The machines supplied were of 1940 civilian specification as the then official military Triumph product was still the Model 3SW. It is likely that the machines supplied were either readily available for delivery from the factory or able to be produced quickly from stocks of parts held at the works, these machines therefore fitted with the civilian specification cylinder head rather than the later military specification 3HW component.

TRIUMPH SWD COMBINATION – 1940/1

Little is known about this model other than it was designed to have a road-speed capability of 55 m.p.h., and was killed off by the arrival of the Lend-Lease Jeep from America, as were similar offerings from Norton, Sunbeam and Royal Enfield. the Machine concerned may possibly have been based on the SV Model 6S, or alternatively a 500 cc Twin.

TRIUMPH MODEL 3HW 343 CC OHV SINGLE-CYLINDER – 1942–5

By the time Triumph had moved into its new premises at Meridan during 1942, military thinking was now favouring 500 cc SV machines and 350 cc OHV machines. Thereon, Triumph embarked on full-scale production of its 350 cc OHV Model 3HW from April 1942 until the end of the war.

The military specification 3HW differed from the earlier civilian 3H model principally in the design of the cylinder barrel and head, an alteration established to simplify production methods. The Model 3HW shared virtually the same cycle components as the earlier 3SW and 5SW models, the early Model 3HWs very similar in appearance to the late 3SWs having two tool-boxes fitted, a small rear carrier with no pillion facility, full rubber fittings and the large 8 in headlight. During 1943 the rubber fittings began to be withdrawn from new machines and

Official photograph of an early Triumph 3HW. (Airborne Forces Museum)

the headlight was specified as the smaller 6 in variety. Further, machines were now factory fitted with pillion-carrying facilities, a large rear carrier and Universal military pattern pannier-frames.

As time progressed, the economies of war forced the aluminium alloy chaincase and oil-pump cover to be replaced with pressed steel items. By early 1945 machines coming off the production line were fitted as standard with Universal pattern Vokes air filters on top of the fuel tank (frequently with a cutaway portion to the off-side rear of the tank to accommodate the filter hose), a revised lighting system incorporating a change-over switch atop the headlight with the main lighting switch now located beneath the saddle.

Following the end of hostilities, the 3HW models were rapidly disposed of by the military authorities, many being purchased by dealers for rebuilding and sale to the public. Triumph itself offered the military specification 3HW model for sale to the public, finished in civilian colours and constructed using stocks of parts available at the factory, although this had ceased by 1947 as stocks were exhausted. The Triumph Model 3HW was a popular machine during the war years, and this popularity continued following the end of the war. The type was held in high esteem by the grass-track, speedway and trials fraternity largely because of the flexible engine design and the compactness of the frame and associated components. Many machines were converted into specialist mounts, or were dismantled for parts to keep such machines running. Consequently, the Model 3HW Triumph is not commonly encountered today and surviving examples are few and far between.

TRIUMPH MODEL 5TW 498 CC SV PARALLEL TWIN – 1942 AND 1944

The Triumph Model 5TW was not simply an enlarged version of the earlier Model 3TW. Apart from having an SV rather than an OHV engine, there were many differences between the two machines.

The 5TW model was designed by Bert Hopwood following Edward Turner's move to BSA, and in certain quarters it has been suggested that the 5TW project was a political move to spite Turner. The machine was, however, considerably different to the earlier 3TW model, particularly in basic engine design. It was also the first Triumph machine to be fitted with telescopic front forks.

Originally constructed for comparison testing against the company's own 3TW model, the model performed well and showed good prospects. However, further development of the model had to be shelved from 1942 onwards in order to concentrate on model 3HW production, then heavily underway.

Resurrected again in 1944 following interest from the War Office, the project dragged on slowly, no doubt due to the imminent end of the war and the desire to avoid having hundreds of unwanted machines suddenly facing the military. Interest in the project waned only to resurface yet again in the early post-war years when the model became the forerunner of the military TRW model.

Official photograph of a Triumph 5TW SV Twin that has many 3TW features about it. This version may well be the resurrected 1944 version. (IWM, MVE 12850/2)

Velocette

Until just prior to the outbreak of the Second World War, Velocette had virtually nothing to do with the military and, as far as motorcycles were concerned, had not sought any involvement. Following the outbreak of war, however, two Velocette machines were purchased by the Ministry of Supply for evaluation purposes by the MEE to assess their suitability for potential military service. The outbreak of war had prompted the requirement for large numbers of machines for the services and almost every potential product from the many motorcycle manufacturers of the time was considered by the military.

The two Velocette models supplied for evaluation during October 1939 were the company's standard 1940 specification 350 cc MAC model and the larger 500 cc MSS model, both OHV types. Soon after, a military contract was placed for the supply of a militarized version of the MAC, although this was by the French Government and not the British War Office. However, the contract was scarcely underway, let alone complete, when France fell to Germany in June 1940. Production was temporarily halted and the completed machines transferred to the British War Office, who eventually purchased under contract some 1,200 of the MAC models.

Following usage of this model by the services, Velocette produced an improved model called the MAF and managed to secure a War Office contract for the supply of 2,000 such models. With the contract placed during 1941, production of the MAF commenced later that year with the first machines being delivered to the War Office during early 1942. Velocette, however, was still faced with the problem of a lack of bulk-production facilities and was hampered to a considerable degree by the wartime demands of other production commitments that had increased as the war progressed. Production of the MAF was slow, delivery sporadic and never in great quantity. The result was that by September 1942 the contract for the MAF was terminated after the production of some 947 machines. At this stage of the war most of the other main motorcycle manufacturers were producing huge quantities of suitable service machines and the comparatively minor Velocette production was deemed unnecessary. Production thus ceased forthwith for the remainder of the war, and the factory was put to use producing other war work.

The absence of surviving War Office Velocettes today has led to an abundance of stories surrounding the fate of the models. These include tales of sunken transport ships in either the Mediterranean destined for Africa, or in the English Channel destined for France, a rumour about quantities of the model going to Russia under Lend-Lease arrangements, and the notion that many of the military MAC and MAF models were returned to the factory following the end of the war and rebuilt to civilian standard, having the original military frame and engine numbers removed and restamped.

VELOCETTE MODEL MSS 500 CC OHV SINGLE-CYLINDER – 1939

A sole example of the Velocette MSS was purchased by the Ministry of Supply for evaluation purposes by the War Office on 20 October 1939. The example supplied was a 1940 specification standard civilian model. Subsequent testing of the type revealed the machine to be rather powerful and a handful for anyone less than an experienced rider. This was probably why the MSS model was not accepted for military use.

It should be noted that the MSS was not simply an increased engine capacity 350 cc MAC. Indeed, there were many differences between the two models including the gearbox, brakes, wheels, frame, petrol and oil tanks.

VELOCETTE MODEL MAC 350 CC OHV SINGLE-CYLINDER – 1939

Five days after the Ministry of Supply had purchased the MSS model for evaluation, a solitary Velocette Model MAC was purchased for similar testing by the MEE. This machine was again a 1940 specification standard civilian model and, following completion of the evaluation period, it was concluded that the MAC compared favourably with the 500 cc SV BSA and Norton models already in service. It was relatively easy to control across country, and it was suggested that if certain modifications were carried out, the type would be suitable for military service.

The testing of the MAC was observed by officials from both the British and French Governments, and resulted in the French Government placing an order for the type, which was never fulfilled.

Of note is that the MAC test model was, in fact, demonstrated to the respective governments by a BSA factory-rider as Velocette could not offer a skilled rider of its own, having no competition department within the company at the time.

Official photograph of a 1940 Velocette MAC (WD), often termed an MDD. (IWM, KID 5198)

VELOCETTE MODEL MAC (WD) 350 CC OHV SINGLE-CYLINDER–1940

Ultimately delivered to the War Office, the militarized version of the civilian MAC was originally built for the French Government. The model supplied was as originally tested by the War Office, but incorporating the various modifications suggested as a result of the previous testing. These modifications included a crankcase protective steel undershield fitted to the frame, a lower compression ratio engine, a lower bottom gear (16.8:1 as opposed to 14:1), a cylindrical fishtail silencer to increase ground clearance, a rear carrying rack in place of a pillion seat and footrests, a non valenced front mudguard, an improved rear brake pedal, and dull chromium plate in place of normal bright chromium.

It is of note that the Velocette MAC (WD) model is sometimes referred to as the MDD, as this was the prefix stamped on to the frames and engines, although the majority of the surviving official references to the model refer to the type as the MAC (WD).

VELOCETTE MODEL MAF 350 CC OHV SINGLE-CYLINDER – 1941/2

The Velocette MAF was the result of development work carried out by the company on the MAC (WD) model then in service. Although this machine was generally well designed and adequately suited to use by the military in the majority of applications, the company felt that it could be improved upon and made considerably more suitable. Usage by the War Office had highlighted several areas that could be improved upon, and Velocette therefore took a standard MAC model, number MAC 6707, and progressively modified and tested it until it evolved into the form that became the MAF. The development work was carried out by Phil Irving (later famous for his Vincent connections) and the completed model ridden during the period by the Velocette factory manager, Bob Burgess. Commencing in July 1941, the development of the MAC (WD) found favour with the War Office and a proposed second contract for MAC (WD)s was changed in favour of the improved MAF, an initial order for the supply of 2,000 being placed.

The modifications to MAC 6707 were as follows: a redesigned frame incorporating a large forging beneath the engine which strengthened the frame and doubled as a protective shield for the crankcase; large rear carrier and standard military pannier-frames plus a pillion seat and folding pillion footrests; one tool-box now fitted on the off-side of the machine in a low position, rather than the previous pair fitted one either side in high-level positions; rubber bump-stops added to the front forks to avoid 'clashing' over rough ground; longer top-links in the girder-forks; the removal of the engine torque-stay; a different cam fitted to the engine; a different carburettor; a different method for anchoring the rear brake-plate (torque-arm); a marginally smaller exhaust pipe diameter; improved routing of the exhaust system; a lower chainguard fitted; a standard throttle-control fitted in place of Velocette's own push-pull design; a clip fitted to the rear mudguard to hold up the hinged tail-piece and facilitate the removal of the rear wheel; a pocket added to the interior of the singular tool-box lid to accommodate the rider's handbook and instruction manual, plus a length of

Official photograph of a 1941/2 Velocette MAF. (IWM, KID 5418)

bowden cable fitted between the box itself and the hinged lid to stop the latter from falling fully open; a revised foot-change lever for the gearbox and linking mechanism which effectively reversed the gear-change operation to bring the type in line with other military motorcycles; a different gearbox end cover design; an revised rotating kick-start lever, which was an improvement on the existing swivelling variety; an even lower first-gear ratio of 18.17:1; a smaller diameter Miller headlight; the substitution of cast-steel for the alloy of the timing cover and the gearbox end-cover plate; and finally, the rear brake foot-control pedal adjustment method was revised.

These numerous modifications, however, had an adverse effect to a degree, as they raised the cost of the model considerably. By 1942 the MAF model was costing the Ministry of Supply at least £68 per machine, compared with, for example, the Matchless G3/L model, the Ariel W/NG, the Royal Enfield WD/CO and the Triumph 3HW, which all cost less than £60. Coupled with Velocette's limited bulk-production facilities, these figures were ultimately considered to be non cost-effective and Velocette's facilities better directed at other forms of war production. The result was that by September 1942 the MAF model's contract was cancelled after the production of some 947 examples of the type. These continued in service along with existing MAC (WD)s, although many of the latter were subsequently transferred to various civil defence formations, including the National Fire Service, following the introduction of the MAF model. As with the MAC (WD), the MAF tended to be employed within the United Kingdom because of the comparatively small number in service. Many were later transferred over to the Air Ministry for service with Royal Air Force formations at various locations throughout the country.

A Norton 16H fitted with a box sidecar. Note that some carried a spare wheel on the rear panel of the sidecar body, and pillion seating on the motorcycle was also often fitted. (IWM, KID 5882)

An early Norton 16H in RAF use, fitted with a passenger-carrying body. Note these bodies were also used on BSA M20 Combinations. (IWM, MH 14645)

Sidecars

During the war a number of contracts were issued for sidecars only (or sidecars and chassis). In early pre-war years most manufacturers made their own sidecar bodies and chassis, and larger manufacturers continued to do so during the Second World War, although many, in fact, sub-contracted to specialists (such as Swallow) for bodies.

Many different styles of sidecar bodies have been used over the years but not all have been for carrying passengers; during the war a number of box bodies were bought to fit BSA's M20, Norton's 16H and the Indian 741B.

On the sidecar development front, besides the well-known SWD outfits from Norton (and the experimental versions from BSA, Triumph, Royal Enfield and Sunbeam), it is known that folding sidecars for carrying drop containers were experimented with, attached to Triumph 3HWs.

A captured Zündapp KS750 Combination, bearing its new British registration number C5321791. This motorcycle was picked up in the Middle East and has a variety of parts missing and a make-shift rear light. (REME Museum)

A captured German motorcycle (DKW) in use with British Airborne Forces. (Airborne Forces Museum)

Colour Schemes

With the exception of certain test models, motorcycles procured by the War Office during the years prior to the outbreak of war in September 1939 were generally finished in the standard colour scheme of the majority of other service vehicles of that period. This comprised an overall colour of bronze-green (a somewhat deep shade of green), with quite a glossy finish. Normally, engine and gearbox casings were left in unpolished bare metal and ancillary components, such as control levers, exhaust systems, nuts, bolts and studs, were in such finish as supplied by the respective manufacturer, usually dull chromium plate, nickel plate, cadmium (dull) plate, enamel or 'coslettised' – a dull black. Certain machines, principally machines for evaluation purposes, were supplied to the War Office in standard civilian colours.

The paint used on War Office machines was manufactured and supplied by external sources and complied with War Office guidelines, although in practice there existed a wide variation of the one specific colour and the shade could vary considerably.

Following the outbreak of war, the peacetime parade-ground finish of vehicles was unsuitable for camouflage and concealment purposes. Manufacturers therefore began to apply paint which incorporated a matt, non-reflective finish. Officially, this paint was a light khaki-green colour. In reality, due to wartime demands, the colour could vary from a distinct brown shade through to dark green. The paint was supplied to individual units for repainting pre-war machines already in use, and was applied either by brush or by spraying, particularly if the quantity of machines to be finished was considerable. Impressed civilian models, machines of 1940 specification waiting at factories, and those in showrooms were grouped together and finished in the wartime service colour. The application of paint was often quite liberal, resulting in the saddle, engine and tyres being painted along with the rest of the machine.

Two-colour camouflage schemes were both officially and unofficially applied to many War Office vehicles during the course of the war, notably between 1940 and 1943. The scheme usually consisted of a light khaki-brown base colour overpainted with random areas of dark brown. Motorcycles were normally exempted from this practice because of their considerably smaller surface area. Examples bearing this two-colour scheme have been noted, notably motorcycle combinations such as the Norton 'Big 4', which was the size of a small vehicle.

During 1942–3 some contracts of machines from manufacturers were finished in an earth-brown colour, a milk chocolate-brown shade, although khaki-green predominated throughout. During 1944, prior to the D-Day landings in June that

Fork jigs for straightening girder forks, at No. 1 Workshop Group (REME), Chilwell. (REME Museum)

Impressed motorcycles performing training duties. All are Royal Enfields, and most are Model Ds. (The National Motor Museum, C16451A)

A Moto Guzzi Alce captured in North Africa in 1943 and brought back to the UK. (REME Museum)

It is possible that some were donated as gifts for the war effort, with the owners not expecting them to be returned. This was certainly true of car owners, and it is reasonable to assume that motorcyclists were equally generous.

As the Second World War progressed the local purchasing and impressing of vehicles slowed down as the large manufacturers got into their stride. By now damaged motorcycles were on the increase and the job of sorting them out fell to REME. They would often strip down the damaged machines, restoring them to working order using parts from various machines. At big depots these rebuilt machines were reissued as such and carried new registration numbers beginning with the number C.1400000. This method of stripping down and reassembling continued after the war, hence very few existent War Office bikes have their original engines.

Any motorcycle that had seen a lot of military service would have had many rebuilds and consequently would have lost its original identity. This is evident today from the number of 'mixed up' machines that can be found, that is machines which have engine and frame numbers from different contracts and/or parts that do not match the original contract.

It has also been known for 'home-made' components, or parts from another manufacturer's model to be fitted to machines. This happened especially when modifications had to be carried out in the field, and sometimes as a preference, for example, Matchless teledraulic forks being fitted on BSA's M20 and Norton's 16H.

During the Desert War and thereafter many captured motorcycles were used, mainly of Italian or German origin. Towards the end of the war, these too were given their own series of registration numbers beginning with the number C.6000000.

Miscellaneous Motorcycles

This chapter looks at machines from miscellaneous sources, which were pushed into service for one reason or another.

In desperate times many unapproved vehicles were drafted into service until the official versions could replace them, this being particularly the case after Dunkirk, when motorcycles were urgently needed. Thousands were put into service after being bought as 'local purchase' from showrooms, and more still taken from the finished goods areas of factories or even private owners, an operation known as 'impressing' equipment.

Frame jigs for rebuilding motorcycles, at No. 1 Workshop Group (REME), Chilwell. Being worked on is an Ariel W/NG frame. (REME Museum)

BSA M20 and Ariel W/NG in the distinctive colour scheme and pattern used only in Malta during the Second World War. (National War Museum Association, Malta (via Clive Micalef) No. 1686)

year, motorcycles arriving from the manufacturers were finished in matt, non-reflective olive-drab. This was a medium depth colour, of a shade midway between brown and green, although there were many variations of the official specification.

Those machines still bearing earlier finishes retained them until repainting was necessary, typically completed following a major overhaul or rebuild at base workshops. The olive-drab shade in reality was little different from the earlier khaki-green.

Following the end of the war, most War Office machines retained their wartime finishes until repainting was necessary or until the instigation of peacetime directives, which demanded a reversion to semi-gloss bronze- or Brunswick-green colours, though of a lighter shade than previously.

Air Ministry (Royal Air Force) Colour Schemes

Prior to 1939 motorcycles employed by the Air Ministry were finished either in a gloss dark blue-grey or the bronze-green colour of the War Office.

The outbreak of war and the consequent reversion to camouflage colours affected the RAF perhaps to a greater extent than the Army, as the airfields where many vehicles were employed were considered prime targets for air attacks. Pre-war finished machines were hurriedly repainted with any suitable camouflage colour available. Frequently, this involved using paint intended for aircraft, usually matt green or matt earth-brown, or dark grey or dark brown paint intended for hangar camouflage. Other paint shades employed were similar, if not identical to those employed by the War Office.

Motorcycles supplied direct to the Air Ministry were finished by the manufacturers in exactly the same colour schemes as those supplied to the War Office, this trend remaining for the duration of the war.

During early 1946 certain RAF units repainted motorcycles and other vehicles in a gloss blue-grey colour, either utilizing old pre-war stocks of paint or locally mixed colours, which led to a wide variation in shade. Other machines retained wartime camouflage colours or were repainted in the post-war War Office bronze-green colour, until such time as glossy blue-grey finishes were officially reintroduced.

Admiralty Department (Royal Navy) Colour Schemes

Prior to 1939 motorcycles employed by the Admiralty Department were finished in several different colour schemes. Whether these were applied by the manufacturer or completed by individual establishments is unclear. The colours noted, all of a gloss finish, were dark navy-blue, varying from a medium shade through to near-black, dark grey and light grey. The latter two colours may well have been the same paint used for warships, applied at the factory or locally. The pre-war War Office colour of bronze-green (most probably Royal Marine motorcycles) has also been noted. In accordance with the other services, machines were kept in a presentable condition.

Following the outbreak of war, machines were repainted in available camouflage colours, although perhaps to a lesser extent than the other services. A paint occasionally used on Naval motorcycles was a dockyard or battleship camouflage-grey colour, although it did not have a true matt finish.

As no special colour was supplied for machines destined for the Navy, motorcycles supplied to the Admiralty Department were finished in the standard camouflage colour of the period, which was whatever the manufacturers had to use.

After the cessation of hostilities Naval motorcycles, along with those from other services, continued to carry their wartime colours until a repaint was necessary. When this happened, the colour was usually changed back to the War Office bronze-green colour, although sometimes pre-war colours were used.

Overseas Colour Schemes for Service Motorcycles

Contrary to popular belief today, it was rare to find a motorcycle manufacturer finishing a machine in a colour scheme for service use outside the European theatre of war. Virtually all motorcycles were either collected from the manufacturer by the service concerned, or delivered to a specific ordnance depot or other such location of that service. Following delivery, the service then allocated specific machines for issue to units where and when required. Very

Norton 16H in service in Malta. (National War Museum Association, Malta (via Clive Micalef) No. 8650)

occasionally, a batch of motorcycles destined for overseas service, for example North Africa, would be re-painted by the distribution depot in the appropriate desert camouflage colour, although urgency of delivery normally prevented this.

Refinishing was occasionally carried out by the unit receiving the machines on arrival overseas, although this time-consuming practice was not as commonly followed as is often thought today. The large proportion of the motorcycles sent to the Middle and Far Eastern theatres of war served there in their standard European colour schemes. In the case of a motorcycle this was considered acceptable because of its small surface area. In North Africa, the European camouflage colour of matt khaki-green soon faded under constant exposure to sunlight and desert elements. Likewise in the Far East the European green colour was equally effective in the tropical environment. Those machines repainted overseas, particularly in the Middle East, were usually painted a camouflage colour, matching the local terrain. In Malta, for example, all motorcycles (including solos) were repainted with the Island's distinctive colour scheme, which incorporated a crazy-paving pattern (see photograph on p.151). Paint was often mixed locally as a result of supply difficulties and was liberally applied to the machine's main surfaces, usually rather crudely. Dust and sand were frequently thrown on to the paint while it was still wet to further dull the finish.

Notes on Tables

The information contained within the tables has come from many sources, namely original manufacturers' drivers' handbooks and parts lists, a B-vehicle Census document dated November 1944, manufacturers' ledgers, Ministry of Supply ledgers and vehicle test reports

Dates in these documents very often conflict, and in the case of delivery dates it is sometimes not clear whether the date given is a commencement date, during or completed contract date. Some dates, although known, have not been filled in as it could not be firmly established to what exactly they were referring.

Inevitably there are gaps in the tables and the authors would be most grateful to hear from anyone with additional information so that any reprints can be up dated. Likewise, the authors would be pleased to hear about any photographs that might exist of the many models not illustrated.

Key	CD	=	Contract date
	COD	=	Central Ordnance Depot (Army)
	CP	=	Completed contract
	DL	=	Delivered
	DM	=	Demand
	EX CAN	=	Ex-Canadian Commonwealth Forces
	MAP	=	Ministry of Aircraft Production
	M/C	=	Motorcycle
	MOWT	=	Ministry of Works Transport
	MU	=	Maintenance Unit
	N/C	=	Not confirmed
	NK	=	Not known
	PL	=	Parts list
	ROD	=	Regional Ordnance Depot (Army)
	SAS	=	Special Air Service (Army)
	VRD	=	Vehicle Receiving Depot (Army)

AJS

MAKERS TYPE	MILITARY CLASS	WD SERIAL NO ALLOCATION	CONTRACT NUMBER	CAT REF	FRAME NUMBER	ENGINE NUMBER	QUANTITY PRODUCED	DATES	PRICE(S)	DELIVERY DESTINATION & NOTES
M6	M/C Solo 350 cc OHV	20533,?,?	C.1933		M106173 , ?, ?	M6/106173 , ?, ?	3	04/05/29 DM 18/06/29 CD 02/08/29 DL	£46.6s.0d	Civilian reg. MG 9001
M6	M/C Solo 350 cc OHV		C.3512				6	09/02/31 DM 06/03/31 CD	£47.15s.0d	Feltham
M6	M/C Solo 350 cc OHV	22304, 22316	C.4259	1			2	1931		
40/8, 8SS, 40/9	M/C Solo 500 cc SV or OHV	4191344–4191347 4191760	C.7373	2			40/8–1 8SS –2 40/9–2	26/05/40	£51.19s.0d 40/8 £55.2s.1d 8SS £47.4s.6d 40/9	Stirling or Catterick
40/26	M/C Solo 350 cc OHV	4191751	C.7353	3			1	26/05/40	£44.17s.2d	Stirling or Catterick

Ariel

MAKERS TYPE	MILITARY CLASS	WD SERIAL NO ALLOCATION	CONTRACT NUMBER	CAT REF	FRAME NUMBER	ENGINE NUMBER	QUANTITY PRODUCED	DATES	PRICE(S)	DELIVERY DESTINATION & NOTES
VA3	M/C Solo 557 cc SV	35797	C7641		Y10075	KA2590	1	09/09/35 DL		Westminster, civilian reg. was CMM750
Square 4	M/C Solo 600 cc OHC				P120	EC102	1	02/10/36 DL	On Loan	Returned to Ariel 02/10/36 (same day!)
Square 4	M/C Solo 1000 cc OHV				P109	DB107	1	02/10/36 DL	On Loan	Returned to Ariel 02/10/36 (same day!)
W/VA	M/C Solo 500 cc SV	4111501–4111600	C5111	1	10001–10019 10022–10048 10050–10100	CH 147, 160, 454, 724, 994, 502–508, 519–528, 603–612, 623–631, 643–682, 684–699.	97*	27/09/39 DM 06/01/40 CD 11/39 DL	£47.10s.2d	Feltham 30, Chilwell 70 *3 frames not alloc.
W/VA	M/C Solo 500 cc SV	RAF			10634, 10940 10895, 10981, 11050, 10773, 11183, 10909, 10740, 11126, 11099, 10771, 10912, 10646.	CH 1102, 1103 1131, 1132, 1133, 1134, 1192, 1193, 1195, 1196, 1197, 1198, 1199, 1200.	14	04/40		Chilwell, Abingdon, ?, Glasgow, Fareham, ?, Middlesex, Shetlands, Liverpool, Sheffield, S ?, Manchester, ?, Plymouth
W/VA	M/C Solo 500 cc SV	MOA			9639, 9777, 10195, 10217, 10639, 10709, 10739, 10766, 10772, 10942, 11006, 11008, 11016, 11018, 11025, 11026, 11028, 11049, 11102, 11106, 11107, 11110, 11112, 11119, 11121, 11131, 13284, 13376, 13381, 13387, 13388, 13397, 13401, 13405, 13407, 13410, 13413, 13414, 13422, 13425, 13442, 13444, 18874.	CH 1468, 1469, 1637–1645, 1647–1661, 1663, 1665–1667, 1672, 1674, 1676, 1678, 1680, 1684, 1696, 1702, 1713–1717.	43	Aug to Oct '40		
?	M/C Comb.		B7402				64	21/03/40 CD	21 at £56.17s.6d 11 at £64.7s.6d 32 at £67.17s.6d	50% Commercial Box sidecars 50% Passenger carrying sidecars

Ariel

Makers Type	Military Class	WD Serial No Allocation	Contract Number	Cat Ref	Frame Number	Engine Number	Quantity Produced	Dates	Price(s)	Delivery Destination & Notes
?	M/C Comb. 500 cc		C8882				1	05/10/40 DM 18/03/41 CD 27/09/40 DL	£73.3s.0d	
?	M/C Solo 500 cc		C9258				3	16/12/40		
VB	M/C Solo 598 cc SV				10795 13292	1475 1457	2	08/40 DL		MOS and M/C section D, Newcastle
VH	M/C Solo 500 cc OHV	4191554–558, 561, 563, 565, 566, 568, 569, 571, 573–578, 581, 583, 629, 631, 633, 634, 636–638, 660, 661, 663, 664, 670, 672, 673, 676–678, 681, 683, 684, 703, 713, 715–717, 721, 722, 724, 726, 730, 733, 734, 737–739, 741, 858, 861, 863, 865, 884, 885, 887, 888, 890, 894, 898, 900–903, 908, 910–912, 915, 919, 924, 926, 929, 940, 941, 945, 946, 948, 950, 957.	C7372	2	733, 9316, 9322 9345–7, 9352, 9356, 9359, 9842, 9847, 9851, 9852, 9871, 9881, 9891–2, 9903, 9906, 9910–1, 9915, 9988, 10605, 10815, 10827, 10834, 10836, 10873, 10885, 10889, 10916, 10927, 10933, 10945, 10964, 10967, 10983, 10991, 11057, 11067, 11132, 11147, 11160, 11182.	CH 515, 1240, 1248, 1250, 1485–94, 1497–1507, 1526–1545.	45	28/05/40 DM 17/04/40 CD	£57	Catterick
VG	M/C Solo 500 cc OHV	4191559, 567, 635, 655, 659, 665–668, 671, 674, 675, 682, 685–688, 690, 691–702, 704, 705, 708, 720, 723, 725, 731, 735, 736, 740, 886, 892, 899, 904, 905, 907, 909, 913, 916–918, 927, 928, 931–936, 939, 947, 953, 954.	C7372	5	9323, 9341, 9344, 9351, 9360, 9819, 9875, 9908, 9912–4, 9973, 10317, 10714, 10829, 10892, 11010, 11021, 11023, 11041, 11043, 11045, 11054–5, 11058–9, 11063, 11068, 11090, 11100, 11117, 13429, 19447.	CH 1252, 1256, 1430, 1432, 1433, 1436–9, 1508–10, 1512–21, 1546–50, 1552, 1554–5, 1591, 1593–4 1596.	34	26/05/40 Deliveries in April, June, and Sept '40, and Jan '41.		Catterick
VA Test Model	M/C Solo 500 cc SV				XG 9567	CH 107	1	02/11/39 DL		Returned to Ariel on 02/12/39
VA Lightened	M/C Solo 500 cc SV				XG 10208	CH 683	1	17/11/39 DL		Returned to Ariel on 21/12/39
NH	M/C Solo 350 cc OHV	4191570, 572, 580, 582, 628, 630, 632, 679, 689, 707, 709, 711, 714, 718, 732, 855–857, 859, 860, 862, 864, 891, 893, 895–897, 906, 930, 937, 938, 943, 944, 949, 951, 952, 955, 956.	C7372	3			38	26/05/40	£55.19s.0d	
NG	M/C Solo 350 cc OHV	4191560, 562, 564, 579, 654, 656–658, 662, 669, 680–706, 710, 712, 719, 727–729, 742, 889, 914, 920–923, 925, 942.	C7372	6			27	26/05/40	£55.15s.0d	
?	M/C Solo 350 cc	1038301	N.K.				1	1941?		
W/NG Proto.	M/C Solo 350 cc OHV				XG12179	BH 1700	1	18/07/40 DL		
W/NG	M/C Solo 350 cc OHV	4311978–4314677	C8302	4	XG11186–13285 13554–14153 with gaps	BH 600–3299	2700	08/08/40 DM 10/12/40 CD 18/07/40 DL	*c.* £55	Chilwell, with 153 to French Government
W/NG	M/C Solo 350 cc OHV	4381388–4381737	C8574	7	XG14154–14503	BH 3300–3649	350	27/08/40 DM 01/11/40 CD	£55.18s.1d	Chilwell
W/NG	M/C Solo 350 cc OHV	4459718–4461717	C8722	8	XG14759–17000 with gaps	BH 4131–6149 with gaps	2000	18/09/40 DM 07/12/40 CD Early '41 DL	£54.10s.6d	Chilwell. C4460559 had cast-iron gearbox casing (XG 15626/

Ariel

MAKERS TYPE	MILITARY CLASS	WD SERIAL NO ALLOCATION	CONTRACT NUMBER	CAT REF	FRAME NUMBER	ENGINE NUMBER	QUANTITY PRODUCED	DATES	PRICE(S)	DELIVERY DESTINATION & NOTES
								Dec '40 PL		BH 5024). C4460175 had engine BH 4423 enlarged to 500 cc
W/NG + Ariel-Matchless + Ariel-BSA	M/C Solo 350 cc OHV	4553325, 4553326, 1034001–1037500	C9387	11	XG15685, 15690, XG17001–20999	BH 6150–9999	3500 1 1	07/03/41 DM 28/01/42 CD Mid '41 DL	£54.10s.0d	Tewkesbury C4553325/XG15685 had Matchless engine fitted on 29/05/41. C4553326/ XG15690 had BSA WB30 Engine/523 fitted on 20/02/41
W/NG	M/C Solo 350 cc OHV	4589426–4590925 1038302–1039801	C10477	9	XG20501–23500	BH10777–13776	3000	26/04/41 DM 24/01/42 CD By Feb '42 DL	£57.15s.0d	Chilwell 1500 and Ashchurch 1500. Some to RAF & RN
W/NG	M/C Solo 350 cc OHV	4692899–4696398	C11103	10	XG23751–27250	BH15001–18500	3500	05/07/41 DM 27/02/42 CD By Aug '42 DL	£57.15s.0d	Chilwell. Fitted with bag racks
W/NG	M/C Solo 350 cc OHV	4850001–4852000	C12450	13	XG29751–31750	BH19001–21000	2000	12/11/41 DM 24/01/42 CD By Aug '42 DL	£57.15s.0d	Tewkesbury at 650/month
W/NG	M/C Solo 350 cc OHV	4812104–4815603	C13871	12	XG31751–35250	BH21501–25000	3500	14/03/42 DM Nov '42 PL By Apr '43 DL		
W/NG	M/C Solo 350 cc OHV	R.N.	S308		XG35251–35300	BH14946–14995	50	02/07/42 DM 08/09/42 CD	£44.14s.9d	Portsmouth 15, Clyde 11, 8 each to Mersey, Rosyth, Chiswick
W/NG	M/C Solo 350 cc OHV	5167181–5170430	S1049	14	XG37281–40530	BH27501–30750	3250 (+162?)	30/09/42 DM 02/04/43 to 15/11/43 DL		
W/NG	M/C Solo 350 cc OHV	5360771–5363020	S2601	15	XG42001–44250	BH32001–34250	2250	03/03/43 DM Sept '43 to Feb '44 DL		
W/NG	M/C Solo 350 cc OHV	5490401–5494400	S4554	16	XG47251–51250	BH35001–39000	4000	20/09/43 DM 31/12/43 to 07/09/44 DL	£62.13s.6d	
W/NG	M/C Solo 350 cc OHV	5363021–5366020	S5514	17	XG44251–47250	BH42001–45000	3000	06/01/44 DM Sept '44 on for DL	£62.13s.6d	
W/NG	M/C Solo 350 cc OHV	6193966–6197465	S6287	18	XG51856–55355	BH45701–49200	3500*	31/03/44 DM Mid '45 DL	£65	See Cont. S6197. No tyres fitted. * Reduced to 2000
W/NG	M/C Solo 350 cc OHV	RN	S6197		XG57221–57520	BH47801–48000	300	12/06/45 to 21/08/45 DL		See Cont. S6287
W/NG	M/C Solo 350 cc OHV	RN	S1494?			BH18924–18963	40	20/11/42 CD	£60	
W/NG	M/C Solo 350 cc OHV		C/S12928				100	26/12/41 DM 28/01/42 CD Jan '42 to mid '42 DL	£57.15s.0d	As per C.12450. Del. at 25/month
W/NG	M/C Solo 350 cc OHV		C/S11464				750	12/08/41 DM 17/01/42 CD	£56.12s.6d	
W/NG	M/C Solo 350 cc OHV		C/S12427				300	10/11/41 DM 20/01/42 CD	£57.15s.0d	As per C/S 11464. Del. at 75/week from Jan '42
W/NG	M/C Solo 350 cc OHV		S788				105?	02/02/42 09/10/42	Total cost £6,383.4s.9d	
W/NG	M/C Solo 350 cc OHV	RAF	C/S14218			BH25201–27000	1800	09/04/42 DM 26/01/43 CD 15/01/43 to 23/12/43 DL	£61	
W/NG	M/C Solo 350 cc OHV	RN 17200 to 17300 with gaps	S2037				50	21/01/43 13/04/43 to 16/07/43 DL	£60	
W/NG	M/C Solo 350 cc OHV	RN 20200 to 20300	S3174				100	05/05/43	£6,162.4s.5d	
W/NG	M/C Solo 350 cc OHV	RN	S4670			BH40001–40250	250	09/10/43 09/02/44 Jan '44 to	£61	

Ariel

MAKERS TYPE	MILITARY CLASS	WD SERIAL NO ALLOCATION	CONTRACT NUMBER	CAT REF	FRAME NUMBER	ENGINE NUMBER	QUANTITY PRODUCED	DATES	PRICE(S)	DELIVERY DESTINATION & NOTES
								Apr '44 DL		
W/NG	M/C Solo 350 cc OHV		S6151				5	25/03/44 19/04/44 CD	£62	
W/NG	M/C Solo 350 cc OHV	RN 35151–35500	S6520		XG51506–51855	BH40251–40600	350	16/06/44	£61	
W/NG	M/C Solo 350 cc OHV	RN 46014–46163 49312–49411	S8049		XG56928–57015 57017–57177	BH40601–40699 45101–45250	249	31/01/45 12/01/45 to 14/05/45 DL	£64.12s.0d	
W/NG	M/C Solo 350 cc OHV	RAF	S7011			BH40701–41822	1572*	15/02/45 25/07/44 to 11/05/45 DL		*Reduced to 1122
W/NG	M/C Solo 350 cc OHV	RN 54096–54138	S8574		XG57175, 57179–57220	BH45251–45293	43	27/01/45 14/02/45 DL	£64.13s.6d	
W/NG	M/C Solo 350 cc OHV	RN	S9167				300	07/04/45		Preserved against rust and tropicalized
W/NG	M/C Solo 350 cc OHV	French (See Cont.C8302)			XG11186–11213, 11217–11230, 11232–11240, 11245, 11248, 11250–11252, 11255, 11257, 11258, 11260, 11264–11265, 11267–11270, 11272, 11276, 11278–11284, 11286–11291, 11293–11295, 11300–11301, 11304, 11306–11308, 11310–11311, 11313, 11315, 11317–11319, 11321–11323, 11327, 11329–11331, 11333–11335, 11337, 11339–11342, 11345, 11347–11349, 11352–11354, 11356, 11358–11359, 11361–11362, 11365–11368, 11371, 11377–11379, 11381, 11385–11389, 11391, 11396, 11397, 11402, 11406, 11407, 11412, 11416, 11421, 11424, 11426, 11431, 11435, 11438, 11446, 11451, 11464, 11470, 11500.		153			
W/NG	M/C Solo 350 cc OHV	RAF	?		XG27501–28083 28085, 28086, 28088–28091, 28093–28095, 28099, 28100, 28102, 28104, 28105, 28107, 28108. 20127, 20129, 20135, 20168, 20181, 20184, 20190–20192, 20194–20197, 20199, 20200, 20202–20206, 20208–20210, 21212, 21213, 21215, 21216.	BH9635, 9637–9644, 9648, 9650–9652, 9655–9657, 9662–9667, 9674, 9677, 9678, 9683, 9684, 9758, 9849, 9896, 9900–9902, 9904–9912, 9914–9916, 9919, 9922–9928, 9930–9944, 9946, 9947, 9952–9956, 9959–9984, 9986–9991, 9993–	625	Aug '41 DL		

Ariel

Makers Type	Military Class	WD Serial No Allocation	Contract Number	Cat Ref	Frame Number	Engine Number	Quantity Produced	Dates	Price(s)	Delivery Destination & Notes
						10004, 10006–10015, 10017–10025, 10028–10032, 10035, 10036, 10039–10042, 10044–10050, 10052–10055, 10057–10060, 10062–10075, 10078, 10080, 10081, 10084–10086, 10088–10098, 10100, 10102–10109, 10111–10116, 10118, 10120, 10121, 10123–10129, 10132–10137, 10139–10146, 10149–10156, 10158–10173, 10175–10181, 10184–10188, 10190–10194, 10196–10199, 10201, 10203, 10209–10210, 10213–10221, 10223–10231, 10235–10243, 10246–10254, 10256–10265, 10268–10276, 10278–10285, 10287, 10290–10298, 10301–10310, 10312–10320, 10323–10331, 10334–10340, 10342–10353, 10356–10364, 10367–10377, 10379–10385, 10388–10396, 10398, 10400–10408, 10411–10418, 10422–10425, 10427–10430, 10433–10441, 10444–10452, 10455–10462, 10466–10474, 10477–10485, 10488–10496, 10499–10518, 10521–10530, 10533–10540, 10543–10551, 10554–10562, 10565–10573, 10576–10584, 10587–10594, 10597–10607, 10610–10618.				
W/NG	M/C Solo 350 cc OHV	RAF	?		XG28110, 28111, 28113–28115, 28118, 28120, 28124, 28125, 28128–28131, 28135–28140, 28142–28146, 28148–28180, 28182–28183, 28185–28188, 28190–28203, 28206–28207, 28209–28212, 28214–28216, 28218–28219, 28221–28223, 28225, 28227–28230, 28233, 28235–28237, 28240–28243,	BH10685–10705, 10709–10733 10736, 10739, 10741–10748, 10752–10760, 10763–10771, 10774–10782, 10785–10788.	107 Frms. 87 Engs.	Sept '41 DL		Some frames with no engines alloc.

Ariel

MAKERS TYPE	MILITARY CLASS	WD SERIAL NO ALLOCATION	CONTRACT NUMBER	CAT REF	FRAME NUMBER	ENGINE NUMBER	QUANTITY PRODUCED	DATES	PRICE(S)	DELIVERY DESTINATION & NOTES
					28265, 28321–28322.					
W/NG	M/C Solo 350 cc OHV	RN	?		XG29059, 29075–29077, 29079–29088, 29090–29012.	BH14220–14246	27	20/02/42 Feb '42 DL		
W/NG	M/C Solo 350 cc OHV	RN	?		XG29103–29105, 29107–29112, 29114–29119, 29121–29125, 29127–29230.	BH14666, 14670, 14686–14692, 14695, 14697, 14699.	24	Mar/Apr '42 DL		
W/NG	M/C Solo 350 cc OHV	RN	?		XG35079, 35301–35353, 35355, 35358–35360, 35362, 35363, 35366, 35368, 35369, 35371–35375, 35378, 35380–35383, 35390, 35399.	BH18824–18882, 18885, 18886.	75	27/08/42 to 19/09/42 DL		

Aveling Barford

MAKERS TYPE	MILITARY CLASS	WD SERIAL NO ALLOCATION	CONTRACT NUMBER	CAT REF	FRAME NUMBER	ENGINE NUMBER	QUANTITY PRODUCED	DATES	PRICE(S)	DELIVERY DESTINATION & NOTES
Exptl. LW	M/C Solo 125 cc 2-Stroke	3921638	V.7235			AAA 8335	1	24/11/38 DL	£250	Farnborough

BMW

MAKERS TYPE	MILITARY CLASS	WD SERIAL NO ALLOCATION	CONTRACT NUMBER	CAT REF	FRAME NUMBER	ENGINE NUMBER	QUANTITY PRODUCED	DATES	PRICE(S)	DELIVERY DESTINATION & NOTES
	M/C Solo	4339541, 4339542	57/Vehs/7487				2	1940 ?		

BSA

MAKERS TYPE	MILITARY CLASS	WD SERIAL NO ALLOCATION	CONTRACT NUMBER	CAT REF	FRAME NUMBER	ENGINE NUMBER	QUANTITY PRODUCED	DATES	PRICE(S)	DELIVERY DESTINATION & NOTES
S 29 D/lux.	M/C Solo 500 cc SV	20530–20532	C1933		XH 213, XH ?, XH 221.	XS 311, XS ?, XS 312.	3	04/05/29 DM 18/06/29 CD 02/09/29 DL	£42.0s.0d	Farnborough. Civilian reg. of one was MT6498
WO Prototype Twin (A14)	M/C Solo 500 cc OHV V-twin				EX 146	Not stated	1	02/05/32 DL		BSA property, only on loan
WO Twin A14	M/C Solo 500 cc OHV V-twin	33206–33271, 33277–33416	C4845	1	A14.101–197, 199–223, 225–226, 228–285, 288–290, 293, 295–314, 316–317	A14	208*	17/10/32 CD 15/07/33 DL		*Not enough serial numbers. Civilian reg. of one was MV5768
WO Twin B15	M/C Solo 500 cc OHV V-twin	33579–33654	C5678	2			76	31/08/33		
?	M/C Solo		DDS.1317	3			?			

BSA

MAKERS TYPE	MILITARY CLASS	WD SERIAL NO ALLOCATION	CONTRACT NUMBER	CAT REF	FRAME NUMBER	ENGINE NUMBER	QUANTITY PRODUCED	DATES	PRICE(S)	DELIVERY DESTINATION & NOTES
WO Twin B15	M/C Solo 500 cc OHV V-twin	34055–34232, 34250–34279	C6264	4			208	18/04/34 26/04/34 CD		
WO Twin B15	M/C Solo 500 cc OHV V-twin	RAF	311916/34 C1(d)		B15–233 to B15–270	B15–185 to B15–222	38			Frame type 'A'
WO Twin E15	M/C Solo 500 cc OHV V-twin	34561–34660	C6264	5	E15–114, 134, ?, ?	E15–119, 101, ?, ?	100	18/04/34		Civilian reg. of one was BMM 431
WO Twin E15	M/C Solo 500 cc OHV V-twin	34963–34999, 341000–341089	C7090	6	E15–251, 299, 272, 229	E15–251, 299, 272, 229	127	14/01/35 CD 05/04/35 DL		C341013 was control m/c in 7-make trial (E15/251), BMM 642. Pillion seating fitted
WO Twin E15	M/C Solo 500 cc OHV V-twin	35586–35765, 35803–35828, 351837–351932, 352140–352187	C7487	7			350	05/06/35		
WO Twin E15	M/C Solo 500 cc OHV V-twin		7876				96	18/10/35 DM		As Contract C7487
WO Twin E15	M/C Solo 500 cc OHV V-twin		8518				48	26/11/35 DM		As Contract C7487
WO Twin E15	M/C Solo 500 cc OHV V-twin	RAF	412315/35 C2(b)		E15–521 to E15–559	E15–521 to E15–559	39			Frame type 'B'
WO Twin E15	M/C Solo 500 cc OHV V-twin	RAF	41235/35 C10(b)		E15–586 to E15–604	E15–586 to E15–604	19			Frame type 'B'
WO Twin E15	M/C Solo 500 cc OHV V-twin	RAF	559903/36 C10(b)		H15–101 to H15–130	H15–106 to H15–135	30			Frame type 'C'
WO Twin E15	M/C Solo 500 cc OHV V-twin	RAF	632331/37 C12		H15–150 to H15–319	H15–150 to H15–319	170			Frame type 'D'
WO Twin Lightened	M/C Solo 500 cc OHV	33969	Dds/1317		B15–J.15X	B15–113	1	11/04/34 DL		Civilian reg. was AMP 366
W.35–6	M/C Solo 500 cc SV	35796	C7641	8	D6–224 and E6–877	D6–684 and E6–966	1	29/05/35 DL		Dunstable. Civilian reg. was CMM 798
M20 Prototype	M/C Solo 500 cc SV	363543	C9131	9	EX 197	EX 197	1	31/07/36 DM 28/08/36 CD 02/06/36 DL	£42.5s.0d.	Farnborough. Civilian reg. was EMV 196
M20 Prototype	M/C Solo 500 cc SV	3711350–3711352	C991	12	EX 232, EX233, EX 234	EX 232, EX233, EX 234	3	13/11/37 DM 15/12/37 CD 19/10/37 DL	£47	Farnborough. Civilian regs were HMP 803, HMP 804 and HMP 805
M20	M/C Solo 500 cc SV	389144–389441, 391733–391832	A9764	14	KM20–318, ?	KM20–318, ?	398	19/07/38 DM 10/10/38 CD 06/12/38 DL	£42	
M20	M/C Solo 500 cc SV	398052–398434	C3139	16	KM20	KM20	383	24/02/39 CD	£42.5s.9d	
M20 Deluxe	M/C Solo 500 cc SV	398435–398733, 3914359–3915660	C3655	18	KM20–3001 to KM20–4602	KM20–2001 to KM20–3602	1602	24/07/39 DM 15/08/39 CD		
M20	M/C Solo 500 cc SV		?		KM20–4603 to 4662, 4676, 4678, 4692, 4695, 4700, 4705, 4709, 4938, 4941, 4958, 4976, 4985, 4986, 4987, 4998, 5000, 5005, 5008–5010, 5012, 5018–5022, 5024, 5025–5027, 5030–5032,	KM20–156, 162, 187, 188, 195, 711, 980, 1022, 1024, 1818, 1819, 1824, 1846, 1889, 1891, 1897, 1900, 1902, 1909, 1911–4, 1917, 1921–9, 1931–3, 1935, 1936, 1939, 1941–1949, 1950–7, 1959–1961, 1963, 1965,	117	Sept '39 DL		

BSA

Makers Type	Military Class	WD Serial No Allocation	Contract Number	Cat Ref	Frame Number	Engine Number	Quantity Produced	Dates	Price(s)	Delivery Destination & Notes
					5672–5674, 5677, 5679, 5680, 5682–5684, 5687, 5693, 5694, 5698, 5699, 5701, 5703, 5708, 5710, 5711, 5720, 5730–5732, 5734	1967–1970, 1972–1975, 4676, 4692, 4695, 4700, 4705, 4709, 4958, 4986, 4987, 5003, 5005, 5008, 5009, 5010, 5012, 5018–5022 5024, 5025, 5030–5032, 5672–5674, 5677, 5679, 5680, 5682, 5683, 5684, 5687, 5693, 5694, 5698, 5699, 5701, 5703, 5707, 5708, 5710, 5711, 5720, 5730–5732, 5734				
M20	M/C Solo 500 cc SV		?		KM20–5712, 5728, 5729	KM20–121, 120, 122	3	Nov '39 DL		
?	M/C Solo 500 cc SV		?		EX 315	WM20–499	1	27/12/40 DL		lightened M20?
M20	M/C Solo 500 cc SV		?		WM20–111 to 122, 124, 125A 125B, 126–132, 134–184, 186–194, 195A, 195B, 196–199, 201–219, 220A, 220B, 221–252, 420, 501–506, 508, 511, 513–515, 517, 520–523, 527, 528, 530, 534, 535, 541, 542, 544, 545, 550, 556, 559, 562, 570, 572, 573, 575–578, 580, 585, 587–592, 596, 733, 1501–1560, 1562–1566, 1568–1572, 1574–1629, 1631–1653, 1655–1664, 1666–1671, 1673–1675, 1677–1680, 1682, 1684–1714, 1716–1718, 1720, 1722–1760, 1762–1769, 1771, 1773–1782, 1784–1792, 1794, 1795, 1797–1800, 4501, 4619, 4689, 4846, 4899	WM20–244 to 249, 251, 252 420, 501–506 508, 511, 513–515, 517, 520–523, 527, 528, 530, 534, 535, 541, 542, 544, 545, 550, 556, 559, 562, 570, 572, 573, 575–578, 580, 585, 587–592, 596, 841, 868, 1501–1560, 1562–1566, 1568–1572, 1574–1629, 1631–1653, 1655–1664, 1666–1675, 1677–1680, 1682, 1684–1714, 1716–1718, 1720, 1722–1760, 1762–1769, 1771, 1773–1805, 1807–1814, 1816–1817, 1822, 1825, 1826, 1828–1832, 1835–1840, 1842–1843, 1845, 1847, 1848, 1850–1856, 1858–1867, 1869, 1872, 1873–1888, 1890, 1892–1896, 1898–1899, 1901, 1904–1908, 1910, 1913, 1915, 1916, 1918–1920, 1930, 1932, 1934, 1940, 1944, 1955, 1963, 1964, 1966, 4501, 4619, 5689, Repeated Nos. 1776, 1778, 1779, 1781,	474	Sept '39 DL		

BSA

MAKERS TYPE	MILITARY CLASS	WD SERIAL NO ALLOCATION	CONTRACT NUMBER	CAT REF	FRAME NUMBER	ENGINE NUMBER	QUANTITY PRODUCED	DATES	PRICE(S)	DELIVERY DESTINATION & NOTES
						1782, 1784–1792, 1794, 1795, 1797–1800, 1813, 1814, 1837, 1840, 1851, 1866. 1869, 1871, 1876, and 1791 yet again!				
M20	M/C Solo 500 cc SV	4191743–4191748, 4191761–4191801	C7370	26			147*	28/08/40 DM 14/09/40 CD	£49.9s.9d	Colchester or Catterick. * Only 47 serial numbers. 145 were demanded
M20	M/C Solo 500 cc SV		?		WM20–256	WM20–256	1	03/11/39 DL		
M20	M/C Solo 500 cc SV		?		WM20–4251	WM20–533	1	31/03/41 DL		
M20	M/C Solo 500 cc SV		?		WM20–255, 239, 2232, 2241, 2264, 2275, 2276, 2280, 2283, 2284, 2289, 2296, 2297, 2299, 2300, 2309, 2312, 2371, 2372, 2373, 2378, 2380, 2795, 2863, 2864, 2868, 2873, 2875, 2876, 2879, 2881, 2887, 2889, 2892, 2898, 2900, 2902, 2908, 2909, 2911, 2914–2917, 2981, 2982, 2987, 2988, 2990, 2993, 2995, 3000, 3074, 3904, 3978, 3982, 3984, 3995, 4001, 4002	WM20–255, 348–359, 361, 362, 364, 366–368, 370, 371, 374–376, 378–381, 384, 385, 387, 388, 390, 391, 394–397, 2232, 2241, 2267, 2275, 2276, 2280, 2283, 2284, 2289, 2296, 2297, 2299, 2300, 2309, 2312, 2371, 2372, 2373, 2378, 2380, 2795, 3904	60	29/30 May and		
M20	M/C Solo 500 cc SV		?		WM20–4240, 4243–4251	WM20–502 to 505, 508–513	10	09/03/41 DL		
M20	M/C Solo 500 cc SV		?		WM20–4216	WM20–42116	1	20/03/41 DL		
M20	M/C Solo 500 cc SV		?		WM20–4222	WM20–42121	1	20/03/40 DL		
M20	M/C Solo 500 cc SV		?		WM20–4253	WM20–630	1	06/02/41 DL		
M20	M/C Solo 500 cc SV	RN	?		WM20–4050 to 4061	WM20–4050 to 4061	11	26/05/40 DL		Bath
M20	M/C Solo 500 cc SV	RN	?		WM20–44161, 4163–4165, 4167, 4173	WM20–473 to 476, 479, 483	6	20/09/40 and 14/10//40 DL		Bath
M20	M/C Solo 500 cc SV	3928419–3931195, 3934710–3935709, 4105401–4107400, 4123773–4125995, 4137042–4137141	C5110	20	WM20–5001 to 7099, WM20–7201 to ?	WM20–5001 to 7099, WM20–7201 to ?	8100?	27/09/39 DM 04/02/40 CD 21/08/40 CP		Chilwell at 600 per week from 16/09/39 Deluxe models
M20	M/C Solo 500 cc SV	4140434–4144433	C5610	21	WM20–14001 to 18000	WM20–14001 to 18000	4000	21/11/39 DM 19/01/40 CD 04/06/40 CP	£44.4s.6d	Chilwell at 450/500 per week from 10/02/40
M20	M/C Solo 500 cc SV	4170215–4173214	C6126	22	WM20–18001 to 21000	WM20–18001 to 21000	3000	25/01/40 DM 14/06/40 CD	£48.5s.0d	Chilwell at 1500 per month after C5610
M20	M/C Solo 500 cc SV	4196513–4199999 4300000–4300512	C6654	23	WM20–21001 to 25000	WM20–21001 to 25000	4000	21/03/40 DM 17/07/40 CD 04/08/40 CP	£49.10s.0d	Chilwell after C6126

BSA

Makers Type	Military Class	WD Serial No Allocation	Contract Number	Cat Ref	Frame Number	Engine Number	Quantity Produced	Dates	Price(s)	Delivery Destination & Notes
M20	M/C Solo 500 cc SV	4341593–4358592	C7287	24	WM20–25001 to 42000	WM20–25001 to 42000	17000	25/05/40 DM 30/11/40 CD 28/08/41 CP	£49.15s.0d	Chilwell at 2000 per month after C6654
M20	M/C Solo 500 cc SV	RAF	C9893				115	17/02/41 DM 29/08/41 CD	£49.12s.0d	Hartlebury at 40 per week
M20	M/C Solo 500 cc SV	RAF	C9892		WM20–42116 to 42121, 42201–44106	WM20–42116 to 42121, 42201–44106	1912	17/02/41 DM 03/01/42 CD	£51.9s.6d	Hartlebury. Fitted with sidecar lugs
M20	M/C Solo 500 cc SV		C10021				2	04/03/41 DM 02/05/41 CD	*c.* £50	
M20	M/C Solo 500 cc SV		C10119				100	18/03/41 DM 20/10/41 CD	£57.11s.6d	Similar to C9310
M20	M/C Solo 500 cc SV		C11440				10	09/08/41 DM 02/12/41 CD	£56.5s.0d	Crated for colonies
M20	M/C Solo 500 cc SV	4553722–4562721	C9310	30	WM20–44213 to 53212	WM20–44213 to 53212	9000	03/12/40 DM 30/12/40 CD 21/01/42 DL	£56.5s.0d	Chilwell. Bag racks fitted
M20	M/C Comb. 500 cc SV	RAF	C10655		WM20–53213 to 53412	WM20–53213 to 53412	200	10/05/41 DM 30/12/43 /01/44 DL	£85.19s.7d	No panniers
M20	M/C Solo 500 cc SV	4635001–4640000 4662156–4667155	C11101	31	WM20–53413 to 61412, 61448–63447	WM20–53413 to 61412, 61448–63447	10000	05/07/41 DM /42 DL	£64.12s.0d	Order originally for 350 cc OHV
M20	M/C Comb. 500 cc SV		C12586				35	24/11/41 DM 06/01/44	£85.19s.7d	
M20	M/C Solo 500 cc SV	4699545–4707544	C12424	32	WM20–63448 to 71447	WM20–63448 to 71447	8000	10/11/41 DM	£64.12s.0d	Order originally for 350 cc OHV
M20	M/C Solo 500 cc SV		C13048				1	06/01/42 DM 24/01/42 CD	£61.3s.6d	
M20	M/C Solo 500 cc SV		C13213				2	21/01/42 DM 18/02/42	£63.0s.0d	
M20	M/C Solo 500 cc SV	4752401–4757400 4860801–4865800	C13290	33	WM20–71818 to 81817	WM20–71818 to 81817	10000	26/01/42 DM	£64.12s.0d	
M20	M/C Comb. 500 cc SV		C13322				50	29/01/42 DM 16/02/44	£96.4s.0d	
M20	M/C Solo 500 cc SV		C13441				2	06/02/42 DM 24/02/42 CD	£63.0s.0d	
M20	M/C Comb. 500 cc SV		C13873				35	14/03/42 DM 31/12/43	£87.3s.7d	
M20	M/C Comb. 500 cc SV		C13909				25	18/03/42 DM 30/12/43	£87.3s.7d	
M20	M/C Comb. 500 cc SV	RAF	C14052		WM20–71509 to 71817	WM20–71509 to 71817	309	31/12/43 01/44 DL	£86.17s.7d	To India? No panniers
M20	M/C Solo 500 cc SV		C14330				2	26/05/42 CD	£58.10s.0d	No pillion equip.
M20	M/C Solo 500 cc SV		S38				2	05/06/42 DM 24/09/42	£63.0s.0d	
M20	M/C Solo 500 cc SV		S364				4	10/07/42 DM 24/09/42	£63.0s.0d	
M20	M/C Comb. 500 cc SV		S649				1?	02/10/42	£93.12s.0d	
M20	M/C Solo 500 cc SV	5115218–5130217	S1048	34	WM20–81818 to 96817	WM20–81818 to 96817	15000	24/09/42 DM? 03/11/43	£62.15s.0d	
M20	M/C Solo 500 cc SV	5207518–5215517	S2603	35	WM20–96818 to 104817	WM20–96818 to 104817	8000	03/03/43 01/07/44	£63.10s.6d	
M20	M/C Solo 500 cc SV	5545518–5557517	S5209	36	WM20–104818 to 116817	WM20–104818 to 116817	12000	02/12/43 28/07/45	£64.10s.0d	
M20	M/C Solo 500 cc SV		S5773				5	26/05/44	£63.10s.6d	
M20	M/C Solo 500 cc SV		S6003				1	31/05/44	£63.10s.6d	

BSA

Makers Type	Military Class	WD Serial No Allocation	Contract Number	Cat Ref	Frame Number	Engine Number	Quantity Produced	Dates	Price(s)	Delivery Destination & Notes
M20	M/C Solo 500 cc SV		S6050				1	31/05/44	£63.10s.6d	
M20	M/C Solo 500 cc SV		S6061				5	31/05/44	£63.10s.5d	
M20	M/C Comb. 500 cc SV		S6506				1	16/06/44	£63.10s.0d	
M20	M/C Comb. 500 cc SV		S6507				4	16/06/44	£63.10s.6d	
M20	M/C Solo 500 cc SV	5885918–5895917	S7218	37	WM20–		10000*	10/08/44 19/01/46	£69.2s.3d	*Reduced to 5870
M20	M/C Solo 500 cc SV		S9330				14	12/12/45	£69.2s.3d	
M20	M/C Solo 500 cc SV		S10277				3	05/08/47	£79.14s.0d	
B20	M/C Solo 250 cc SV	377600–377629	C174	10	HB20–4086, 4088–4090, 4092, 4093, 4098–4100	HB20–2009 to 2017	30*	04/05/37 DM 15/06/37 CD 20/07/37 CP	c. £30	Chilwell at 20 per week. *Only 9 machines listed in B.S.A. ledgers. 07/07/37 delivery
B20	M/C Solo 250 cc SV	383859–383982	C912	11	JB20–3101 to 3224	JB20–901 to 1024	124	14/10/37 DM 06/12/37 CD 05/02/38 CP	£31.0s.0d	Chilwell at 20 per week
C10	M/C Solo 250 cc SV	399327–399926	C3739	17	KC10–3015 to 3600	1415–2000	585*	03/05/39 DM 10/06/39 CD	£29.5s.0d	Chilwell at 125 per week. Deluxe model. *600 serials issued
C10	M/C Solo 250 cc SV	3922946–3924295	C4452	19	WC10–101 to 1451	WC10–101 to 1451	1350	15/08/39 1940 DL		Chilwell
C10	M/C Solo 250 cc SV	RN	?		WC10–3804 to 3807	WC10–3804 to 3807	4	02/04/40 DL		Deptford
?	M/C Solo 250 cc		C11135				3	09/07/41 DM 26/08/41 CD	£34.7s.6d	Bromsgrove. Civilian model
C11	M/C Solo 250 cc OHV	India Office	Y8142/9064		WC11–4001 to 4531	WC11–4001 to 4531	530	20/02/40		India
C12	M/C Solo 350 cc SV	RN			C12–3848 to 3852, 3854–3864	C12–401, 403, 404, 405, 408, 410, 413, 421, 426, 429–432, 434, 435, 439	16	Sept '40 DL		Bath
WB30 Prototype	M/C Solo 350 cc OHV	436975	C6623		EX290	EX291	1	30/03/40 DM 12/06/40 CD 25/01/40 DL	£50 ?	Farnborough. 288 lbs Tyres were 300–21 front 325–19 rear
WB30 Pre- production	M/C Solo 350 cc OHV		C7975		EX309	EX309	1	13/07/40 CD 16/07/40 DL	£50.3s.6d	313 lbs 315–19 tyres
WB30 + BSA–Matchless	M/C Solo 350 cc OHV	4379578–4379627 (less 4379619) 4379619	C8330	28	WB30–101 to 139, 101A, 140, 141, 143–150. Also as part of this contract frame EX289 fitted with AMC engine 23297	WB30–503, 505– 511, 513–521, 523–527, 529–533, 535–539, 541–555, 557–560	50 + 1	09/08/40 DM 02/01/42 CD 18/12/40 DL onwards	£57.16s.7d	As contract C7975. Chilwell – 25, Canada – 2, Feltham – 19, U.S.A. – 3, and 1 to A.M.C.
WB30	M/C Solo 350 cc OHV	G.P.O.	C13683		WB30–501 to 600	WB30–501 to 600	100*	27/02/42 DM		*Possibly not delivered if BSA ledgers correct
?	M/C Solo 350 cc		C13872				100	14/03/42 DM		
WB29	M/C Solo 350 cc OHV	4191834–4191854, 4191866	C7370	27			167*	28/08/40 DM 14/09/40 CD	£42.8s.3d	Colchester or Catterick. *Only 22 serial numbers, but 170 originally demanded
M24	M/C Solo 500 cc OHV	387078–387080	C2007	13	385, 398, 404	JM24–344, 369, and 365	3*	04/07/38 DM 30/07/38 CD 19/08/38 DL	£64.0s.0d	Civilian regs EOF 200, 201 and 202. *Another three also purchased by M.E.E. Frames 362, 367, 386. Engines 345, 347, 358. Civilian regs EOG 20, 21 and 22

BSA

Makers Type	Military Class	WD Serial No Allocation	Contract Number	Cat Ref	Frame Number	Engine Number	Quantity Produced	Dates	Price(s)	Delivery Destination & Notes
M24	M/C Solo 500 cc OHV		?		5003, 5004, 5006, 5014–5016, 5029, 5228	KM24–425–427, 429, 432, 435, 437, 439	8	Sept '39 DL		
M22	M/C Solo 500 cc OHV		?		4694, 4706, 4764, 4796, 4829, 4831	KM22–109, 119, 137, 172, 177, 181	6	Sept '39 DL		
M21	M/C Solo 600 cc SV	4191485–4191553, 4191584–4191627, 4191959–4192302	C7370	25	WM20–1440, 1457, 1494, 1819, 1822, 1827, 1845, 1871, 1880, 1939, 1941, 1945, 1957, 2354, 2360, 2367, 2368, 2382, 2383, 2387, 2395–2397, 2403, 2405, 2408, 2412, 2413, 2415, 2417, 2419, 2420, 2422–2429, 2431–2433, 2439, 2440, 2443, 2444, 2446–2450, 2452, 2454, 2456, 2458–2463, 2465, 2466, 2469–2480, 2483–2500, 2721, 2722, 2768, 2771, 2781, 2782, 2784–2793, 2796–2800, 2825–2832, 2834–2841, 2843, 2844, 2846, 2848–2852, 2854–2861, 2865, 2867, 2869–2872, 2877, 2878, 2882, 2886, 2888, 2893–2895, 2897, 2904, 2905, 2912, 2918–2920, 2923–2931, 2934, 2936–2967, 2969, 2970, 2972–2975, 2978–2980, 2983, 2986, 2989, 2991, 2992, 2994, 2996, 3862, 3975, 3976, 3985, 3986, 3989, 3997, 3998	WM21–354, 356, 357, 360, 362–371, 373, 374, 376, 378, 379, 381–385, 393, 395, 402, 1440, 1457, 1494, 1819, 1822, 1827, 1845, 1871, 1880, 1939, 1941, 1945, 1957, 2354, 2360, 2367, 2368, 2382, 2383, 2387, 2395–2397, 2403, 2405, 2408, 2412, 2413, 2415, 2417, 2419, 2420, 2422–2429, 2431–2433, 2439, 2440, 2443, 2444, 2426–2450, 2452, 2454, 2456, 2458–2463, 2465, 2466, 2469–2480, 2483–2500, 2721, 2722, 2771, 2781, 2782, 2784–2793, 2796–2800, 2825–2830, 2832, 2834–2841, 2843, 2844, 2846, 2848–2850, 2852, 2854–2857, 2859–2861, 2869, 2870, 2882, 2893, 2897, 2904, 2918–2920, 2923–2931, 2934, 2936–2967, 2969, 2970, 2972–2980, 2982, 2994	212*	28/08/40 DM 14/09/40 CD 28/29/30 May DL	£48.4s.3d	Colchester or Catterick. *211 demanded, 457 serial numbers, 233 frames and engines
M21	M/C Solo 600 cc SV		?		4929	1382	1	04/10/39 DL		
M21	M/C Solo 600 cc SV		?		WM20–2732	WM21–288	1	23/12/40 DL		
M21 s.w.d. prototype	M/C Comb. 600 cc SV		?		EX 311	EX 311	1	11/07/40 DL		Experimental frame and engine
Prototype parallel twin	M/C Solo 500 cc SV		?				1?			
M20	M/C Comb. 500 cc SV	RAF					?			
M23	M/C Solo 500 cc OHV		?		KM20–4681, 4696, 4698, 4711, 4713,	KM23–941, 970, 976, 977, 985, 994, 995, 998,	19	Sept '39		

BSA

Makers Type	Military Class	WD Serial No Allocation	Contract Number	Cat Ref	Frame Number	Engine Number	Quantity Produced	Dates	Price(s)	Delivery Destination & Notes
					4714, 4720, 4730, 4740, 4741, 4775, 4921, 4934, 4971, 5002, 5007, 5011, 5017, 5023	1004, 1005, 1009, 1013, 1015, 1017, 1019, 1021, 1023, 1025, 1027				
B23	M/C Solo 348 cc SV				111	HB23–101		21/09/36 DL		Returned same day
B–2 *or* B–18 *or* B–3	M/C Solo 249 cc OHV				103	104		21/09/36 DL		Returned same day
B26	M/C Solo 348 cc OHV				HB24–104	HB26–106		21/09/36 DL		Returned same day
M22	M/C Solo 496 cc OHV				HM19–833	HM22–309		21/09/36 DL		

Douglas

Makers Type	Military Class	WD Serial No Allocation	Contract Number	Cat Ref	Frame Number	Engine Number	Quantity Produced	Dates	Price(s)	Delivery Destination & Notes
L29	M/C Solo 350 cc SV Flat twin		C.1933	1			150	04/05/29 DM 18/06/29 CD	c.£40	
L29/2	M/C Solo 350 cc SV Flat twin	20518, 20430	C.2922	2	WF 1925, 1838, ?	EN 1703, ?	27	20/07/29 DL		Civilian reg. of one was MT 6461
L29/2	M/C Solo 350 cc SV Flat twin	21125, 21107, 21097, 21158	C.3644	3	WF 2014, 1697, 1347, 1663, ?	EN 2508, 2502, 2491, 2559, ?	70	07/04/31 DM 05/06/31 CD 10/04/31 DL	£41.7s.0d	Farnborough. Civilian reg. of one was MG 9719
L29/3	M/C Solo 350 cc SV Flat twin	21697, 21714, 21758, 21757, 21752, 21753, 21755, 21754, 21709	C.4259	4	FA 963, 1309, 1530, 1451, 1038, 1446, 1344, 1480, ?	EN 2331, 2320, 2332, 2203, 2212, 2330, 2171, 2222, ?	30?	15/09/31 DL		Civilian reg. of one was HX 6383
L29/4	M/C Solo 350 cc SV Flat twin	22410, 22420	C.4443	5	2148 WF, ?	2820, ?	30?	1933		Civilian reg. of one was MV 5267
5Y2 Blue chief	M/C Solo 500 cc SV Flat twin		–			5/H/103	1	22/11/34 DL		Douglas Property 3-Speed. Civilian reg. was DC 5187
5Y2 Blue chief	M/C Solo 500 cc SV Flat twin		–			5.B/2	1	22/11/34 DL		Douglas Property 4-Speed
5Y2 Blue chief	M/C Solo 500 cc SV Flat twin	341192	C.7122	6	FZ 135 then FZ 256	5/H/148	1	25/01/35 CD 22/11/34 DL		Civilian reg. was BMM395
A31	M/C Solo 348 cc SV Flat twin				FC 1141	EV 1202	1	1931 09/04/31 DL		
DV60 Proto.	M/C Solo 600 cc SV Flat twin						2	1944/5		Farnborough
Experimental	M/C Solo				FH 119	35/C.101	1	04/01/32 DL		

Excelsior

Makers Type	Military Class	WD Serial No Allocation	Contract Number	Cat Ref	Frame Number	Engine Number	Quantity Produced	Dates	Price(s)	Delivery Destination & Notes
Army Prototype	M/C Solo 98 cc 2-Stroke		–	–			1			
Prototype Welbike	M/C solo 98 cc 2-Stroke		?				6?	1942		
Mk.1 Welbike	M/C Solo 98 cc 2-Stroke	4658474–4659673	S.789	1	4–1186	XXE– ? to ?	1183*	26/08/42		*1200 serial numbers issued
Mk.2 Series 1 Welbike	M/C Solo 98 cc 2-Stroke	5152014–5153413	S.1649	2	1214–2613	XXE– ? to ?	1400	19/11/42		
Mk.2 Series 1 Welbike	M/C Solo 98 cc 2-Stroke	5153414–5154654	S.1946	3	2614–3954	XXE– ? to ?	1340	27/12/42		
Universal	M/C Solo 125 cc 2-Stroke		S.545	–			1?		£31.3s.7d	

Francis Barnett

Makers Type	Military Class	WD Serial No Allocation	Contract Number	Cat Ref	Frame Number	Engine Number	Quantity Produced	Dates	Price(s)	Delivery Destination & Notes
Exptl. Military LW (Model 9)	M/C Solo 172 cc 2-Stroke	19257			16211	TL 1391	1	15/06/28 DL		Farnborough. Civilian reg. was MP 8175
Model 12 (Modified)	M/C Solo 350 cc 2-Stroke	20407			E1644	CZA.2959	3	04/05/29 DM 18/06/29 CD 02/09/29 DL	£38.15s.0d	Farnborough
Plover	M/C Solo 150 cc 2-Stroke		C12029				25	02/10/41 DM 01/11/41 CD	£33.5s.5d	

Gillet Herstal

Makers Type	Military Class	WD Serial No Allocation	Contract Number	Cat Ref	Frame Number	Engine Number	Quantity Produced	Dates	Price(s)	Delivery Destination & Notes
	M/C Comb. 728 cc 2-Stroke parallel twin		—				1	22/05/39 DL		Farnborough. Had SWD fitted + reverse gear. Returned 24/05/39

Harley-Davidson

Makers Type	Military Class	WD Serial No Allocation	Contract Number	Cat Ref	Frame Number	Engine Number	Quantity Produced	Dates	Price(s)	Delivery Destination & Notes
WLC	M/C Solo 750 cc SV V-Twin	4782631, 4782632	S/M2164	–	–	42 WLC - - - -	2	1942		Received at the same time as two Indian 640Bs
WLC	M/C Solo 750 cc SV V-Twin	RAF			–	43 WLC - - - -	?	1942/3 DL		Canadian specification
UA	M/C Comb. 1200 cc SV V-Twin					42 U - - - -	?	1942/43		Fitted with left-hand sidecars. British used
ELC Test Comb.	M/C Comb. 1000 cc OHV V-Twin				42 LLE.1347	42 ELC.1600	1	29/12/41		Fitted with left-hand sidecar. Ex-Canadian Army
WLC Test Model	M/C Solo 750 cc SV V-Twin	C.M.D.I.			–	42 WLC.1436	1	25/09/41		Slough
US	M/C Comb. 1200 cc SV V-Twin		LL-NDS-105.A		42 LLE. - - - -	42 US - - - -	1597	Nov '42		Sent to South Africa via British Supply Council (no. 9259)

Indian

Makers Type	Military Class	WD Serial No Allocation	Contract Number	Cat Ref	Frame Number	Engine Number	Quantity Produced	Dates	Price(s)	Delivery Destination & Notes
340B	M/C Comb. 1204 cc SV V-twin	4369589–4369674, 4370932–4370981, 4372332–4372518, 4448086, 4448087	Dds. 1624 V4042	1	CAV - - - -	CAV - - - - B	325	29/07/40 12/08/40 DL		Chilwell, Test model C4370969 was Frame CAV4510 and Engine CAV4510 B 4.00 – 18 tyres fitted
340B	M/C Comb. 1204 cc SV V-twin	4501466–4501601	S/M2039	2			136	20/02/41 30/02/41 Feb to Apr '41 DL		
340B	M/C Comb. 1204 cc SV	4648240–4648339	S/M2289	3	340–4275 to 4374	CDO–4275 to 4374	100	19/12/41 CD Oct '42 CP		12 to Polish, rest to British. Sidecar chassis Nos. were FC263010 to

Indian

MAKERS TYPE	MILITARY CLASS	WD SERIAL NO ALLOCATION	CONTRACT NUMBER	CAT REF	FRAME NUMBER	ENGINE NUMBER	QUANTITY PRODUCED	DATES	PRICE(S)	DELIVERY DESTINATION & NOTES
										FC263109
741B	M/C Solo 500 cc SV V-twin	4896842–4898825, 4953034–4955034, 5574052–5575051	S/M2404	5	741– ?	GDA– ?	10248	13/02/42 CD Nov 1942 DL		UK 4272, India 1000, India Admiralty 6, Australia 1816, West Africa Admiralty 4, Trinidad 6, Poland 671, New Zealand 1066, Crown Agents British Honduras 2, Crown Agents Mauritius 16, Crown Agents Ceylon 25, West African Air Ministry 80, Middle East Air Ministry 868, Belgian Congo 259, Jamaica 5, South Rhodesia 94, South Caribbean 8, UK (MOWT) 50
741B	M/C Solo 500 cc SV V-twin	4782691–4784490	S/M2220	6	741–?	GDA–?	4900*	19/06/43 CP		UK 1888, New Zealand 2500, Australia 500, Poland (Canada) 12. *Only 1800 serial nos. Also, 50 fitted with Norton handlebars.
741B	M/C Solo 500 cc SV V-twin	4895721–4896841	S/M2384	7	741–?	GDA–?	2624*	13/02/42 CD 26/07/43 CP		UK 1390, Australia 1162, Admirality of South Africa 72. *Only 1121 serial nos.
741B	M/C Solo 500 cc SV V-twin		S/M2193	–	741–?	GDA–?	1100	26/07/43 CP		Malaya 370, Australia 680, New Zealand 50
640B	M/C Solo 750 cc SV V-twin	4782629, 4782630	S/M2164	8	640–4445, and 640–4446	FDO–4445, and FDO–4446	2	Oct '42		UK
?	M/C Comb.		S/M2300				2182	19/12/41 CD		Cancelled July 1942
344B ?	M/C Comb. 1204 cc SV	India	S/M6451		344–1001 to ?	CDD–1001 to ?	360*	21/12/44		UK. *Originally was 385. Left-hand sidecar on '344'

James

MAKERS TYPE	MILITARY CLASS	WD SERIAL NO ALLOCATION	CONTRACT NUMBER	CAT REF	FRAME NUMBER	ENGINE NUMBER	QUANTITY PRODUCED	DATES	PRICE(S)	DELIVERY DESTINATION & NOTES
ML (Prototype)	M/C Solo 125 cc 2-Stroke	5146001	S.1718		11896	20105	1	23/01/43 CD	£39.15s.9d	ML lightweight prototype model. Possibly ended up in East Africa
K17	M/C Solo 125 cc 2-Stroke		S.1549				2	05/02/43 CD	£34.0s.0d	
K15/K16	M/C Solo 150 cc 2-Stroke		S.1698				10	30/04/43 CD	£34.10s.0d	Exact model not known
ML (Prototype)	M/C Solo 125 cc 2-Stroke		S.1833				12	11/05/43 CD	£32.10s.6d	Further improved evaluation models
ML	M/C Solo 125 cc 2-Stroke	5146002–5149541	S.1972	1	ML 2–3541	AAA - - - - A -	3540	03/43 DL	£31.17s.6d	Delivery commencing March 1943 at 300 per month, May 1943 at 400 per month, after then 500 per month
ML	M/C Solo 125 cc 2-Stroke	5522209–5522308	S.5571	2	ML 5209–5409	AAA - - - - A - ?	200	1943	£32.7s.0d	Delivery of 1st 100 machines to Army. Remainder to the Admiralty (Navy)
ML	M/C Solo 125 cc 2-Stroke	5830501–5831400	S.6603	3	ML 6001–6900	AAA - - - - A - ?	900	1943–1944	£32.6s.4d	
ML	M/C Solo 125 cc 2-Stroke	5854601–5856100	S.7113	4	ML 7001–8500	AAA - - - - A - ?	1500	1944	£33.15s.0d	Contract originally for 3,000 machines but cancelled after 1,500 delivered
ML	M/C Solo 125 cc 2-Stroke		S.8236				200	05/02/45 CD	£34.6s.6d	No details known. Possible contract for Admiralty

Levis

MAKERS TYPE	MILITARY CLASS	WD SERIAL NO ALLOCATION	CONTRACT NUMBER	CAT REF	FRAME NUMBER	ENGINE NUMBER	QUANTITY PRODUCED	DATES	PRICE(S)	DELIVERY DESTINATION & NOTES
Model M	M/C Solo 250 cc 2-Stroke		8345				1	03/10/28 DM 13/10/28 CD 23/10/28 DL	£38.10s.0d	Farnborough
Model 6-Port	M/C Solo 250 cc 2-Stroke	19725, ?	8789		20079, ?	24380, ?	2	30/11/28 DM 05/12/28 CD	£38.10s.0d	Farnborough and Feltham (for Egypt). Standard trim with electric lights. Civilian registration MT9344
Model 6-Port	M/C Solo 250 cc 2-Stroke		1126				10	28/08/29 DM 05/12/29 CD	£37.0s.0d	Feltham
Model 6-Port	M/C Solo 250 cc 2-Stroke		3520				9	12/08/30 DM 02/09/30 CD	£37.0s.0d	Feltham
?	M/C Solo 350 cc		C10484				2000	26/04/41 DM		Cancelled on 28/06/41

Matchless

MAKERS TYPE	MILITARY CLASS	WD SERIAL NO ALLOCATION	CONTRACT NUMBER	CAT REF	FRAME NUMBER	ENGINE NUMBER	QUANTITY PRODUCED	DATES	PRICE(S)	DELIVERY DESTINATION & NOTES
T/4	M/C Solo 350 cc SV	20351, ?, ?	C1933	1	10397, ?, ?	T/4 4419, ?, ?	3	04/05/29 DM 18/06/29 CD	£42.10s.0d	Civilian reg. of one was MT 6345
Silver Arrow	M/C Solo 400 cc SV V-Twin	20974, 20966	P.2.T. 4145	3	1390, 967, ?	1299, 1022, ?	?	1930 20/02/30 DL		Civilian reg. of one was MT 9485
Silver Arrow	M/C Solo 400 cc SV V-Twin	21821, 21813	C3644	5	2098, 2103	A1991, 1961	37	07/04/31 DM 05/06/31 CD 11/09/31 DL and into 1932	£49.7s.8d	Farnborough. Civilian reg. of one was HX 6501
?	?		P.2.T. 3932	2						
?	?		P.2.T. 4219	4						
G7	M/C Solo 246 cc SV	363870–364021	C9221	7	1744, ?, ?	37/G7 526, ?	152	17/08/36 DM 26/09/36 CD	£30.1s.4d	Chilwell at 13/16 per week. Civilian reg. of one was EMV 635
G80, G90, G5. (All civilian spec.)	M/C Solo 500 cc SV or OHV	4191348–4191353 4191749–4191750 4191752–4191755 4191757–4191759	C7373	8			12 – G80 1 – G90 2 – G5	26/05/40	£50.0s.1d £53.0s.10d £44.0s.0d	Catterick or Stirling
Exptl. LW	M/C Solo 250 cc OHV	4187516	C6674		550	W40/G2M 4237	1	16/04/40 DM 03/06/40 CD 19/03/40 DL	£49.19s.0d	Farnborough
?	M/C Solo 350 cc	37180, 37181					2			
?	M/C Solo		?		D.E.6	4247	1	10/06/40 DL		
Exptl. LW	M/C Solo 250 cc OHV		C8019		578	4249	1	19/07/40 DM 17/08/40 CD 20/06/40 DL	£49.18s.9d	Chilwell
G3	M/C Solo 350 cc OHV	35795	C7641	6	617	36/G3 630	1	15/08/35 11/09/35 DL	£44.4s.0d	Civilian reg. CMM749. Evaluation Model
G3	M/C Solo 350 cc OHV	36260–36270	C8968	24			11	02/07/36 DM 19/08/36 CD	£42.17s.9d	Feltham. Fitted with air cleaners
G3	M/C Solo 350 cc OHV	353512–353555 354624–354689	C8239	25	1001, 990, ?	36/G3 767, 777, ?	110	22/11/35 DM 31/12/35 CD 30/03/36 CP	£38.18s.0d	Feltham at 10 per week. C353544 had air cleaner. Civilian reg. of one was DMF 42
G3	M/C Solo 350 cc OHV		C422				2	13/07/37 DM 13/08/37 CD 16/10/37 CPs	£45	Feltham
G3	M/C Solo 350 cc OHV	3811084–3811347	C2073	21	3257–3520	39/G3–2715 to 39/G3–2978	264	30/06/38 DM 26/09/38 CD 25/11/38 CP	£42	Feltham at 50 per week. (Panel in tank) Civilian reg. of one was RHX 643

Matchless

MAKERS TYPE	MILITARY CLASS	WD SERIAL NO ALLOCATION	CONTRACT NUMBER	CAT REF	FRAME NUMBER	ENGINE NUMBER	QUANTITY PRODUCED	DATES	PRICE(S)	DELIVERY DESTINATION & NOTES
G3	M/C Solo 350 cc OHV	3916253–3916452	C3360	18			200	27/04/39 CD	£43	Feltham at 50 per week
G3	M/C Solo 350 cc OHV	39515–39534	C3398	28			20	20/12/38 DM 09/08/39 CD	£45.2s.10d	
G3	M/C Solo 350 cc OHV	3917752–3918091	C4608	13	502–841	40–G3WO–3516 to 40–G3WO–3855	340	26/07/39 DM 02/10/39 CD		Chilwell at 50 per week. (Panel in tank) as C3360
G3	M/C Solo 350 cc OHV	63586–65551 65553–65569 65571–65583 65586–67585 78041, 78058, 78061, 78065, 78068, 78069, 78078	C5247	10	845–4844	40–G3WO–3862 to 40–G3WO–7861	4000	25/10/39 DM 18/01/40 CD 23/03/40 CP	£49.18s.9d	Feltham at 200 per week from 25/11/39. (Panel in tank)
G3	M/C Solo 350 cc OHV	65552, 65570, 65584, 65585, 78038–78040 78042–78057, 78059, 78060, 78062–78064, 78066, 78067, 78070–78077, 78079–80037, 80764–80766	C6094	11	5000–6999	40–G3WO–8226 to 40–G3WO–10225	2000	25/01/40 DM 24/06/40 CD 15/11/40 CP	£49.18s.4d	Olympia at 180 per week from 01/06/40. (Panel in tank)
G3	M/C Solo 350 cc OHV	92889–93358, 95889–96828, 934001–938590	C7183	17	7000–12999	40–G3WO–10226 to 40–G3WO–16225	6000	23/05/40 DM 29/03/41 CD	£49.13s.11d	Ashchurch and Feltham. (Dest. for Mid-East) 150 per week rising to 450 per week. Deliveries starting from 29/03/41
G3	M/C Solo 350 cc OHV	4335008–4337785, 938591–938900 938930–938940	C8078	12	13000–16399	40–G3WO–17226 to 40–G3WO–20325	3000* *gaps in frame/eng + serial numbers	01/08/40 DM 29/07/41 CD	£49.12s.4d	321 to Slough, rest to Chilwell by April 1941. 256 have panel in tank. C4337785 had BSA WB30 engine fitted (WB30–556)
G3	M/C Solo 350 cc OHV	938901–938929 938941–941911	C8934	14	16300–19299	41–G3WO–20000 to 41–G3WO–22999	3000	15/10/40 DM 26/04/41 CD	£49.12s.11d	Feltham and Slough. Deliveries at 300 per week. 50 fitted with teles
G3	M/C Solo 350 cc OHV	RAF								
G3	M/C Solo 350 cc OHV	4191756	C7373	9			1	26/05/40	£46.5s.6d	Catterick or Stirling. Standard Specification
G3L Proto.	M/C Solo 350 cc OHV				16100, ?	20326, ?	2	21/11/40 DL	£49.18s.9d	Farnborough. 328 lbs. Civilian regs EED 869 and GPP 869. Frame from contract C8078
G3L	M/C Solo 350 cc OHV	4588175–4589424	C9506	15	19400–20649	41–G3L–23800 to 41–G3L–25049	1250	02/01/41 DM 26/09/41 CD	£52.15s.0d	Chilwell
G3L	M/C Solo 350 cc OHV	4649425–4651174 less cat. ref 20 941912–943911 less cat. ref 20	C9841	16	20650–24399 including cat. ref. 20	41–G3L–25050 to 41–G3L–28799 including cat. ref. 20	3608*	15/02/41	£52.15s.0d	Chilwell or Liverpool. *3643 serial numbers. Lucas lighting fitted
G3L	M/C Solo 350 cc OHV	4649432, 438, 466, 470, 481, 528, 719, 764, 765, 768–770, 772–775, 795, 796, 798, 805, 882, 883, 886, 891, 4650032, 056, 077, 105, 112, 115, 130, 136, 140, 142, 144, 146, 161, 162, 170, 171, 174, 177, 187, 199, 203, 204, 209, 238, 310, 464, 507, 510, 511, 610, 618, 707, 941961, 963, 988, 991–994, 997, 942000, 002–005, 007–010, 013, 015, 018–023, 026–029, 032, 033, 035, 038, 043, 044, 050, 055, 057, 060, 118–120, 254, 256, 257, 260,	C9841	20	See cat. ref. 16	See cat. ref. 16	142	15/02/41		Chilwell or Liverpool. Miller lighting fitted

Matchless

MAKERS TYPE	MILITARY CLASS	WD SERIAL NO ALLOCATION	CONTRACT NUMBER	CAT REF	FRAME NUMBER	ENGINE NUMBER	QUANTITY PRODUCED	DATES	PRICE(S)	DELIVERY DESTINATION & NOTES
		261, 263–265, 268, 271, 273, 277, 278, 280, 282–284, 287, 289, 290, 292, 293, 295, 297, 299, 319, 326, 335, 340, 345, 356, 369, 943048, 058, 062, 065, 068, 076, 091, 092, 124, 153, 198, 206								
G3L	M/C Solo 350 cc OHV		C/S11462				500	12/08/41 DM 17/09/41 CD 09/41 CP	£52.15s.0d	
G3L	M/C Solo 350 cc OHV	RAF	C/S12428		25000–25199	41-G3L-40000 to 41-G3L-40199	200	10/11/41 DM 28/01/42 CD	£55.17s.0d	To MUs throughout country at 50 per week starting in January
G3L	M/C Solo 350 cc OHV	RAF	C/S12800		25200–26011	41-G3LWO-40200 to 41-G3LWO-41011	812	12/12/41 DM 28/03/42 CD	£55.19s.0d	Quedgeley, Milton, Stafford, Hartlebury, Carlisle, and Haywood
G3L	M/C Solo 350 cc OHV	943912–945110, 155–158, 160, 161, 166–171, 173–176, 180, 182, 183, 185, 191–771, 922–941, 952–966, 972–991, 946007–946041, 047–066, 072–096, 102–116, 946120–947521	C11102	30	26012–29363	41-G3L-41012 to 41-G3L-44363	3352*	21/07/41	£56.18s.3d	Chilwell and Tewkesbury. Miller lighting fitted. *Only 3252 serial nos
G3L	M/C Solo 350 cc OHV	945111–154, 159, 162–165, 172, 177–179, 181, 184, 186–190, 772–921, 942–951, 967–971, 945992–946006, 042–046, 067–071, 097–101, 117–119, 4688899–4692898, 4777736–4778125	C11102	19	29364–34011	41-G3L-44364 to 41-G3L-49011	4647	05/07/41 DM 11/04/42 CD	£56.18s.0d	Chilwell and Tewkesbury. Lucas lighting fitted
G3L	M/C Solo 350 cc OHV	4837001–4842500	C12632	23	34012–39511	41-G3L-49012 to 41-G3L-54511	5500	26/11/41 DM	£62.13s.1d	Lucas lighting fitted
G3L	M/C Solo 350 cc OHV	4842501–4844000 947522–947921	C12633	22	39512–41011	41-G3L-54512 to 41-G3L-56011	1500	26/11/41 DM	£65.16s.0d	Miller lighting fitted
G3L	M/C Solo 350 cc OHV	4990101–4997100	C14499	27	41012–48011	41-G3L-56012 to 41-G3L-63011	7000	01/05/42	£65.17s.10d	Chilwell
G3L	M/C Solo 350 cc OHV	5255460–5264459	S.1050	29	48060–57059	41-G3L-63060 to 41-G3L-72059	9000	01/10/42	£60	Army, but some to RAF Regiment
G3L	M/C Solo 350 cc OHV	5477370–5484369	S.2604	31	57070–64069		7000	03/03/43	£67.15s.10d	
G3L	M/C Solo 350 cc OHV	5800000–5807999	S.4555	32	64070–72069	79070–87069	8000	20/09/43	£60.15s.0d	Delivery at 1300 per month
G3L	M/C Solo 350 cc OHV	6112000–6121999	S.6150	33	73000–79088	90000–96088	6089 (Orig. 10000)	15/03/44		All fitted with air cleaners
proto.	M/C Solo OHV						1	1944		Rear Springing fitted

Moto-Chenille

MAKERS TYPE	MILITARY CLASS	WD SERIAL NO ALLOCATION	CONTRACT NUMBER	CAT REF	FRAME NUMBER	ENGINE NUMBER	QUANTITY PRODUCED	DATES	PRICE(S)	DELIVERY DESTINATION & NOTES
'Mercier'	M/C Solo 350 cc OHV		V7223				1	08/06/39 DM 07/06/39 CD 06/06/39 DL	£75.0s.0d	Farnborough, from W.R. Chadborn of Victoria Street, SW1

New Hudson

MAKERS TYPE	MILITARY CLASS	WD SERIAL NO ALLOCATION	CONTRACT NUMBER	CAT REF	FRAME NUMBER	ENGINE NUMBER	QUANTITY PRODUCED	DATES	PRICE(S)	DELIVERY DESTINATION & NOTES
83 E	M/C Solo 350 cc SV	20374, ?, ?	C.1933		L.16631, ?, ?	H.T. 313, ?, ?	3	04/05/29 DM 18/06/29 CD 02/08/29 DL	£42	Civilian reg. on one was MT 6368

New Imperial

MAKERS TYPE	MILITARY CLASS	WD SERIAL NO ALLOCATION	CONTRACT NUMBER	CAT REF	FRAME NUMBER	ENGINE NUMBER	QUANTITY PRODUCED	DATES	PRICE(S)	DELIVERY DESTINATION & NOTES
Model 40	M/C Solo 350 cc OHV	35794	C.7641		28230	35976	1	1935 10/09/35 DL	£42	1935 evaluation model. Civilian reg. was CMM 748
Model 76	M/C Solo 500 cc OHV	4191311–343	C.7377	1			33	07/06/40 DM 16/08/40 CD		To Stirling

Norman

MAKERS TYPE	MILITARY CLASS	WD SERIAL NO ALLOCATION	CONTRACT NUMBER	CAT REF	FRAME NUMBER	ENGINE NUMBER	QUANTITY PRODUCED	DATES	PRICE(S)	DELIVERY DESTINATION & NOTES
'The Lightw't'	M/C Solo 125 cc 2-Stroke		S.1916				161	25/05/43	£32.9s.10d	
'The Lightw't'	M/C Solo 125 cc 2-Stroke		S.6960				55	10/10/44	£32.9s.10d	

Norton

MAKERS TYPE	MILITARY CLASS	WD SERIAL NO ALLOCATION	CONTRACT NUMBER	CAT REF	FRAME NUMBER	ENGINE NUMBER	QUANTITY PRODUCED	DATES	PRICE(S)	DELIVERY DESTINATION & NOTES
16H	M/C Solo 500 cc SV	Not registered			7868	54410	1	25/10/32 DL		On loan. Returned on 15/11/32
16H	M/C Solo 500 cc SV	35801	C.7641	1	57283	62012	1	16/09/35 DL		Model 16H evaluation machine. 'CMM 754'
16H	M/C Solo 500 cc SV	352836–353146	C.8245	2	61206–64510 (with gaps)	65501–65809	308	13/12/35 DM 21/01/36 or 02/36 CD	£39.18s.2d	To Chilwell at 50 per week. As C.7641 but modified
16H	M/C Solo 500 cc SV	361206–361514	C.8496	3	63808–64108	67700–68019	309	11/03/36 DM 20/04/36 CD	£41.3s.11d	To Chilwell at 50 per week
16H	M/C Solo 500 cc SV				66625	70069	1	04/09/36 DL		Odd machine. Possibly lightened 16H
16H	M/C Solo 500 cc SV	362679–362897	C.8753	4	64127–64199 66000–66136 66145–66153	69100–69309 70060–70068	219	08/05/36 DM 17/06/36 CD 16/09/36 CP	£41.3s.11d	To Chilwell at 50 per week. Air cleaner fitted. Civilian reg. of one was EMG 221
16H	M/C Solo 500 cc SV	364737–364844	C.9438	5	73301–73406	72200–72307	108	20/10/36 DM 12/11/36 CD 02/01/37 CP	£44.15s.8d	To Chilwell at 30 per week. 72308 & 72309 are spare engines
16H	M/C Solo 500 cc SV	373731–375334 375336–375354 375356–375358 375360–375365 375367–375369 375371–375373 375375–375376 375380–375385 375387–375388 375391 375395–375397 375399–375401	C.9681	6	75149, 78767, 79554, 87047, 88498, 91618, ?	72829, 77166 77988, 84083 86144, 83589, ?	1792*	28/12/36 DM 02/03/37 CD 19/03/38 CP	£44.15s.8d	To Chilwell at 73 per week dropping to 30. *2223 serial numbers allocated & quantity amendment on 27/08/37

Norton

MAKERS TYPE	MILITARY CLASS	WD SERIAL NO ALLOCATION	CONTRACT NUMBER	CAT REF	FRAME NUMBER	ENGINE NUMBER	QUANTITY PRODUCED	DATES	PRICE(S)	DELIVERY DESTINATION & NOTES
		375403 375406–375407 375410–375411 375415 375417 375419 382717–383196 384330–384409								
16H Light-weight	M/C Solo 500 cc SV				66154	70869	1	15/10/36		
16H	M/C Solo 500 cc SV				79063	77557	1	12/10/37 DL		Fitted with twin seat
16H	M/C Solo 500 cc SV					73400–73535 (less 73521)	135	?/02/37 CD		India Office contract
16H	M/C Solo 500 cc SV				85480, 85608, 85606, 85604, 85605, 85606* 85607	82136, 81305, 81301, 81303, 81302, 81300, 81304	7	?/11/37 CD		Delivery to NIZAM (?) – forces. Fittings incl. sand Amal carb; pillion seat; modified Vokes air cleaner & lifting-handle to front guard. *Frame 85606 quoted twice. Probable error
16H	M/C Solo 500 cc SV		C.1202				200	30/12/37 DM 30/11/38 CD		Spares to Chilwell. Not confirmed if 200 spare machines or part of such to produce complete machines as required by workshops
16H	M/C Comb. 500 cc SV						1	1937–1938		16H combination with SWD. Probable experimental machine
16H	M/C Solo 500 cc SV	386444–386943	C.1666	8	95000–95499	88000–88499	500	02/04/38 DM 25/05/38 CD 02/11/38 CP	£47	To Chilwell
16H	M/C Solo 500 cc SV	3810603–3810702 388449–388948	A.9764	10			500*	19/07/38 CD	£46	To Chilwell at 50 per week. *600 serial numbers allocated
16H	M/C Solo 500 cc SV	395732–396081	C.3139	12	101534	10495	350	24/02/39 CD 27/11/39 DL	£45.11s.6d	To Chilwell
16H	M/C Solo 500 cc SV	3910768–3912368	C.3655	13	104700–106300	95100–96700	1601	20/06/39 DL		
16H	M/C Solo 500 cc SV	3932709–3934708 4101401–4105400	C.5109	15	W 1000–6999	W 1000–6999	6000	16/03/39 CD		
16H	M/C Solo 500 cc SV	3943989, ?	C.3309				7	22/03/39 DM 24/03/39 CD	£45.11s.6d	Ex-works (?)
16H	M/C Solo 500 cc SV	4152168–4156167 4163938–4163939	C.5612	18	W 7000–10999	W 7000–10999	4000*	21/11/39 DM 24/04/40 CD 15/11/40 CP	£48.14s.6d	To Chilwell at 300 per week. *4002 serial numbers allocated
16H	M/C Solo 500 cc SV	4191202 4191204 4191206 4191209–4191211 4191215 4191221–4191222 4191226 4191231 4191234–4191239 4191242–4191263 4191265 4191267–4191269 4191271 4191274–4191275 4191278–4191280 4191282–4191310	C.7371	23	W 10292 used by Sir (Capt.) Malcolm Campbell		78	07/06/40 DM 03/08/40 CD	£48.13s.4d	To Stirling
16H	M/C Solo 500 cc SV	4191203 4191205 4191207–4191208 4191212–4191214 4191216–4191220 4191223–4191225 4191227–4191230 4191232–4191233 4191240–4191241	C.7371*	23			31	1940 As above		*LP civilian models embraced under contract C.7371

Norton

MAKERS TYPE	MILITARY CLASS	WD SERIAL NO ALLOCATION	CONTRACT NUMBER	CAT REF	FRAME NUMBER	ENGINE NUMBER	QUANTITY PRODUCED	DATES	PRICE(S)	DELIVERY DESTINATION & NOTES
		4191264 4191266 4191270 4191272–4191273 4191276–4191277 4191281								
16H	M/C Solo 500 cc SV	4192303–4196302	C.6127	19	W 14001–18000	W 14001–18000	4000	01/02/40 CD		To Canadian forces also
16H	M/C Solo 500 cc SV	4316278–4320277	C.6653	25	W 18001–22000	W 18001–22000	4000	10/04/40 DM 17/07/40 CP	£54.9s.10d	To Chilwell at 300 per week after contract C.6127
16H	M/C Solo 500 cc SV	4386027–4403026	V.7353	22	W 26001–43000	W 26001–43000	17000	03/06/40 DM 25/07/40 CD 28/07/40 CP	£54.9s.10d	To Chilwell at 2000 per week after contract C.6653. Many machines allocated to Egypt
16H	M/C Solo 500 cc SV	4490148–4492040	C.9062	27	W 43001–44893	W 43001–44893	1893	30/10/40 DM 22/04/41 CD	£55.5s.11d	
16H	M/C Solo 500 cc SV	4583129–4588128	C.10217	28	W 45001–50000	W 45001–50000	5000	26/03/41 DM 03/09/41 CD	£64.17s.2d	Chilwell
16H	M/C Solo 500 cc SV	4595601–4605600	C.11082	30	W 60001–70000	W 60001–70000	10000	03/07/41 DM 19/11/41 CD	£65.6s.10d	Contract included 1000 spare engines/frames + 250 gearboxes
16H	M/C Solo 500 cc SV	4678658–4684657	C.12426	31	W 70001–76000	W 70001–76000	6000	10/11/41 DM 28/01/42 CD Del from 8/42	£65.3s.1d	Contract was initially 250 x 350 cc machines. Chilwell at 1600/month
16H	M/C Solo 500 cc SV	4773811–4773860	C.14274	33			50	15/04/42 DM		
16H	M/C Solo 500 cc SV		C.12524				3	18/11/41 DM 02/12/41 CD	£65.2s.1d	
16H	M/C Solo 500 cc SV	4671302, ?	C.12872				39	22/12/41 DM 12/01/42 CD	£65.3s.1d	Royal Marines, Hayling
16H	M/C Solo 500 cc SV		C.13845				35	12/03/42 DM 27/03/42 CD	£61.0s.1d	
16H	M/C Solo 500 cc SV		C.13908				25	18/03/42 DM 02/04/42 CD	£65.3s.1d	
16H	M/C Solo 500 cc SV	RAF	C.9891				20	15/02/41 DM 05/06/41 CD	£51.12s.6d	
16H	M/C Solo 500 cc SV		S7743				1	05/10/44	£67.8s.5d	
16H	M/C Solo 500 cc SV		S7927				12	02/12/44	£67.8s.5d	
16H	M/C Solo 500 cc SV		S9175				200	03/05/45	£69.3s.1d	
16H	M/C Solo 500 cc SV	RAF			W 22250–22780	W 22250–22780				
16H	M/C Solo 500 cc SV	4188854–4188991					138			India
16H	M/C Solo 500 cc SV	6191545–6191556	Ex-Min O.W.T.				12			
16H	M/C Comb. 500 cc SV	53288–53323	C7371	36	92046	86787	36			Converted from solo
16H	M/C Comb. 500 cc SV	RAF	S921				522	10/05/43	£92.2s.3d	
16H	M/C Comb. 500 cc SV	RAF	S3959				120	26/08/43	£93	
16H	M/C Comb. 500 cc SV		S4460				150	06/11/43	£93.3s.7d	
16H	M/C Comb. 500 cc SV	RN	S4669				75	07/01/44	£89.17s.0d	
16H	M/C Comb. 500 cc SV		S2704				30	17/04/44	£88.15s.5d	
16H	M/C Comb.	RAF	S2762				212	19/06/44	£92.2s.3d	

Norton

Makers Type	Military Class	WD Serial No Allocation	Contract Number	Cat Ref	Frame Number	Engine Number	Quantity Produced	Dates	Price(s)	Delivery Destination & Notes
	500 cc SV									
16H	M/C Solo 500 cc SV				25354	Not stamped	1	04/04/41 DL		Civilian reg. was FOJ 890
16H	M/C Solo 500 cc SV	4183563–4183595	Ex. Can E1081/CD/817				34			
16H	M/C Solo 500 cc SV	4183675	BM/2783 WS 6 (d)				1			
16H	M/C Solo 500 cc SV	4184030–4184032	EX CAN				3			
16H	M/C Solo 500 cc SV	4473264–4473297	EX CAN				34			
16H	M/C Solo 500 cc SV	4183951	N.C.				1			
16H	M/C Solo 500 cc SV	4858001–4859250	S.150	34			1250	14/06/42 DM 19/12/42 CD	£65.12s.0d	
16H	M/C Solo 500 cc SV	4865801–4870800	C.14498	35	W 78001–83000	W 78001–83000	5000	04/02/42 DM 01/05/42 CD	£66.15s.3d	
16H	M/C Solo 500 cc SV		S.1046				2	13/04/43	£66.16s.11d	
16H	M/C Solo 500 cc SV	RN	S.3103				150	08/08/43	£66.18s.8d	
16H	M/C Solo 500 cc SV	RN	S.4723				125	16/11/43	£67.15s.4d	
16H	M/C Solo 500 cc SV	5266965–5271964	S.2602	37			5000		£67.8s.4d	
16H	M/C Solo 500 cc SV	4958019	S.2942				1	21/05/43	£66.16s.11d	
16H	M/C Solo 500 cc SV	5484401–5490400	S.5161	38	W 90001–96000	W 90001–96000	6000*	27/11/43	£67.8s.4d	*Quantity reduced to 4600
16H	M/C Solo 500 cc SV		S.3103				150	11/08/44	£67.11s.0d	
16H	M/C Comb. 500 cc SV		S.7584				2	29/09/44	£67.7s.5d	
16H	M/C Comb. 500 cc SV		S.8048				200	18/01/45	£69.5s.11d	
16H	M/C Comb. 500 cc SV		S.8047				50	13/01/45	£97.16s.7d	
16H	M/C Comb. 500 cc SV		S.7671				1	22/11/45	£95.18s.1d	Passenger sidecar
16H	M/C Comb. 500 cc SV		S.7671				1	22/11/45	£90.6s.8d	Box sidecar
?	M/C Comb.	4163937	A/248/16				1			
?	M/C Comb. 600 cc		C.3309				4	22/03/39 DM 27/01/40 CD	£97.1s.11d	
Exptl.	M/C Comb. 1096 cc V-twin				Not marked	LTZ/P.67714/S	1	1940 19/05/41 DL		SWD. JAP engine
50	M/C Solo 350 cc OHV	387072–387077 4184317, 4184318	C.2007	9	39285, ?, ?	4305, ?, ?	6	04/07/38 DM 30/07/38 CD 22/06/38 DL	£75.0s.0d	
Exptl.	M/C Solo 350 cc SV		C.6775				2	12/04/40 DM 07/11/40 CD	£231.0s.0d	To Chilwell as part of C.5612. Aluminium substitutes
Exptl. L.W.	M/C Solo 346 cc SV	3938953	C.3585	14	LW 100	LW 100	1	04/04/39 DM 25/05/39 CD 25/08/39 CP	£300.0s.0d	Farnborough
18	M/C Solo 500 cc SV	4381738–4381744 4337786–4337790	C.8461	26			12*	17/08/40 DM 09/11/43 CD	£58.19s.10d	Chilwell. *Possible quantity 7. 12 serial nos. alloc.
Exptl. L.W.	M/C Solo 500 cc SV		C.8031		LW 103	LW 103	1	18/07/40 DM 16/09/40 CD	£100.0s.0d	Farnborough

Norton

MAKERS TYPE	MILITARY CLASS	WD SERIAL NO ALLOCATION	CONTRACT NUMBER	CAT REF	FRAME NUMBER	ENGINE NUMBER	QUANTITY PRODUCED	DATES	PRICE(S)	DELIVERY DESTINATION & NOTES
								26/06/40 DL		
Big 4	M/C Comb. 633 cc SV	385691–385705	C.1561	7	92872, 93460–93474	86558, 84876–84890	1 on 14 on	29/03/38 DM 30/04/38 CD 13/05/38 DL 21/08/38 DL	£120.0s.0d	Chilwell. C 385691 had civilian reg. JMF 192
Big 4	M/C Comb. 633 cc SV	399012–399326	C.2925	11			315	02/12/38 DM 25/01/39 CD 30/05/39 CP	£97.1s.11d	Chilwell at 25 per week
Big 4	M/C Comb. 633 cc SV	4112258–4112602	V.3565	16	S 1000–1344	S 1000–1344	345	28/08/39 DM 02/11/39 CD 25/03/40 CP	£97.1s.11d	Chilwell at 15/20 per week
Big 4	M/C Comb. 633 cc SV	4148480–4148696 4163994	C.5333	17	S 1345–1562	S 1345–1562	218	21/10/39 DM 23/01/40 CD 14/06/40 DL	£98.11s.8d	Chilwell at 50 per week
Big 4	M/C Comb. 633 cc SV	4185623–4185782	C.6831	20	S 2117–2276	S 2117–2276	160	23/04/40 DM 05/09/40 CD	£96.7s.11d	Chilwell at 25 per week from 16/09/40
Big 4	M/C Comb. 633 cc SV	4185069–4185622	V.3849	21	S 1563–2116	S 1563–2116	554	22/02/40 DM 29/04/40 CD 13/06/40 CP	£98.9s.11d	Chilwell at 50 per week C 4185089/S 1582 to SAS at Netheravon C 4185606/S 2099 sent to AMC. C 4185179/S 1672 to SAS
Big 4	M/C Comb. 633 cc SV	4384906–4386026 4427053–4427072	C.7576	24	S 2276–3396 S 3397–3416	S 2276–3396 S 3397–3416	1141	19/06/40 DM 02/05/41 CD 31/05/41 DL	£99.0s.0d	Chilwell at 25 per week
Big 4	M/C Comb. 633 cc SV	4591410–4593218	C.11297	29	S 3500–5308	S 3500–5308	1809*	28/07/41 DM 25/09/41 CD		Chilwell at 400 per month. *Could also be 2238
Big 4	M/C Comb. 633 cc SV	4707738–4707949	C.13056	32	S 5309–5521	S 5309–5521	212*	07/01/42 DM 11/02/42 CD		Chilwell. *Could also be 180
Big 4	M/C Comb. 633 cc SV	RAF	C.9914				10	01/07/41 CD	£72.19s.8d	Hartlebury. No SWD
?	M/C Comb. ?		C.10435				1	23/04/41 DM 22/05/41 CD	£73.14s.6d	Chislehurst, fitted Box sidecar
Box s'car body and chassis for 16H			C.13158				1	16/01/42 DM 07/02/42 CD		
?	M/C Solo + Combs		C.9693				1985*	14/02/39 07/03/39 CD	£51.12s.0d	*Some with sidecars. 12 with Commercial Box sidecars at £21.1s.3d and 959 sidecars at £21.7s.8d
?	M/C Solo 500 cc OHV		?		100998	91820	1	Mid '39 06/07/39 DL		Fitted with Exptl. spring frame. Civilian rg. EOP 68
?	M/C Solo 500 cc SV		?		106982	98012	1	Late '39 30/10/39 DL		Fitted with Exptl. spring frame.
Model 19	M/C Comb. 596 cc OHV		?		25171	92866	1	Mid '40 13/06/40 DL		Had SWD
Prototype	M/C Solo 500cc SV Parallel Twin							1944		
Norton–Matchless	M/C Solo 350 cc OHV	4389812			29786	23267	1	To AMC on 26/04/41		Fitted with AMC engine
Norton–BSA	M/C Solo 350 cc OHV	4389667			Not stamped	WB30–522	1	To BSA on 20/02/41		Fitted with BSA engine
Model 18	M/C Solo 500 cc OHV	Not registered			47861	54440	1	25/10/32 DL		On loan
Model 19	M/C Solo 596 cc OHV	Not registered			47869	54291	1	25/10/32 DL		On loan

OEC

Makers Type	Military Class	WD Serial No Allocation	Contract Number	Cat Ref	Frame Number	Engine Number	Quantity Produced	Dates	Price(s)	Delivery Destination & Notes
?	M/C Solo 342 cc 2-Stroke	RAF	?				?	Late 1920s		
3-Wheeler	M/C Solo 490 cc SV	19247	C886		37227	99558	1	27/04/28 DL		Aldershot. Weight 453 lb. JAP engine. Civilian reg. was MP 8161
3-Wheeler	M/C Solo 350 cc SV	19621	C886		DS/8/3103	FJ 4879	1	04/06/28 DM 02/07/28 CD 18/09/28 DL	£150	Farnborough. Weight 354 lb. Blackburne engine. Civilian reg.was MT 9186
3-Wheeler	M/C Solo 250 cc SV	19622	C886		DS/8/3104	JP 1255	1	18/09/28 DL		Farnborough. Weight 310 lb. Blackburne engine. Civilian reg.was MP 9187
?	M/C Solo 350 cc SV	20467, ?, ?	C1933		5DL/9/405013, ?, ?	JPE 2540, ?, ?	3	04/05/29 DM 18/06/29 CD	£54.6s.6d	Blackburne engine fitted. Farnborough. Weight 338½ lb

Royal Enfield

Makers Type	Military Class	WD Serial No Allocation	Contract Number	Cat Ref	Frame Number	Engine Number	Quantity Produced	Dates	Price(s)	Delivery Destination & Notes
Model C Test model	M/C Solo 350 cc SV	35799	C7641?		31295	15174*	1	Oct '35 10/09/35 DL		Civilian reg. was CMM 751. *New cases fitted in Oct '35. New number 15179
Model B Test model	M/C Solo 250 cc SV	35800	C7641?		2833	1855	1	10/09/35 DL		Civilian reg. was CMM 752
Model D	M/C Solo 250 cc SV	399927–399999, 3910000–3910526	C3739	1	2275–2874	D 1001–1600	600	04/05/39 DM 10/06/39 CD	£33.8s.0d	Chilwell. For RAF
Model D	M/C Solo 250 cc SV	3922045–3922944	C4452	3	3001–3900	2001–2900	900	24/07/39 DM 15/08/39 CD	£33.8s.0d	Chilwell at 100 per week
Model D	M/C Solo 250 cc SV	4191639–4191653, 4191802–4191883, 4303647–4303901, 4191454–4191484	C7374	5	4337, 4343, 4379, 4396, 4406, 4408, 4414, 4535, 4565, 4571, 4576, 4579, 4580, 4584, 4588–4590, 4593, 4594, 4596–4598, 4602, 4605, 4609, 4610, 4636, 4643, 4648, 4651, 4653, 4655, 4666, 4667, 4669–4672, 4676–4681, 4683–4685, 4687, 4689, 4691, 4696, 4699, 4701, 4702, 4704–4720, 4722, 4726, 4733, 4734, 4736, 4737, 4741, 4748, 4749, 4755, 4757, 4760, 4763, 4764, 4767, 4769, 4775, 4779, 4782, 4785, 4786, 4791, 4794, 4800, 4801, 4804, 4805, 4809, 4811–4813, 4815–4824, 4827–4835, 4837–4842, 4844, 4845, 4848,		350	07/06/40 DM 24/09/40 CD	*c.* £40	Chilwell, Stirling or Catterick

Royal Enfield

Makers Type	Military Class	WD Serial No Allocation	Contract Number	Cat Ref	Frame Number	Engine Number	Quantity Produced	Dates	Price(s)	Delivery Destination & Notes
					4850, 4853, 4855, 4857, 4859, 4861, 4868, 4871, 4876, 4880, 4885, 4887, 4893, 4894, 4897, 4899, 4902–4904, 4907, 4909, 4911, 4912, 4914, 4916, 4924, 4930, 4931, 4936, 4937, 4939, 4945, 4947–4949, 4956, 4959, 4961, 4962, 4964, 4966–4969, 4971, 4973, 4977–4979, 4982, 4984–4986, 4993, 4996, 4997, 5001, 5003–5005, 5007, 5011–5013, 5015, 5016, 5018–5020, 5022, 5024–5026, 5028–5030, 5033, 5034, 5036–5042, 5044–5046, 5049, 5510–5514, 5516, 5519, 5520, 5523, 5526, 5527, 5532, 5533, 5538, 5540–5542, 5550, 5551, 5554, 5556–5559, 5563, 5565, 5566, 5568–5570, 5576, 5578, 5579, 5581, 5585, 5590, 5595, 5603, 5605, 5606, 5609, 5611–5615, 5619, 5622, 5624, 5629, 5632, 5634, 5639–5652, 5654, 5656, 5658–5664, 5666, 5667, 5669–5685, 5688–5700, 5702–5705, 5708, 5710, 5713–5715, 5717, 5718, 5725, 5728, 5730–5737, 5739, 5744					
Model D	M/C Solo 250 cc SV	4327418–4327497, 4327574–4327801, 4327924–4327935, 4327941–4327978	C7945	10	4599, 4600, 4617, 4618, 4624, 4640, 4645, 4646, 4654, 4688, 4729, 4732, 4843, 4877, 4879, 4884, 4888, 4890, 4918–4920, 4925, 4928, 4932, 4942, 4960, 4999, 5006, 5008, 5014, 5021, 5027, 5031, 5032, 5043,		300	27/07/40 DM 07/10/40 CD	£42.6s.9d	Burscough, Woking, Tidmouth and Catterick

Royal Enfield

Makers Type	Military Class	WD Serial No Allocation	Contract Number	Cat Ref	Frame Number	Engine Number	Quantity Produced	Dates	Price(s)	Delivery Destination & Notes
					5047, 5051, 5053, 5056–5060, 5062, 5064–5066, 5068–5070, 5072–5077, 5079–5094, 5097, 5098, 5100, 5101, 5103, 5104, 5107, 5112–5160, 5162–5170, 5172–5178, 5180–5184, 5186–5201, 5203–5241, 5243, 5244, 5246–5249, 5251–5256, 5258–5267, 5269–5274, 5286, 5293, 5377–5385, 5502, 5529, 5537, 5567, 5582, 5593, 5595–5597, 5599, 5602, 5604, 5607, 5608, 5610, 5616–5618, 5620, 5621, 5623, 5625–5628, 5633, 5635–5638, 5657, 5665, 5668, 5686, 5687, 5701, 5706–5708, 5711, 5712, 5716, 5719, 5720, 5723, 5724, 5727, 5729, 5738, 5740, 5741, 5743, 5745–5747, 5749, 5750					
Model D	M/C Solo 250 cc SV		C8664				2	04/09/40 DM 22/11/40 CD	£42.6s.9d	Woolwich Arsenal
Model D	M/C Solo 250 cc SV		C8881				2	05/10/40 DM 19/03/41 CD	£43.11s.3d	RA Woolwich
Exptl. LW (1st)	M/C Solo 350 cc SV	3925599	C3585	2	101	101	1	04/04/39 DM 25/05/39 CD 17/08/39 CP	£200.0s.0d	Farnborough
Exptl. LW (2nd)	M/C Solo 350 cc SV	4328451	C7972		303	D.C. 303	1	13/07/40 DM 15/08/40 CD 25/06/40 DL	£48.12s.1d	Chilwell
Exptl. LW	M/C Solo 350 cc SV		C6718				2	01/04/40 DM 01/04/40 CD	£48.12s.0d	Feltham
WD/C	M/C Solo 350 cc SV	67586–68280, 68286–68883, 68898, 68903, 68904, 68907–68927	C5107	6	101 to 1100	101 to 1100	1000*	27/09/39 DM 12/02/40 CD	£41.7s.7d	Feltham at 100/150 per week from 06/01/40. *Too many serial numbers
WD/C	M/C Solo 350 cc SV	4328291–4328353, 4328393, 68884–68897, 68899–68902, 68905, 68906, 68928–69585, 75250–75557, 75648, 75649, 75654–75659, 75663–75665	C5654	7	1101 to 2100		1000*	28/11/39 DM 13/02/40 CD	£43.9s.0d	Feltham and Olympia at 75 per week after C5107. *Too many serial numbers
WD/C	M/C Solo 350 cc SV	4328354–4328392, 4328394–4328398, 75558–75647, 75650–75653, 75660–75662,	C6125	8	3001 to 5000	3001 to 5000	2000*	25/01/40 DM 28/03/40 CD 03/08/40 CP Feb '40 PL	£45.0s.0d	Olympia at 150 per week from 03/05/40. *Too many serial numbers issued for frames

Royal Enfield

Makers Type	Military Class	WD Serial No Allocation	Contract Number	Cat Ref	Frame Number	Engine Number	Quantity Produced	Dates	Price(s)	Delivery Destination & Notes
		75666–77567								
WD/C	M/C Solo 350 cc SV	4327498–4327573, 4327887–4327907	C7945	11	2176–2183, 5334, 5339, 5344, 5347–5349, 5369–5371, 5373, 5374, 5377, 5379–5382, 5385, 5386, 5395–5397, 5411, 5412, 5415, 5418–5421, 5431, 5434, 5435, 5440, 5443–5445, 5447–5451, 5454–5456, 5459–5466, 5468–5484, 5486–5495, 5497–5512, 5514–5549, 5551–5559, 5567–5569	2176–2183, 5334, 5339, 5344, 5347–5349, 5369–5371, 5373, 5374, 5377, 5379–5382, 5385, 5386, 5395–5397, 5411, 5412, 5415, 5418–5421, 5431, 5434, 5435, 5440, 5443–5445, 5447–5451, 5454–5456, 5459–5466, 5468–5484, 5486–5495, 5497–5512, 5514–5549, 5551–5559, 5567–5569	150*	27/07/40 DM 07/10/40 CD	£46.9s.3d	Burscough, Woking, Tidmouth, and Catterick. *Not enough serial numbers. French specification
WD/C	M/C Solo 350 cc SV	984216, 984217, 984219, 984222, 984251–987400, 987426–989562, 989614–989750, 989801–989900, 989926–990402	C7182	17	5901–11900	5901–11900	6000*	16/05/40 DM 23/11/40 CD 29/08/40 CP		Olympia at 250 per week after C6125. *Too many serial numbers
WD/C	M/C Solo 350 cc SV	99139–99291, 984001–984215, 984218, 984220, 984221, 984223–984250, 987401–987425, 989751–989800, 989901–989925	C7890	20	11901–12400	11901–12400	500	10/07/40 DM 15/08/40 CD	£44.12s.0d	Slough, after C7182
WD/C	M/C Solo 350 cc SV	4361416–4364196, 990403–990723	C8136	9	12401–15500	12401–15500	3100*	13/08/40	£47.18s.9d	*Too many serial numbers
WD/C	M/C Solo 350 cc SV	4437509–4439008, 990727–992227	C8732	15	15501–18500	15501–18500	3000*	18/09/40 DM 23/11/40 CD	£44.14s.10d	1500 to Chilwell and 1500 to Feltham. *Too many serial numbers
WD/C	M/C Solo 350 cc SV		C11463				600	12/08/41 DM 30/09/41 CD 30/09/41 CP	£48.16s.0d	
WD/C	M/C Solo 350 cc SV	RAF	C12429				250	10/11/41 DM 07/02/42 CD		Milton, Quedgeley, Carlisle, Stafford, Hartlebury, and Haywood
Model L	M/C Solo 570 cc SV		On loan		28921	11206	1	19/04/40 04/12/39 DL		
WD/L	M/C Solo 570 cc SV	4191354–4191453	C7374	4			100	07/06/40 DM 24/09/40 CD	*c.* £62	Chilwell, Stirling and Catterick
WD/L	M/C Solo 570 cc SV	4478583–4478832	C8620	13	29201–29450	29201–29450	250	29/08/40 DM 26/03/41 CD	£48.7s.6d	Chilwell
WD/G Prototypes	M/C Solo 350 cc OHV				G101, G102	WDG 101, 102	2	16/01/41 DL		
WD/G	M/C Solo 350 cc OHV	4327802–4327886, 4327908–4327923	C7945	12			118*	22/07/40 DM 07/10/40 CD	£52.13s.3d	Burscough, Woking, Tidmouth, and Catterick. *Not enough serial numbers
WD/G	M/C Solo 350 cc OHV	4478833–4479082 990724–990726	C8621	14	29701–29950	29701–29950	250*	17/08/40 DM 03/02/41 CD	£48.13s.6d	Chilwell
WD/G	M/C Solo 350 cc OHV	4553327, 4553328	C9311	16	1042, ?	WB30–540, ?	2	04/12/40 DM Early '41 DL		C4553327 fitted with BSA engine. C4553328 may be Matchless engined machine
WD/G	M/C Solo 350 cc OHV	99389–99488	C8200	21			100	02/08/40 DM 08/11/40 CD 25/10/40 CP	£52.13s.3d	Feltham

Royal Enfield

Makers Type	Military Class	WD Serial No Allocation	Contract Number	Cat Ref	Frame Number	Engine Number	Quantity Produced	Dates	Price(s)	Delivery Destination & Notes
KX	M/C Comb. 1140 cc SV V-twin		C11467				4	12/08/41 DM 10/09/41 CD	£90.0s.0d	Thorp-Arch, York. Supplied without bodies
Exptl. V-twin	M/C Comb. 1140 cc SV		?				1	1941		Had SWD
?	M/C Comb.		V3609				2	26/09/39 DM		Chislehirst
Model CO	M/C Solo 350 cc OHV	RN	C10175				50	22/03/41 DM 24/04/41 CD 22/04/41 CP	£50.10s.9d	Chatham, Portsmouth, Devonport, and Rosyth
Model CO	M/C Solo 350 cc OHV	RN	C10850				50	05/06/41 DM 15/07/41 CD	£50.17s.6d	Chatham, Portsmouth, Devonport, and RN Store Dept. at Preston, Staffs
WD/J2	M/C Solo 500 cc OHV	RAF	C10103				6	15/03/41 DM 18/06/41 CD	£55.16s.0d	M.A.P. Pool, Horseferry Road, London
WD/CO	M/C Solo 350 cc OHV	4605601–4610600	C11081	18	1001–6000	1001–6000	5000	03/07/41 DM 22/10/41 CD	£50.3s.6d	1055 to Tewkesbury, rest to Chilwell
WD/CO	M/C Solo 350 cc OHV	5104201–5109200	C12425	19	6001–11000	6001–11000	5000	10/11/41 DM 07/02/42 CD	£50.3s.6d	
WD/CO	M/C Solo 350 cc OHV	4940701–4943700	C13869	24	11001–14000	11001–14000	3000	14/03/42 DM		Paisley War Office
WD/CO/B	M/C Solo 350 cc OHV	4847001–4850000	C13870	22	14001–17000	14001–17000	3000	14/03/42 DM		Burman gearbox fitted
WD/CO	M/C Solo 350 cc OHV	RAF	S14219	–	17001–19826	17001–19826	2826	09/04/42 DM 1944 DL		Sandtoft, Yorkshire
WD/CO	M/C Solo 350 cc OHV	5162167–5167166	S1546	26	19827–24826	19827–24826	5000	14/11/42 DM Late '44 DL		Vokes filter fitted
WD/CO	M/C Solo 350 cc OHV		S4606	–	24910–25019	24910–25019	110	1944		
WD/CO	M/C Solo 350 cc OHV	5529038–5534037	S3357	27	25038–30037	25038–30037	5000	21/05/43 1944/5 DL		
WD/CO	M/C Solo 350 cc OHV		S9635 and S9669				58	1945	£76.1s.9d	
Model RE	M/C Solo 125 cc 2-Stroke		S831				1	06/01/43	£41.17s.0d	Possibly prototype
WD/RE	M/C Solo 125 cc 2-Stroke	4893237–4893256	C14775	23	2792, 2799, 2802, 2807, 2814, 2817, 2854, 2856, 2857, 2793, 2798, 2805, 2813, 2816, 2850, 2860, 2872, 2878	2792, 2799, 2802, 2807, 2814, 2817, 2854, 2856, 2857, 2793, 2798, 2805, 2813, 2816, 2850, 2860, 2872, 2878	18*	29/05/42 DM 26/06/42 CD 22/07/42 DL and 25/07/42 DL	£23.0s.0d	Coventry and Leicester. *Delivered in two batches of nine. Too many serial numbers
WD/RE	M/C Solo 125 cc 2-Stroke	5111171–5115170	S1945	25	4171–8170	4171–8170	4000	02/01/43 DM Nov '43 DL into 1944	£29.0s.0d	
WD/RE	M/C Solo 125 cc 2-Stroke	5816151–5816885	S6602	28	8171–8905	8171–8905	735	04/05/44 09/44 DL Nov '44 PL	£30.0s.0d	Delivery at 350 per month from September
WD/RE	M/C Solo 125 cc 2-Stroke	5859206–5862429	S7112	29	8906–12129*	8906–12129*	3224*	10/07/44 14/12/44 1945 DL	£32.0s.0d	*Factory ledgers show only to 11129, so last 1000 motorcyles were probably not taken
Exptl. Twin (prototype)	M/C Solo 350 cc SV		?				1	1944		
RE/Matchless	M/C Solo 350 cc OHV				874	23305		29/05/41 DL to AMC		Fitted with Matchless engine

Rudge Whitworth

Makers Type	Military Class	WD Serial No Allocation	Contract Number	Cat Ref	Frame Number	Engine Number	Quantity Produced	Dates	Price(s)	Delivery Destination & Notes
Rapid (modified)	M/C Solo 250 cc OHV	364845	W.7917	1	57906	A.477	1	09/10/36 DM 23/11/36 CD 08/07/36 DL	£44.0s.0d	Farnborough. Civilian reg. was EHX 707
Ulster (modified)	M/C Solo 500 cc OHV	364846	W.7917	2	57907	S.3006	2	09/10/36 DM 23/11/36 CD 08/07/36 DL	£52.0s.0d	Farnborough. Civilian reg. was EHX 708
Service Model	M/C Solo 250 cc OHV	3810114–3810125	C.1927	3	64533–64544	1871–1882	12	11/06/38 DM 26/08/38 CD 29/10/38 CP	£45.0s.0d	Chilwell

Stewart-Ehrlich

Makers Type	Military Class	WD Serial No Allocation	Contract Number	Cat Ref	Frame Number	Engine Number	Quantity Produced	Dates	Price(s)	Delivery Destination & Notes
Prototype	M/C Solo 350 cc 2-Stroke (Split-single)						1	15/10/41 DL		Returned same day

Sunbeam

Makers Type	Military Class	WD Serial No Allocation	Contract Number	Cat Ref	Frame Number	Engine Number	Quantity Produced	Dates	Price(s)	Delivery Destination & Notes
Model 6	M/C Solo 500 cc SV		?				?	1927 DL		
'Lion'	M/C Solo 500 cc SV		?		MM 774	29/238	1	09/10/36 DL		Farnborough. Civilian reg. was ADA 508
Prototype SWD Combination	M/C Comb. 1000 cc OHV V-twin		?		Not stated	Not stated	1	27/10/41 DL		Had SWD. (Also referred to as Matchless Heavy M/C combination in some War Office literature)

Triumph

Makers Type	Military Class	WD Serial No Allocation	Contract Number	Cat Ref	Frame Number	Engine Number	Quantity Produced	Dates	Price(s)	Delivery Destination & Notes
Model P	M/C Solo 494 cc SV		?				?	1925 to 1927		
Model P	M/C Comb. 494 cc SV		?				?	1925 to 1927		
Model N	M/C Comb. 494 cc SV	19240	?		1011233	257071	?	09/06/28 DL		Farnborough. Civilian reg. was MP 8114
Model N	M/C Solo 494 cc SV	19189, 19401, 19467	C839		1011133, 1009639, 1010754	257073, 256128, 254837	?	1927		Farnborough
Model N	M/C Solo 494 cc SV	19956	C1417		2007152	507550	30	19/12/28 DM 28/12/28 CD		Farnborough
Model NL3	M/C Solo 494 cc SV	19895, 19855, ?	C1417		?, 2009098, ?	?, 507472, ?	80	19/12/28 DM 28/12/28 CD 12/02/29 DL		Farnborough
Model N	M/C Solo 494 cc SV		C1412				3	30/11/28 DM 20/12/28 CD	£39.15s.0d	Feltham. As C839
Model P 3-Wheeler	M/C Solo 494 cc SV	16247	–		931179	237951	1	09/05/28 DL		Civilian reg. was MK 5625. Originally a 1926 m'cycle

Triumph

MAKERS TYPE	MILITARY CLASS	WD SERIAL NO ALLOCATION	CONTRACT NUMBER	CAT REF	FRAME NUMBER	ENGINE NUMBER	QUANTITY PRODUCED	DATES	PRICE(S)	DELIVERY DESTINATION & NOTES
?	M/C Solo	33275, 33276	C5244				2	1933/4 ?		
Model ND	M/C Solo 549 cc SV	33424–33466	C5467	17			43			
Model ND	M/C Solo 549 cc SV	33713–33743	C5678	16			31			
Model ND	M/C Solo 549 cc SV	34748–34760	C6877	15			13			
3/1 (Test model)	M/C Solo 350 cc SV	35798	C7641?		SL.3315	1.T6.1537	1	1935 18/09/35 DL		Civilian reg. was CMM 799
3SW (Test model)	M/C Solo 350 cc SV	373232	C9800	3	1630	7/3S/216	1	04/02/37 DM 01/03/37 CD 25/11/36 DL	£41.7s.0d	Farnborough. Civilian reg. was FMG 604
3SW	M/C Solo 350 cc SV	38614–38999 3811000–3811039	C2073	11	TL 7773, 7893, ?	14822, 14783, ?	426	30/06/38 DM 26/09/38 CD 21/01/39 CP	£40.0s.0d	Feltham at 50 per week
3SW	M/C Solo 350 cc SV	3812675–3812715	C3398	19			41	20/12/38 DM 07/11/39 CD	£39.7s.0d	Feltham
3SW	M/C Solo 350 cc SV	3916045–3916247	C3360	14			203	28/02/39 DM 27/04/39 CD	£39.13s.9d	Feltham at 25 per week
3SW	M/C Solo 350 cc SV	3917452–3917751	C4631	18			300	26/07/39 DM 02/10/39 CD	£39.19s.0d	Chilwell at 50 per week. As C3360
3SW	M/C Solo 350 cc SV	60788–61000, 62686–62885, 62916–63085, 63144–63585, 69586–70088, 70586–72365	C5108	10	14612, ?	27606, ?	3300*	27/09/39 DM 19/01/40 CD 07/11/40 DL	£43.16s.6d	Feltham at 150 per week from 28/10/39. *27/9/39 for 300, 21/10/39 for 3000
3SW	M/C Solo 350 cc SV	72366–72585, 80038–80763, 4359296	C6128	6	TL 17300 to 18299	40–3SW–34401 to 35400	1000	25/01/40 DM 28/03/40 CD 13/08/40 CP	£43.16s.6d	Olympia at 300 per week. After C5108. Not enough serial numbers. 17366 was converted to carry Bren Gun. 11/7/40
3SW	M/C Solo 350 cc SV	4358641–4359295	C8079	7			3000*	27/07/40 DM 28/09/40 CD	£47.18s.11d	Feltham and Slough at 150 per week. *Reduced to 649
3SW	M/C Solo 350 cc SV	80889–81274, 83889–84230, 84786–84829, 884001–886686	C7162	13	TL 18300 to 18329, 20834–24812, 24814–29997, 29999, 30001–30265, 30416–30700. With gaps	3SW–35401 to 44500. With gaps	5000*	20/05/40 DM 07/08/40 CD 08/01/41 CP		3000 to Slough at 300 per week, and 2000 to Feltham at 75 per week. As C6128. *Further quantity added, all sent to Ashchurch
3SW	M/C Solo 350 cc SV	RAF	C11465		TL 30266 to 30415	3SW–40266 to 40415	150	12/08/41 DM 18/09/41 CD Aug '41 to Sept '41 DL	£55.0s.0d	Quedgeley, Carlisle and Stafford. From temporary factory at Cape Warwick
?	M/C Solo 350 cc		C12177				1	16/10/41 DM		From Cape Warwick
?	M/C Solo	4133005–4133011	?				7			
?	M/C Solo	4187767	C5247				1			
5SW	M/C Solo 500 cc SV	4320278–4321625	C7828	5	TL 18330 to 20833. With gaps	5SW–31897 to 34400. With gaps	1322*	18/07/40		*1655 ordered
5SW	M/C Solo 500 cc SV		C7827				9	18/07/40 DM 21/02/41 CD		
5SW	M/C Solo 500 cc SV	4403027–4403171	C8575	8			145	27/08/40 DM 26/11/40 CD	£48.18s.6d	Chilwell
Speed Twin	M/C Solo 500 cc OHV Parallel Twin	4133940–4133941	C5819				2	18/12/39 DM 22/01/40 CD 22/12/39 DL	£57.1s.4d	Chilwell
5TW (Prototype)	M/C Solo 500 cc SV Parallel Twin		?				1	1942		

Triumph

MAKERS TYPE	MILITARY CLASS	WD SERIAL NO ALLOCATION	CONTRACT NUMBER	CAT REF	FRAME NUMBER	ENGINE NUMBER	QUANTITY PRODUCED	DATES	PRICE(S)	DELIVERY DESTINATION & NOTES
?	M/C Comb.		?				1	1940/1		Had SWD
3TW (Prototype)	M/C Solo 350 cc OHV Parallel Twin	3937042	C3585	4	?	3TW EXP 1	1	04/04/39 DM 25/05/39 CD 27/07/39 DL	£250.0s.0d	Farnborough. 1st prototype. Both GLU 653 and ERW 784 accredited to this motorcycle!
3TW (2nd version)	M/C Solo 350 cc OHV Parallel Twin		C6523		F.1083, ?	3TW EXP 5, ?	2	09/03/40 DM 17/06/40 CD 13/06/40 DL	£238.10s.0d	Feltham, incorporating aluminium substitutes
3TW (3rd version)	M/C Solo 350 cc OHV Parallel Twin		C8020		F.1965, ?	E 1742, ?	2	Sept/Oct '40 11/09/40 DL		
3TW (Prod. version)	M/C Solo 350 cc OHV Parallel Twin	4854130–4854179	C8331	9	LT 101 to 150	3TW–41401 to 41450	50*	09/08/40 DM		As C8020 with modifications. *Possible only 10 taken
3H	M/C Solo 350 cc OHV	See C7162 of 3SW	C7162	13	TL 24813, 29998, 30000 30701–30840	3H 37899	143	20/05/40 DM 07/08/40 CD		EWTDD, Feltham and Ashchurch
3HW	M/C Solo 350 cc OHV	RAF	C12492		TL 30841 to 30922	3HW–30841 to 30875, 40876–40922	82	14/11/41 DM		Hartlebury. From Cape Warwick
3HW	M/C Solo 350 cc OHV	886687–890052, 4852001–4854129	C13948	20	TL 30923 to 36417	3HW–40923 to 46417	5495	21/05/42 DM 03/04/42 to June '43 DL		Tewkesbury, Slough, Ashchurch and No. 7 VRD Glasgow
3HW	M/C Solo 350 cc OHV	5205018–5207517	S1246	22	TL 36418 to 38917	3HW–46418 to 48917	2500	June '43 to Sept '43 DL		Littlewoods at Liverpool, Vauxhall Motors at Hendon, and R.A. Brand Co.
3HW	M/C Solo 350 cc OHV	5271968–5274467	S2114	23	TL 38918 to 41417	3HW–48918 to 51417	2500	Sept '43 to Dec '43 DL		As above
3HW	M/C Solo 350 cc OHV	5423418–5428417	S2956	24	TL 41418 to 46417	3HW–51418 to 56417	5000	Dec '43 to June '44 DL		Littlewoods at Liverpool, Mars factory at Slough, and VRD's
3HW	M/C Solo 350 cc OHV	5566918–5570917	S5340	25	TL 46418 to 50417	3HW–56418 to 60417	4000	15/12/43 June '44 to Oct '44 DL		As above
3HW	M/C Solo 350 cc OHV	4854180–4857179	C8886	21	TL 50418 to 50431, 50439–53417	3HW–60418 to 60431, 60439–63417	3000	07/10/40 DM* Oct '44 to Feb '45 DL	£63.14s.10d	*Original demand not delivered. Pearson's Garage and Littlewoods in Liverpool, and Morris Motors in Wales
3HW	M/C Solo 350 cc OHV	6101418–6109417	S6680	26	TL 53418 to 58617	3HW–63418 to 68617	8000*	15/05/44 Feb '45 to Sept '45 DL	£63.9s.8d	S.G.B. (Dudley) Ltd and ?. Some supplied without tyres. *Reduced to 5200

Velocette

MAKERS TYPE	MILITARY CLASS	WD SERIAL NO ALLOCATION	CONTRACT NUMBER	CAT REF	FRAME NUMBER	ENGINE NUMBER	QUANTITY PRODUCED	DATES	PRICE(S)	DELIVERY DESTINATION & NOTES
MAC	M/C Solo 350 cc OHV				MDD 10430	MAC 6476	1	25/10/39 23/10/39 DL	£67.10s.0d	MAC evaluation model
MSS	M/C Solo 500 cc OHV				Not stated	MSS 4447	1	20/10/39 23/10/39 DL	£77.0s.0d	MSS evaluation model
MAC (WD)	M/C Solo 350 cc OHV	4321935–4323134	C.7974	1	MDD 11001–12200	MDD 11001–12200	1200	29/06/40 or 10/41 CD	£50.15s.0d	Ex-French Government contract. 100 to York (ROD), remainder to Chilwell
MAC (WD)	M/C Solo 350 cc OHV	4323135–4323334					200	22/07/40 CD		To Chilwell Central Ordnance Depot. This not confirmed, as serial number block not noted as allocated. Possible cancelled contract or for Air Ministry?
MAF	M/C Solo 350 cc OHV	4653101–4654048	C.10973	2	MAF 1001–1948	MAF 1001–1948	947	21/06/41 CD 03/42 DL 09/42 CP	£68	Contract originally for 2000 machines but cancelled after 947 produced

Sidecars

MAKERS TYPE	MILITARY CLASS	WD SERIAL NO ALLOCATION	CONTRACT NUMBER	CAT REF	FRAME NUMBER	ENGINE NUMBER	QUANTITY PRODUCED	DATES	PRICE(S)	DELIVERY DESTINATION & NOTES
Swallow Box	sidecar		B/S9413				2	12/09/41 DM 24/10/41 CD	£20.14s.11d	For BSA's
Norton Box	sidecar + chassis		C/S13158				1	16/01/42 DM 07/02/42 CD		For Norton 16H
Watsonian	chassis		C/S14583				300	12/05/42 DM		For Indian 500 cc
Swallow Model 8 Bodies	sidecar		C/S14585				100	12/05/42 DM 14/05/42 CD		Passenger carrying (Standard)
Swallow Box	sidecar		C/S14584				200	12/05/42 DM		For Indian M/Cs. Standard WD type

LP Impressed Rebuilt and Captured

MAKERS TYPE	MILITARY CLASS	WD SERIAL NO ALLOCATION	CONTRACT NUMBER	CAT REF	FRAME NUMBER	ENGINE NUMBER	QUANTITY PRODUCED	DATES	PRICE(S)	DELIVERY DESTINATION & NOTES
various makes	M/C Solo	46001–47551	imp.	–			1551			
various makes	M/C Solo	47801–48081	imp.	–			281			
various makes	M/C Solo	48301–53287	imp.	–			4987			
various makes	M/C Solo	53324–58301	imp.	–			1978			
various makes	M/C Solo	58322–60787	imp.	–			2466			
various makes	M/C Solo	61001–62360	imp.	–			1361			
various makes	M/C Solo	62415–62685	imp.	–			271			
various makes	M/C Solo	63086–63143	imp.	–			58			
All AJS	M/C Solo 350 cc	72586–72639	imp.	–			54			
various makes	M/C Solo	73586–73603	imp.	–			18			
various makes	M/C Solo	73686–73986	imp.	–			301			
R. Enfield	M/C Solo 500 cc	78037	imp.	–			1			
various makes	M/C Solo	99489–99490	imp.	–			2			
various makes	M/C Solo	1400000–1499999	rebuilt	–			100000*			*Reserved numbers
Velocette MAC	M/C Solo	4123209–4123231	LP	–			23	1940		
various makes	M/C Solo	4138882	NC(?)	–			1			
various makes	M/C Solo	4191203, 4191205, 4191207, 4191208, 4191212–4191214, 4191216–4191220, 4191223–4191225, 4191227–4191230, 4191232, 4191233, 4191240, 4191241, 4191264, 4191266, 4191270, 4191272, 4191273, 4191276, 4191277, 4191281	LP	–			32			
various makes	M/C Solo	4191749–4191801, 4191884–4191957	LP	–			127			
various makes	M/C Solo	4333316–4333653	LP	–			338			
various makes	M/C Solo	4657352–4657369	ex-RAF	–			18			
various makes	M/C Solo	6000000–6009999	captured	–			10000*			*Reserved numbers
various makes & types	Some motorcyles	5307001–5327000	captured	–						All serials used and issued in North Africa